THE GREAT INKA ROAD

PUBLISHED BY THE

National Museum of the American Indian

IN ASSOCIATION WITH

Smithsonian Books

WASHINGTON, DC, AND NEW YORK

THE GREAT INKA ROAD

ENGINEERING AN EMPIRE

Ramiro Matos Mendieta & José Barreiro, *Editors*

This book may be purchased for educational, business, or sales promotional use. For information, please write: Smithsonian Books, Special Markets, PO Box 37012, MRC 513, Washington, DC, 20013.

The National Museum of the American Indian (NMAI), Smithsonian Institution, is committed to advancing knowledge and understanding of the Native cultures of the Western Hemisphere—past, present, and future—through partnership with Native people and others. The museum works to support the continuance of culture, traditional values, and transitions in contemporary Native life.

For more information about the Smithsonian's National Museum of the American Indian, visit the NMAI's website at www.AmericanIndian.si.edu. To support the museum by becoming a member, call 1-800-242-NMAI (6624) or click on "Support" on the website.

Director: Kevin Gover (Pawnee)
Associate Director for Museum Programs: Tim Johnson (Mohawk)
General Editors: Ramiro Matos Mendieta (Quechua) and José Barreiro (Taíno)
Publications Manager: Tanya Thrasher (Cherokee Nation)
Assistant Publications Manager: Ann Kawasaki
Project Editors: Sally Barrows, Christine T. Gordon, Cecilia I. Parker
Editorial, Research, and Translation Assistance: Eriksen Translations, Inc.; Diana Marcela Hajjar; Indexing Partners, LLC; Katharine Martinek; Jane McAllister; Samantha Pary Ghayour McKnew; Arwen Nuttall (Four Winds Band of Cherokee); Jessica Phippen
Permissions: Diana Marcela Hajjar, Wendy Hurlock Baker, Ann Kawasaki, Jessica Phippen
Object Photography, Photo Services, and Media Group: Ernest Amoroso, Mark Christal, Daniel Davis, Katherine Fogden (Akwesasne Mohawk), Doug McMains, Erin Weinman, R.A.Whiteside
Map Illustrations: Nancy Bratton Design; Daniel G. Cole, Smithsonian Institution
Design: Julie Allred, BW&A Books; Steve Bell

Published by Smithsonian Books
Director: Carolyn Gleason
Production Editor: Christina Wiginton

First Edition
10 9 8 7 6 5 4 3 2 1
Printed in Canada

Library of Congress Cataloging-in-Publication Data
The great Inka road : engineering an empire / José Barreiro and Ramiro Matos, editors.
    pages cm
Includes bibliographical references and index.
ISBN 978-1-58834-495-3
1. Qhapaq Ñan. 2. Inca roads. 3. Incas—Civilization.
I. Barreiro, José, editor. II. Matos Mendieta, Ramiro, editor. III. Title: Great Inca road, engineering an empire.
F3429.1.R6G73 2015
909".0498323—dc23   2015005190

page i: The Inka Trail through Colca Canyon. Colca Canyon, Peru, 2014. Photo by Doug McMains, NMAI

page ii: A llama caravan travels the Inka Road. Warautambo, Peru, 1990. Photo by Ramiro Matos Mendieta, NMAI

page iii: This *illa*, or amulet, is typical of offerings that were left along the Inka Road to ensure a safe journey. Inka llama amulet, AD 1400–1500. Peru. Gold. 4.9 × 4 × 0.6 cm. 13/1591. Photo by Ernest Amoroso, NMAI

page iv: The *arybalo* is a distinctly shaped vessel found in every Inka territory. Arybalos were used to store *a'qa* (also known as *chicha*, or maize beer), and their pointed ends were stuck into the earth to keep them upright. All arybalos have a small protrusion on the front and two handles. Inka *arybalo*, AD 1450–1532. Juan Benigno Vela (Pataló), Ecuador. Ceramic, paint. 21.6 × 17.2 × 13.3 cm. 1/2780. Photo by Ernest Amoroso, NMAI

page v: The intricate designs embossed on this gold disc have calendric or religious significance. Pre-Inka–style chest ornament, known colloquially as the Echenique Disc, AD 1000–1500. Cusco, Peru. Gold-silver-copper alloy. 13.7 × 13.3 × 0.2 cm. 3/4785. Photo by Ernest Amoroso, NMAI

pages vi–vii: Q'eswachaka suspension bridge. Apurímac River, 2014. Canas Province, Peru. Photo by Doug McMains, NMAI

page ix, facing: An Inka irrigation channel. Tipon, Peru, 2014. Photo by Doug McMains, NMAI

CONTENTS

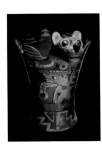

The essays in this book demonstrate that what inspired the Inka and their great road was not only the concept of a transportation network but also an idea and a belief system. The Inka instinctively understood that this road—like none seen before or since—could inspire awe, connect the disparate cultures of their empire, allow prompt communication, enable their military forces to deploy rapidly, and link iconic sites that were both spiritual and functional.

This road, passing through the tropical forests of the Amazon and the high elevations of the Andes, inspires awe—and connects cultures—to this day. As a geotechnical engineer by training, I marvel at the stonework and built-in drainage systems along the Inka Road, which I saw firsthand on a trip to Peru with colleagues from the National Museum of the American Indian (NMAI). One trail in particular stays with me. Built to connect people in areas west of Machu Picchu, it is carved directly into a vertical rock face. The view from the road is breathtaking, the Inka engineering technique even more so.

My colleagues and I were privileged to walk a rocky and picturesque stretch of the historic Inka Road with a group of Quechua people, descendants of the Inka, in a llama procession. The local leaders graciously greeted me using a Quechua title that was translated as "grand chief." This experience underscored for me how directly the Inka Road links present to past and teaches all of us about the culture of an ancient empire. This volume, a product of the collaboration between NMAI and Smithsonian Books, does the same; my congratulations to all involved. An excellent complement to a major NMAI exhibition of the same title, this thought-provoking collection of essays sparks our sense of wonder at a monumental accomplishment by Native peoples of the Western Hemisphere.

G. WAYNE CLOUGH
Secretary Emeritus, Smithsonian Institution

Two men walk the Inka Road. Charazani, Bolivia, 2011. Photo by Ramiro Matos Mendieta, NMAI

FOREWORD

We at the National Museum of the American Indian strongly believe that knowledge is to be gained from examining indigenous cultures with the particular purpose of gathering and enhancing ancient lessons that can have practical applications in our contemporary lives. In building and expanding the largest empire in the fifteenth-century Americas—one that covered parts of present-day Colombia, Ecuador, Peru, Bolivia, Chile, and Argentina—Inka rulers linked thriving peoples, communities, and nations that extended the length of a continent. The Inka's attention to empirical knowledge, and their organizational capacity, understanding of their environment, agriculture, and engineering—all remain infinitely interesting and instructive, particularly in a contemporary world that is grappling with similar existential challenges of sustainability. There are no perfect cultures, but all cultures offer their particular superlatives. The attention paid by the Inka to long-term inhabitation and natural forces parallels modern thinking and offer important lessons.

The Inka Road, or Qhapaq Ñan, in the Quechua language, is a primary example of the achievements of indigenous people in the Western Hemisphere. The product of a culture of reciprocity that survives in the Andes, the road system—the length of which totals more than twenty-four thousand miles—also has survived the ravages of time, including thousands of seismic events. A significant achievement, it is now celebrated by UNESCO as a World Heritage site. A major research and documentation effort by scholars in six Andean countries coincided with the NMAI's own research and is much appreciated for its scientific and cultural contributions to the understanding of the road, which remains a monument to Inka ingenuity and purpose.

With *The Great Inka Road: Engineering an Empire*, we welcome everyone to consider and explore the wonderful subject of the Qhapaq Ñan—the Inka Road—and we honor the Andean peoples for this unique contribution to human achievement.

KEVIN GOVER (Pawnee)
Director, National Museum
of the American Indian

A paved stretch of Inka road extending through the upper Amazon from Chachapoyas to Moyobamba. Near Chachapoyas, Peru, 2014. Photo by Inge Schjellerup

Overleaf: This figure depicts a man on one side and a woman on the other, reflecting the importance of duality in the Andean world view.

Inka double-sided figurine. AD 1470–1532. Lima, Peru. Silver-copper alloy. 9.9 × 6.8 × 3.5 cm. 19/9105. Photo by Ernest Amoroso, NMAI

Pasto

Manta

Ingapirca
Tomebamba

Cabeza
de Vaca

Chachapoyas
Cajamarca

Chan Chan

Chavín de Huantar • Huánuco Pampa
Curamba
Machu Picchu
Ollantaytambo
Pachacamac
Ushkus • Cusco Wanakauri
Q'eswachaka
Raqchi
Vilcashuaman
Quebrada de las Vacas
Colca Canyon

Lake Titicaca
Tiwanaku
Inkallacta
Samaipata
Arica Paria
Salar de Uyuni Potosí

Catarpe
San Pedro de Atacama Tilcara

Jujuy

Copiapó
Shinkal
Catamarca

Maule River Talca

AMAZON RIVER

SOUTH AMERICA

ANDES

PACIFIC
OCEAN

ATLANTIC
OCEAN

Tawantinsuyu's Four Regions

Antisuyu

Chinchaysuyu

Contisuyu

Collasuyu

STRONG IN OUR HEARTS

The Legacy of the Inka Road

vivid Andean legend tells how the ancient Inka ancestors would crack their whips, and massive stones would fall into line, stacking themselves up miraculously. Sixty-four-year-old Nazaria Meza, from the Quechua community of Chawaytiri, related the story to me and a group of travelers as we hiked along one of the main trails leading out of the city of Cusco, Peru. "We don't know anymore just how they [the Inka people] made such a road," explained Nazaria, elder and grandmother. "But when we walk our llamas along the Inka Road, we feel strong in our hearts." Many wonderful and generous people like Nazaria have informed this publication and its accompanying exhibition. We have sought the expertise of those who have long studied the diversity and wonder of the Inka world, from community-based keepers of oral traditions and practices as well as academic scholars such as the authors of this volume.

The Qhapaq Ñan, the sacred road of the ancient Inka sovereign and an intricate forty-thousand-kilometer system, stands as the physical remnant of a highly organized American empire—both politically and economically. Unparalleled in hemispheric history for its capacity to integrate a wide range of people and resources over a huge and difficult geography, the Qhapaq Ñan ("road of power" in the Quechua language) still functions as a series of living roads traveled by indigenous peoples over long stretches of Andean landscape.

The magnificent Andean mountain ranges run the length of western South America, from southern Chile to Colombia. Dropping east to the jungles and west to the sea, the Andes are a monumental and aggressive terrain, difficult to traverse and even harder to integrate into large-scale human endeavor. Altitudes in the Andes range from thirty-five hundred to five thousand meters above sea level. A vertical world of extensive, abrupt, often impassable ranges, it is also a world of promise. The Andes enjoy four vegetational floors and many ecological zones. A generous variety of horticulture is possible, where terraces can be built into the landscape and the transport of goods can be safely organized.

The great human effort required to organize the Andean world was most expansively and adeptly accomplished by the Inka. On the heels of earlier civilizations the Inka created a road network that crossed high sierras, punas, deserts, and coasts—and even penetrated deep into the

The name Tawantinsuyu means "the four parts together," referring to the empire's four *suyus*. Antisuyu and Chinchaysuyu were considered the upper (*hanan*) half. Collasuyu and Contisuyu were considered the lower (*hurin*) half. These dual and quadripartite divisions were grounded in Inka cosmology.

Map by Daniel G. Cole, Smithsonian Institution, and Nancy Bratton Design with core data from ESRI and NaturalEarth. © 2015 Smithsonian Institution.

jungle. As scholar Victoria Castro describes in Chapter 1, the road was an ingenious humanization of a "fractured geography." Much of the Inka's hallmark agricultural knowledge has been sustained in oral tradition and continuously useful practice. Castro points out: "Native Andeans distinguish perfectly the differences in soil types, geomorphology, microclimate, and vegetation . . . distinctions [that] correspond well to the physiognomic zones described by botanists."

The Andes nurtured numerous nations and several civilizations before the Inka emergence. The Inka are particularly recognized for integrating knowledge from earlier civilizations, such as the Wari and Tiwanaku, for incorporating ancient trails into their road systems, and for concentrating the ancestral knowledge of many cultures in the Andean region. The integration took place at many levels: the interpretation and practice of cosmology, local social organization, and state administration.

A monumental geography that impresses itself upon the human psyche, the Andes communicate a power of presence that renders landscapes sacred. Thus many mountaintops are by long tradition identified with *apus*, or mountain deities of varied personalities and spiritual powers. So venerated was the landscape that even human life was offered to its magnificence. A Capacocha, the ceremonial sacrifice of an unblemished child, was an offering made atop the highest peaks, likely to appreciate and ensure continued success in expanding the empire.

This volume gathers cutting-edge scholarship and commissioned writings on varied aspects of the Inka Road from twenty-eight contributors representing five countries and numerous disciplines. This distinguished roster of scholars examines the nature of Inka expansion—which tapped into the rich customs and culture of the Andean highlands' kinship-based communities, the *ayllus*—showing how

major state institutions incorporated community cultural concepts. The deep sense of duality and symmetry inherent in community life and ritual also was useful in designing the state. The equally acute sense of balance expressed in the Andean concepts of *ayni* (reciprocity) and *minka* (exchanging labor) was the basis of a highly productive social organization, which could support a major achievement in civil engineering. A vast empire, meeting the essential definitions of the term—a central sovereign state dominating many regions and cultures—Inka governance was also unique in developing a polity informed substantially by these Andean reciprocity protocols.

The Inka accomplished these feats of empire building by founding and expanding from a central administrative and religious center, the capital city of Cusco. In this book, Inka-era Cusco is skillfully rendered in a fine new approximation of its layout at the moment of

contact with Francisco Pizarro and the Spanish empire. Cusco is *chawpi*, or the center, of the Inka Empire. It is the home region, marked by a deep and abiding mytho-historical narrative and forever identified with the brilliant figure of the greatest of the Inka rulers, Pachacutic, who reigned from 1438 to 1471. The long-lived Pachacutic, a legend in his own time, engineered much of the style and form of his world. Credited with saving Cusco from an invasion from the enemy Chanka, whom he later vanquished, Pachacutic went on to redesign the city and its valleys, forging rivers into water canal systems, carving horizontal terraces into steep mountains to recover agricultural land, and establishing an Inka mastery of engineering and architecture that organized the labor and military service of many thousands.

The legend and physical presence of Pachacutic carry the dynasty of Inka sovereigns from the mythological narratives of oral memory into modern history. In the creation stories, the Ayares—the original four couples from one *panaca*, or extended family—emerged from caves at Pacariqtampu and, before that (in a different version), from the waters of Lake Titicaca. These principals, Manco Capac and Mama Ocllo in particular, gathered the ten first communities (ayllus) and began a journey, the first journey on the Inka Road. They carried a mandate from Inti, the Sun. Inka legend tells that before their emergence, chaos and violence ruled the Andes; according to the Inka historian Garcilaso de la Vega, people "lived like fierce and brutish animals" (Garcilaso [1609] 2008, 55). He recounts, "Our Father, the Sun . . . having pity upon them, sent from the sky to the earth a son and a daughter of his, to teach them . . . precepts and laws to live in reason." According to Garcilaso (56), Inti instructed these primordial Inka that they should conquer and incorporate human beings into a "system

Agricultural terraces at an Inka royal estate. Pisac, Peru, 2014. Photo by Doug McMains, NMAI

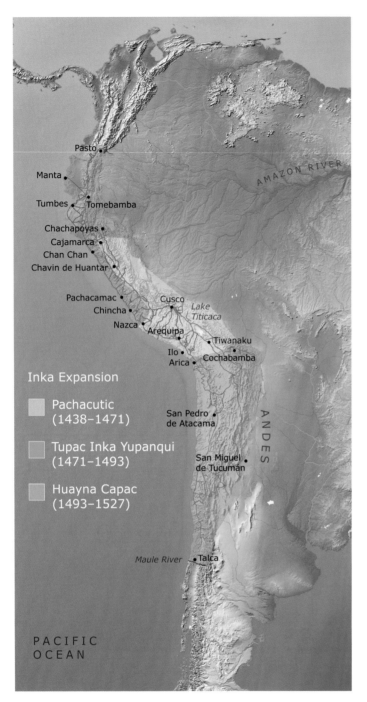

The approximate territories conquered by Pachacutic, Tupac Inka Yupanqui, and Huayna Capac, the ninth, tenth, and eleventh Inka rulers.

Map by Daniel G. Cole, Smithsonian Institution, and Nancy Bratton Design with core data from ESRI and NaturalEarth. © 2015 Smithsonian Institution.

Labels on map:
Pasto
Manta
Tumbes · Tomebamba
Chachapoyas
Cajamarca
Chan Chan
Chavin de Huantar
Pachacamac · Cusco
Chincha · Lake Titicaca
Nazca · Arequipa
Ilo · Tiwanaku
Arica · Cochabamba

AMAZON RIVER
ANDES

Inka Expansion

Pachacutic
(1438–1471)

Tupac Inka Yupanqui
(1471–1493)

Huayna Capac
(1493–1527)

San Pedro de Atacama

San Miguel de Tucumán

Maule River · Talca

PACIFIC OCEAN

of reason and justice, with pity, clemency and calm . . . as with tender and well-loved children."

Garcilaso is not always the most accepted of early witnesses, writing some sixty years after the Spanish Conquest, but the Inka state's impetus to organize is widely accepted in the scholarship. Historians often comment on Inka organizational skill. "In everything from the most important to the most trifling, there was order and methodical arrangement. . . . Men had honorable and useful occupations. . . . Lands, mines, pastures, hunting lands, woods; and all kinds of employments were so managed that each person knew and held his own state" (Hanke 1967, 78).

Through the *chaski*, or runner-messenger, system, and in the accounting of materials and people through a knotted-string device called a *khipu*, the Inka imperial capital had accurate and timely intelligence. In this sense, all roads led to Cusco.

> In each district of the four in which they divided their empire, the Inka had councils of war, justice, treasury. Each of these councils had their ministries and ministers and subordinates from major to minor . . . from decurions that handled ten to others who handled hundreds, thousands and tens of thousands. From grade to grade, these levels gave count of everything there was in the empire to the supreme councils. . . . The council presidents of each district received the sum of reason of everything that happened in the empire, to give count of it to the Inka. (Hanke 1967, 117)

Over time, the eight successive Inka rulers descended from the primordial Ayar couple, Manco Capac and Mama Ocllo, gradually conquered the immediate Cusco region, establishing Inka dominance over its highly productive, sacred valley. According to legend, through this first line of Inka sovereigns, the instruction and organization of conquered peoples was integral to the expansion of the Inka polity. The Inka systematically integrated new populations and in the process standardized their arts and trades, agricultural practices and crops, architectural skills, and other knowledge.

With the advent of Pachacutic—as well as his son, Tupac Inka Yupanqui, and grandson, Huayna Capac—an American indigenous population of between eight and twelve million people was integrated under a single political system, an empirical feat of governance unequaled in that vast region before or since. Pachacutic and two subsequent generations of his descendants—during the course of one incredibly ambitious century—organized and built major urban centers, terraces, canals, aqueducts, storehouses, and roads. They built or rebuilt citadels such as Machu Picchu, Ollantaytambo, Huánuco Pampa, Cajamarca, Tomebamba, Wakrapukara (the list is long).

Inka achievements in civil engineering are visually and technically stunning. Given the aggressive terrain, consistent seismic events, and annual floods, the design and construction of Inka roads and of so many intricately composed buildings, walls, and terraces impress even modern engineers. Construction engineer and professor Cliff Schexnayder has marveled at the Inka's acute attention to nature's powers. "They worked with nature rather than against it" (n.d., personal communication). Engineers today are particularly fascinated by Inka water dissipation and water-channeling techniques. That they accomplished this, as Ramiro Matos Mendieta, archaeologist and co-editor of this book, often points out, with no iron tools, no wheel, no writing system, and no stock animals, tells us of a major achievement of human intelligence and endeavor.

The Inka rulers deployed the most skilled diplomacy, directed the most strategic wars (excelling at provisioning troops), built

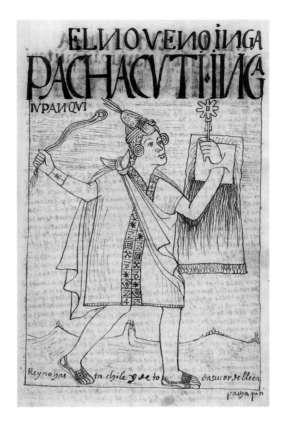

Portrait of Pachacutic, the ninth Shapa Inka (r. 1438–71). Felipe Guaman Poma de Ayala (Quechua, 1535–1616). Pen and ink drawing published in *El primer nueva crónica y buen gobierno* (1615). Royal Library, Copenhagen GKS 2232 4°

countless bridges and roads, and trained and commanded administrators and engineers, huge numbers of skilled artisans, agriculturalists, and construction workers. The three generations of Pachacutic's family expanded to the four directions, or *suyus*, of the Tawantinsuyu, as the Inka called their empire, developing highly complex systems of architecture, agriculture, and social organization. Wrote the earliest Spanish chronicler: "The Christians were amazed to see such great reason in the Indians, the vast amounts of provisions of all kinds that they had, and the extent of their highways and how clean and filled with lodgings they were" (Cieza de León [1553] 1998, 228).

Pachacutic took his conquests first west and then far to the north and south. He fully consolidated Inka hold of the sacred Urubamba River valley, the empire's agricultural bread basket. Countless *caciques* (chiefs) fell to his campaigns as he punished all weak and treacherous

Symbolically linked with water and fertility, the snake was a sacred animal in the Andean universe.

Wari vessel in the form of a snake, AD 800–1000. Chancay Valley, Peru. Ceramic, paint. 21.9 × 18.1 × 13.2 cm. 23/1070. Photo by Ernest Amoroso, NMAI

neighbors. According to the chronicler Bernabé Cobo ([1653], 1979, 140) Pachacutic took the ancient complex of Tiwanaku, subjugating "all the towns and nations surrounding the great Lake Titicaca," and sent expeditions north to the region of present-day Cuenca, Ecuador. Cobo records that so quick and efficient were Pachacutic's bridge-building engineers that at least once their wondrous constructions impressed resisting nations into surrender. Vast herds of llamas and alpacas, major agricultural valleys, rich mining and salt deposits, and other economic rewards increased the power of the Inka sovereign.

Pachacutic's succession was as orderly and efficient as his reign. As he aged, he slowly introduced a favored and proven son, Tupac Inka Yupanqui (also known as Topa Inka), to the reins of government. Topa Inka (r. 1471–93) consolidated his father's dominions, quashing rebellious provinces as he expanded the empire to the north and east, traveling and building on the Antisuyu road to secure the precious woods, fine feathers, coveted plant medicines, and gold of the tropical Amazonian foothills. He then went north beyond his father's Tomebamba to the "edge of the kingdom of Quito," which he besieged and conquered. He consolidated the central coast by conquering the Chimú empire. Topa Inka also took his exploits south to the Maule River, building roads deep into today's central Chile. At the Maule, the Inka army met its match in the fierce resistance of the Mapuche warriors, defining "the edge of his [Topa Inka's] empire; and the dominions of the Inka never passed that line, then or after" (Cobo [1653] 1979, 147).

Topa Inka's son, Huayna Capac, the last true Inka according to Cobo, took seriously the patrilineal mandate to expand his own portion of the empire. He did so by "incorporating much of what is now modern Ecuador as well as the northeastern Peruvian Andes" (McEwan

2006, 77). A brilliant general, Huayna Capac spent so much time on his northern military campaigns that the fabric of the central government was seriously strained. The now-vast empire suffered from his distance from Cusco, while the Inka appeared to be setting up a rival court in the northern center of Tomebamba.

Huayna Capac's absence from Cusco, the sacred city and the center of administrative equilibrium, signaled a power vacuum that would usher in the empire's destruction. In 1527, a new disease (likely smallpox) reached his northern court, just ahead of the Spanish conquistadors. It rapidly killed the Inka along with many high-ranking generals and officials, and, most tragically for the empire, Huayna Capac's designated heir. The lack of an orderly succession opened the doors to chaos and a ruinous civil war—into which walked the Spanish conquistador Francisco Pizarro, and his band of soldiers.

Cusco continues to command great respect and acclaim for its centrality to the Inka, and the marked entrances to the city, which face the four corners of the empire, still garner ceremonial respect from present-day Peruvians. Cusco was *chawpi*, the fulcrum of energy, but in its time it was not the only destination. Territorial extensions of the Inka polity reach all parts of the Andean world. In each of the four directions, roads traversed a diverse landscape of contesting regions and ethnicities. At selected points throughout the Inka territory, the roads converge on various *ushnus*, sacred altars of the sun, where offerings were made at religious gatherings.

The roads to each of the four suyus, or provinces—Chinchaysuyu, Collasuyu, Contisuyu, and Antisuyu, each with its specific bounties and justifications for Inka expansion—carried the economic, religious, military, and political traffic of millions of people. As described in fascinating detail by Gary Urton

in Chapter 2, all these activities were controlled, recorded, and documented with the *khipu*, the ingenious and mysterious mnemonic device of knotted strings.

The Inka Road is a network, "an articulated circuit," writes Victoria Castro, "that leaves no point of the territory without access to the Qhapaq Ñan." Inka planners connected thousands of local communities via a highly efficient system of roads, bridges, *tampus* (way stations), *colcas* (state warehouses), and chaskis (runner messengers). Exhibiting a keen and imaginative sense of engineering, the Inka created works that continue to amaze for their monumentality and durability.

This *paqcha* (ritual vessel) takes the shape of a plowing tool and an *arybalo* jug. Arybalos filled with *a'qa* (also known as *chicha*, or maize beer) were provided by the Inka state to its people in return for their labor.

Inka *paqcha*, AD 1470–1532. Peru. Ceramic. 17.2 × 32.4 × 7.3 cm. 22/2431. Photo by Ernest Amoroso, NMAI

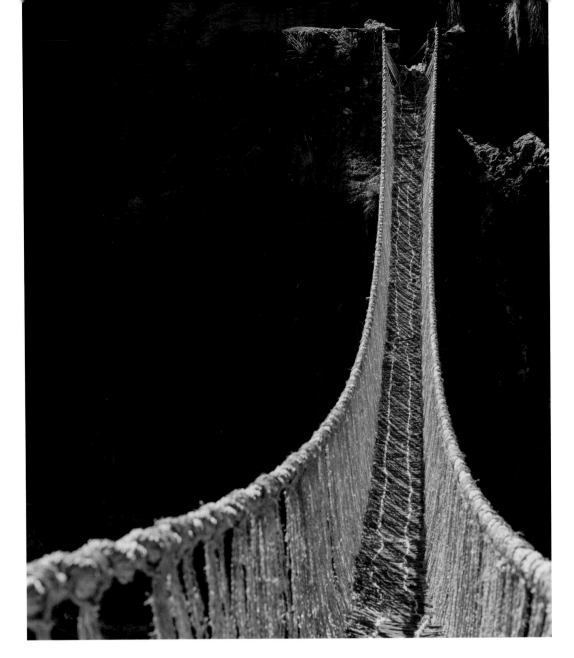

A view of the *kall-apo*, or floor, of the Q'eswachaka suspension bridge. Apurímac River, Canas Province, Peru, 2014. Photo by Doug McMains, NMAI

facing: A family travels on an Inka road. Jujuy, Argentina, 2007. Photo by Axel E. Nielsen

Among noted destinations of the Andean world, Machu Picchu stands out as a five-hundred-year-old architectural wonder that has survived the pressures of nature, firmly defended by the principles and feats of Inka engineering. Kenneth R. and Ruth M. Wright, present-day master engineers and among the most senior scholars of the Inka citadel, describe in this volume the recent uncovering of another Inka trail of exquisite and enduring construction. Its water management, fountains, and retaining walls, they report in their fascinating chapter, "exceeded expectations."

Each road and direction of the Inka suyus takes a traveler to marvels of monumental construction, and each holds the promise of needed and coveted natural treasures: in Antisuyu, gold, precious woods, feathers, medicines; in Collasuyu, precious metals and salt; in Contisuyu, ocean products and sacred sands. One of the most compelling engineering treasures of the four regions can still be seen in Chinchaysuyu, to the north: the famous Inka hanging bridge over the Apurímac River. Known as the Q'eswachaka, the rope bridge is still in use five centuries later, reconstructed ceremonially by

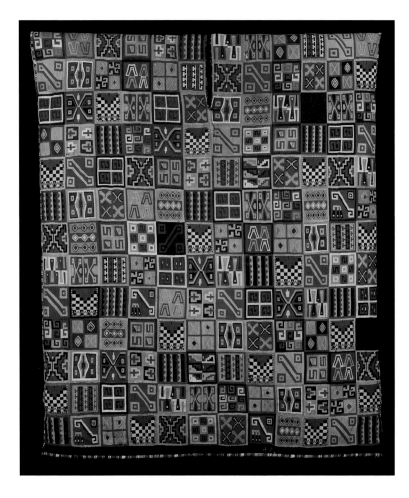

An example of *cumbi* cloth, this tunic is made from the finest alpaca and vicuña wools, with *tucapus* (abstract, square designs) woven in. Such a tunic would only have been worn by a member of the Inka elite.

Inka tunic, AD 1470–1532. Peru. Camelid wool, cotton. 90.2 × 77.1 cm. Dumbarton Oaks, Washington, DC PC.B-518

grew with every generation, in time encompassing some one hundred nations that were lured and sustained by continuous advances in the organization and engineering of agriculture, road and building construction, and military operations. For a dozen Inka reigns, the empire grew—always building and expanding, integrating a vast domain.

Ever since gifted photographer Megan Son suggested an exhibition, and museum associate director Tim Johnson asked Andeanist Ramiro Matos Mendieta of the National Museum of the American Indian to take up the challenge, I have been fortunate as co-curator to join a wonderful caravan of experts in the compilation of this unique study. Beyond our circle of collaborating authors, we are thankful also for the generations of culture bearers and scholars who walked and documented the Inka Road. Of particular note for this project is the remarkable mapping of the road system by John Hyslop, on whose 1984 work we have based the exhibition's maps as well as many of the maps in this book.

We invite everyone to join us in exploring the minds of the Inka leaders, as they sought to fulfill their solar mandate to bring order out of chaos and implement a brilliant, stark, and highly integrated vision of the Andean world.

local Native communities each year. Massive cords twisted from local *ichhu* grasses are hung by masters (with no margin for failure) across a steep gorge in the mountains—a seemingly simple, yet deeply complex, technology that was first skillfully deployed by the Inka ancestors.

Our purpose in examining the Qhapaq Ñan has been to contemplate the sophisticated splendor of the Inka road system, focusing on the masterful civil and social engineering that went into its design and construction. The history of the Inka—their imperial achievements and foibles—while of interest, are beyond the scope of this book. We are more than impressed and intensely intrigued, however, by the Inka development of a confederated society on some of the harshest terrain on earth, a society that

JOSÉ BARREIRO (Taíno Nation)
Assistant Director for Culture and History Research and Director of the Office for Latin America, National Museum of the American Indian

facing: These beads are made from the shell of *Spondylus*, a genus of mollusk found off the coast of Ecuador. Called *mullu* in Quechua, the shell was a sacred material closely controlled by the Inka state.

Shell beads, AD 1000–1500. Tembladera, Cajamarca region, Peru. *Spondylus* shell. Left: 6.2 × 2 × 0.9 cm; right: 4.8 × 1.8 × 0.9 cm. 24/1017. Photo by Ernest Amoroso, NMAI

VICTORIA CASTRO

THE QHAPAQ ÑAN AND ITS LANDSCAPES

Creo yo desde que ay memoria de jentes no se a leydo de tanta grandeza como tuvo este camino hecho por valles hondos y por sierras altas, por montes de nieve, por tremadales de agua, por peña viva y junto a ríos furiosos; por estas partes yva llano empedrado, por las laderas bien sacado, por las syerrasdesechado, por las peñas socavado, por junto a los rios sus paredes entre nieve con escalones y descanzos; por todas partes limpio, barrido, desconbrado, lleno de aposentos, de depósitos, de tesoros, de tenplos del Sol, de postas que avía en este camino !O! Qué grandeza se pu[e] de dezir de Alexandro ni ninguno de los poderosos reyes que el mundo mandarin que tal camino hiziesen, ni enventasen el proveymiento que en él avía? Ni fue nada la calzada que los Romanos hizieron, que pasa por España, ni los otros que leemos, para que este se compare. Y hízose harto en más poco tienpo de lo que se puede ymajinar, porque los Yngas más tardavan ellos en mandarlo que sus jentes en ponerlo por obra.

I believe that, since the history of man has been recorded, there has been no account of such grandeur as is to be seen in this road which passes over deep valleys and lofty mountains, by snowy heights, over falls of water, through live rocks, and along the edges of furious torrents. In all of these places it is level and paved, along mountain slopes well excavated, by the mountains well terraced, through the living rock cut, along the river banks supported by walls, in the snowy heights with steps and resting places, in all parts clean swept, clear of stones, with post and store-houses, and temples of the Sun at intervals. Oh! What greater things can be said of Alexander, or of any of the powerful kings who have ruled in the world, than that they had made such a road as this, and conceived the works which were required for it! The road constructed by the Romans in Spain, and any others of which we read, are not to be compared with it.

—Pedro Cieza de León, 1553

An Inka road with sidewalls cuts through an agricultural valley. Colca Canyon, Peru, 2014. Photo by Doug McMains, NMAI

A paved Inka road skirts Lake Junín, just south of the remains of Pumpu, a large Inka administrative center. Lake Junín, Peru, 2006. Photo by Megan Son and Laurent Granier

Argentina, Bolivia, Chile, Colombia, Ecuador, and Peru share a cultural heritage of exceptional value: the Qhapaq Ñan, or the Main Andean Road (www.unesco.org). Most of this road is between thirty-five hundred and five thousand meters above sea level, with some stretches that are twenty meters wide.

The road, which linked populated areas, administrative centers, agricultural areas, mines, and ceremonial spaces, was the major technological work of the pre-Hispanic Americas. Throughout the road network, the knowledge of preexisting ethnic groups was exploited, and the Qhapaq Ñan succeeded in integrating a vast territory with extremely complex geography, connecting towns and territories with great biological and cultural diversity. Nevertheless, since the Inka period,

the region has been socioeconomically and culturally vulnerable, which requires that current generations respond appropriately, just as their ancestors did, to the conditions they face, such as the need to preserve a harmonious relationship between humans and nature and to use resources in sustainable ways (Banderin 2004).

The Andean region is marked by a fractured geography. The ingenuity that shaped the natural environment, from the system of cultivation in the valleys and the Andean buttresses to sanctuaries in the high mountains, molded the cultural contours of the Andes over many centuries of technological and sociopolitical change. Such a strong cultural tradition demands that close ties with the pre-Columbian past be maintained even today.

Deciphering and understanding the diversity of that tradition require the appropriate methodologies (Sanz 2004).

The Qhapaq Ñan is by nature pan-Andean, owing to both the territory it covers and the rich and diverse cultural substratum that the Tawantinsuyu was able to organize by taking advantage of the different institutions arising from the ancient Andean *ayllus* (extended family groups). This great network of roads extends from the southern part of Colombia to Chile, crossing through deserts, mountains, and the Andean altiplano. In some places, it cuts through the valleys of the Pacific coast, where it is called the Camino Inka Costero (Coastal Inka Road).[1] Requiring even more human effort, the system penetrates the forest with broad, paved roads such as the Camino del Choro in Bolivia (Avilés 1998) and with roads extending into the Zenta Mountains in the western forests of Argentina (Nielsen 2003).

Completing this vast road network involved an enormous engineering enterprise. The Qhapaq Ñan road system organized local settlements, *chaskiwasis* (relay posts for message runners), *tampus* (accommodations for travelers), and *paskanas* (resting places), marking the landscape and making it sacred with cave paintings, mountain sanctuaries, and *apachetas* (offering places) (Castro 2004).

The Inka Road in Bolivia extends through a vast range of environments, passing over plateaus, valleys, altiplanos, and mountains as it wends its way to the hot, humid, tropical valleys, thus encompassing a mosaic of peoples grouped together under the name Collasuyu. The main stretch of the Inka Road in Bolivia is the Desaguadero-Viacha section, which circles the shores of Lake Titicaca and passes through major ritual sites. These religious sites are part of an oral memory and even today are areas of ritual activity for the Native people of the Collao plateau. The Aymara people of the altiplano, for example, preserve the dual conceptualization of the road that encircles Lake Titicaca: they call the eastern branch Umasuyu (feminine, east), while using the name Orqosuyu (masculine) for the western branch. Then the road continues through Chuquiabo (La Paz) and crosses the Chilean and Argentinean plateaus, passing over the long deserts of the Tropic of Capricorn, until it reaches the woods and scrublands of the south, between Diaguitas, Picunches, and Huarpes, in present-day Argentina.

In the north, the Inka Road extends as far

Agricultural terraces on a steep hillside. Colca Canyon, Peru, 2014. Photo by Doug McMains, NMAI

Terraces have allowed the Inka and their descendants to transform steep terrain into viable agricultural land. Pisac, Peru, 2014. Photo by Doug McMains, NMAI

as the Pasto region, on the Colombian border with Ecuador, after passing the equatorial volcanoes beyond the Nudo de los Pastos and the vast, cold, humid highlands (Lumbreras 2006). In Argentina the Inka established military and cultural control of the political borders, and introduced a unique religious tradition: worshipping the mountains and carrying out rituals and sacrifices in temples constructed on glacier-encrusted mountaintops (five thousand meters above sea level), as can be seen on Llullaillaco (Vitry 1999).

In Chile the road network crosses a parched, high-altitude landscape, which shows the Inka strategy of expanding their control into areas with mining resources, such as those in the regions of Arica-Parinacota, Tarapacá, Atacama, and Antofagasta. Aconcagua and Mapocho offer examples of Inka occupation of transverse valleys. It is here that the site of a Capacocha (child sacrifice) is located on a mountaintop at El Plomo.

The Antisuyu branch of the road descends to the rainforests to the east of Cusco—where it disappears among the tributaries of the Amazon—while the Contisuyu branch descends

A llama caravan carrying salt from the altiplano to exchange for maize in Bolivia's Tarija Valley. Altiplano de Sama, Tarija, Bolivia, 1995. Photo by Axel E. Nielsen

to the sea in a westerly direction. Although the Qhapaq Ñan is longitudinal, going from north to south and parallel to the cordillera, the road network is integrated with transverse arteries that extend eastward and westward, creating an articulated circuit that leaves no point of the territory without access to the Qhapaq Ñan. From anywhere, after taking the main road, it is possible to get to Cusco and other destinations within the empire (Lumbreras 2006).

Far more than a road system, the Qhapaq Ñan was a complex network of services and signs, with points for securing provisions and resting. The road was provided with bridges for crossing rivers or ravines, tunnels for shortening distances, and even paving tiles and stones for crossing rainy territories. It also featured elevated sections for crossing swamps and areas marked by seasonal flooding. In places where the route could not be easily preserved, as in deserts, other markers such as buried posts were used to indicate its course.

The road network served not only pedestrians but also caravans of pack llamas, and it continues to be used as a collective system (Lumbreras 2006; Fresco 2004). Solitary travelers such as the *chaskis*, who were part of a messenger system that served the empire, used the road, and the army traveled it, too. Manufactured products, food, and raw materials from the mines, the woods, sea, and desert also were transported along the road. Frequently, caravans of merchants from the northern Andes called *mindalaes* encountered Chimú, Chincha, and other groups from the central Andes. The Kallawaya, traveling doctors from Bolivia, and other itinerant workers from the southern desert also used the road system (Lumbreras 2006; Fresco 2004).

The Andean landscape represents a symbiotic synthesis of nature and humanity. With a historical and political understanding of a landscape, it is possible to account for human perceptions of nature as well as the modifications they have made to it on both material and intangible levels (Skewes et al. 2011). It

The Inka Road made it possible for precious metals to be transported from distant mines to workshops. Metals often were mixed to create colors with specific, sacred meanings.

Inka figurine of a woman, AD 1470–1532. Coast of Peru. Gold-silver alloy. 24.5 × 6.4 × 7 cm. 5/4120. Photo by Ernest Amoroso, NMAI

become familiar with it, they can create and re-create different strategies for being part of the world and for relating to other humans. Humans provide the landscape with a unique toponymy, one that is full of meanings and that becomes interrelated and integrated by roads, mobile populations, and narratives that express perceptions and emotions. The human topography transforms the landscape into a cultural code related to life. For the Andean people, the landscape is endowed with spiritual powers. Humanized in this way, it represents a system of great importance, through which society reproduces and transforms itself (Tilley 1994).

The present-day high Andean communities have inherited from their ancestors a way of understanding their environment that allows them to integrate multiple facets of their reality and incorporate nature into their culture, re-creating it in harmony with Mother Earth. According to their conceptualization, this world is alive and inhabited by positive and negative forces. The land, mountains, and water are sacred: they are the elements that make the reproduction of life possible and, consequently, must be respected and invoked in rituals and offerings. The everyday landscape has a sacred dimension as well. In its different ecological zones, dwellers not only find forage for their flocks but also obtain numerous plants that have medicinal or symbolic powers, among other uses (Castro 2004).

For these reasons, the term "cultural landscape" refers to a variety of manifestations of the interaction between human beings and their environment. The cultural landscape of traditional societies often reflects specific, sustainable techniques for land development and a specific spiritual relationship with nature. Protecting the techniques for sustainable development can contribute to improving land use and to maintaining and fostering positive values with respect to the landscape.

is possible to assume that any landscape is the result of the value systems of the human groups that inhabit it. In this sense, one of the most important approaches to studying the Qhapaq Ñan is to appreciate the landscape as a cultural construction. As such, the landscape can be seen as providing its own standards and conventions, through which human beings give meaning to their world. As a cultural construction, the landscape is part of space-time relationships in which individuals develop, understand, and recognize one another (Hodder 1987). The landscape is so fundamental to social configuration that once humans

The landscape is a topography that is populated by humanity, which invests it with cultural codes related to human life. The landscape is endowed with spiritual and supernatural powers. For thousands of years, the original inhabitants of the South American Andes lived in a markedly heterogeneous high Andean landscape. Because of its extremes in altitude, the Andes chain manifests a variety of ecological zones, and each one offers different possibilities for the well-being of its inhabitants. The people, in turn, have been able to exploit these ecological niches, establishing traditional pan-Andean cultural and economic patterns. These ways of life are directly associated with a vertical perception of the landscape (Murra 1972). In the high Andes most of the landscape traversed by the Qhapaq Ñan is a plateau, the result of successive igneous events during the Miocene and Pliocene epochs of the Quaternary period, when the volcanoes were formed. The landscape above three thousand meters is mid-altitude steppe, the vegetation of which is dominated by dry scrubland, grassland (*ichhu*), and cushion plants (*Azorella*). In the southern Andes, four altitudinal zones support different vegetation.[2]

- The pre-puna zone (2,700 to 3,000 meters above sea level): semiarid, characterized by scattered scrubland.
- The puna zone (3,000 to 3,850 meters above sea level): more extensive and greater density of plants.
- The high Andean zone (3,850 meters to 4,200 meters above sea level): characterized by grass—primarily ichhu, *Stipa venusta*, *Festuca*, and *Azorella*.
- The subnival zone (4,200 to 4,350 meters above sea level): the upper limit for vascular plants (Villagrán and Castro 2004).

Native people recognize several ecological zones within their regional landscape. These units are components of others, which are more important in the use of the landscape and are directly associated with subsistence. Native Andeans distinguish perfectly the differences in soil types, geomorphology, microclimate, and vegetation. It is worth noting that the distinctions made by Native people correspond well to the physiognomic zones described by botanists, which, in turn, are analogous to Peruvian ethnogeography (Pulgar Vidal 1972).

For the Native population, the elements of nature are potentially sacred and can be charged with negative or positive energy; that is the way they construct their landscape. Nevertheless, for the purpose of this essay, it is important to examine more closely the subject of the sacred mountains—*mallkus* (Berenguer et al. 1984; Castro and Varela 1992; Castro and Martínez 1996; Castro 1997), *apus*, or Achachilas—since they have been objects of veneration from ancient times until the present day and are identified with the layout and order of the Qhapaq Ñan (Berenguer et al. 1984).

Testimonies and documents from the sixteenth and seventeenth centuries bear witness to the sacredness of mountains in Inka ideology and in the cultures of the peoples of Tawantinsuyu, as evidenced in such works as *Dioses y Hombres de Huarochirí*, compiled at the end of the sixteenth century by Francisco de Ávila ([1598?] 1966); *Extirpación de la idolatría del Perú*, written by Joseph de Arriaga in the early seventeenth century ([1621] 1968); as well as the texts of Felipe de Guaman Poma de Ayala ([1615] 1980), Bernabé Cobo ([1653] 1890–93), and José de Acosta ([1590] 1962). The sacredness of mountains in Andean civilization extends back to distant times (Benson 1972; Donnan 1978).

The indigenous perception of the landscape is tied to daily life and intimate knowledge. Often imbued with a sense of mystery, the knowledge of Native people incorporates the sacred nature of the landscape, which provides

This *cocha* (ritual vessel) symbolizes the still waters of Lake Titicaca. The snake designs signify water and fertility, and the spiral represents Pachamama (Mother Earth).

Inka *cocha*, AD 1450–1500. Peru. Stone. 12.7 × 45.1 × 40 cm. 23/6192. Photo by Ernest Amoroso, NMAI

human beings with privileged levels of classification and importance (Martínez 1976, 1989). For example, the mountains are considered the home of the spirits—the apus—and personify local or regional sacred entities. Some are divinities linked to livestock fertility or farming, and others can be linked to atmospheric phenomena such as thunder and lightning. Other deities protect life, health, and prosperity.

In the Peruvian mountains, these divinities are also known as *gentiles.* Martínez (1983) briefly refers to the vague and confusing boundaries between the image of the "god of the mountains" and that of the gentil, "sometimes to the point where both figures are almost superimposed." On other occasions, he notes, the "distinction is quite clear." Although their identities may be confused, in many places the god of the mountains and the gentil are recognized by both Quechua and Aymara people

as "grandfather" or "ancestor" (Berenguer et al. 1984).

This Andean concept of the landscape, formed and organized over the course of its millennial history, presents a challenge for archaeologists and historians. Every aspect of the daily life of Native people is imbued with the importance of sacred things. Images from the natural environment are used as signs to indicate true content within a metalinguistic system that makes it possible to conceptualize the world (Castro 1990). In the collective memory of the Andean people, it is possible to visualize the Qhapaq Ñan and its landscapes. In the living Andean cultures, the landscapes of the Qhapaq Ñan—the Main Andean Road —continue to be the bearers of a universal message: the human ability to transform one of the harshest geographies of the Americas into an environment full of life (Castro 2006).

The Inka Road System in the Valley of Cusco

DONATO AMADO GONZALES

T HE URBAN CORE OF CUSCO, recognized as the "honorific center" of the city, was bordered above by the heights of the Temple of the Sun, or Saqsaywaman, and below by the convergence of the Saphi and Choquechaca (also called Tullumayu) Rivers. This place where the rivers meet, known as Pumachupan (tail of the puma), was the political and religious administrative seat of the great state of Tawantinsuyu.

Several *kanchas* (walled ceremonial spaces)—Pucamarca, Hatunkancha, Amarukancha, Qora Qora, Qassana, and Kiswarkancha—were divided into two sectors: Hanancusco, which was made up of Chinchaysuyu and Antisuyu; and Hurincusco, which encompassed Collasuyu and Contisuyu. This was the home of the ruling Inkas, the royal *ayllus* (communities of extended families) and *panacas* (royal family groups) of Inka nobility. The sacred space was accessed through the *wakapunkus* (doors of the *wakas*,

View of the Cusco Valley, with several sacred mountain peaks visible in the distance. Wanakauri, Cusco, Peru, 2011. Photo by Ramiro Matos Mendieta, NMAI

21

Travelers often leave stones or other offerings at sites along the road called *apachetas*. Some of the stones here form Christian crosses as well as more traditional pyramidal shapes. Near Marcapata, Cusco, Peru, 2011. Photo by Ramiro Matos Mendieta, NMAI

or sacred spaces), which were located in strategic places such as Wakapunku de Saphi, Cuichipuncu, Arcopuncu de Ripacpampa, and Arcopuncu de Santa Clara.

This Inka city formed a central axis from which radiated a vast system of roads that integrated and linked wakas, ceremonial places, administrative sites, and production areas in the different ecological zones.

The valley of Cusco was surrounded by sacred mountains such as Wanakauri; Pachatusan; Picol; Catunqui; Senca; Mama Simona, or Yavira; Puquin; Occopata; Arahuay; and Anahuarqui, which were considered to be the city's *apus* (mountain spirits) and wakas. The valley was organized by an entire system of roads: the main roads, which were well designed and constructed, had an average width of four meters, with lateral walls. Depending on the terrain, some also had retaining and containment walls. These roads extended from the city and beyond the valley, connecting settlements throughout the four *suyus* (regions or quarters) and were therefore considered to be the actual vertebrae of the empire, with each section branching off into other roads, as required for integrating other peoples and settlements.

The entrances and exits to the roads were marked with piles of stones similar to those at *apachetas* (travelers' offering places), which also served as access portals (the Spaniards called them "Puerto [sic] del Ynga,"), where a person gave notice as people entered and exited. Such portals can still be seen in Puquin, Casaurco (Arch of Ticatica), Catunqui, and Pachatusan, among other places. On the other hand, ritual roads,

which had the Qorikancha (the Temple of the Sun) as a point of departure, were characterized by a narrow rectilinear design (2.8 centimeters wide) and were used as boundaries for crop- and grazing lands. Lateral walls associated with water channels and systems of platforms integrated and linked the wakas along the way.

The ritual roads ultimately reached a main waka, such as Wanakauri; Mama Simona, or Yavira; Pachatusan; Toma de Agua de Chacan; Muyourco; or Anahuarqui. Maintenance and care were in the hands of ayllus and panacas, following a hierarchical social order: *qollana* (those related to the Inka ruler), *payan* (the "grandfathers" and their descendants), and *cayao* (a parent or sibling of the Inka ruler).

It should be noted that small rectangular or circular platforms can be seen in the layouts of both the main and the ritual roads. These were strategically located in places with a view toward the city or the important apus, and they provided resting places (*paskanas*) for those who led or accompanied the Inka or the main priests.

above: The Rumi Colca, the entrance to Cusco on the Collasuyu road. Cusco Valley, Peru, 2014. Photo by Doug McMains, NMAI

left: Inside Cusco's Qorikancha, the lower temple of the sun, several original Inka stone *kanchas* (enclosures or compounds) remain. A contemporary painting can be seen in the passage between two of the kanchas. Convent of Santo Domingo, Cusco, Peru, 2014. Photo by Doug McMains, NMAI

© R.MAR - BELTRÁN-CABALLERO

0   100   500M

N

PANACA COMPOUNDS
A. Hanan Cusco Panancas
B. Hurin Cusco Panancas

HOUSES OF THE SUN
1. Saqsaywaman
2. Qorikancha, Cusikancha
   and other compounds

STATE COMPOUNDS AND WAKAS
   a. Hatunkancha
   b. Amarukancha
   c. Hatunrumiyoc
   d. Cuyus Manco
   e. Qora Qora
   f. Sapantiana

**SACRED GARDENS
AND AGRARIAN TERRACES**

To Chinchaysuyu

To Antisuyu

Choquechaca River

1

f

A

e

d

c

Hawkaypata

a

b

Saphi River

To Collasuyu

2

B

Tullumayu River

To Contisuyu

Chunchulmayu River

RICARDO MAR MEDINA & JOSÉ ALEJANDRO BELTRÁN-CABALLERO

Inka City Planning in Cusco

The morphology of the Cusco valley is the product of thousands of years of glacial advance and retreat. During the late Pleistocene, after the disappearance of the glaciers, the Cusco valley was flooded by three terraced lagoons that extended over more than thirty kilometers. The first of these, known as Lake Morkill, formed the basin now occupied by the present-day city of Cusco. It extended to the south as far as the Angostura, a narrow, closed pass that functioned as a natural dam. The second lagoon extended from Angostura to Kunturqaqa, and the last in its full extension covered Muyna, Huacarpay, Lucre and the surrounding area. It is thought that Lake Morkill dried up for geological reasons relating to the rupture of a dam in the Angostura area. This collapse led to the formation of a number of marshy meadows, and a similar process undoubtedly took place in the other lagoons. The present-day Lucre-Huacarpay meadow bears witness to this process in the area of the third lagoon.

Because of the flooding in the valley during the Pleistocene, the first humans who crossed the area in about 3000 BC navigated the slopes of the surrounding mountains. In addition to the hunters and gatherers who moved about on the shores of the lakes, the evolving Chanapata culture that established the first towns was followed by other cultures of equal importance, such as the Lucre. Sometime after the disintegration of the Wari administration in the region in AD 1000, the Cusco basin apparently became densely inhabited (Bauer 2008, 154–56). In the central area of the present-day city, small fragments of walls from Killke structures, which are different from and predate those of the Inka period, have been found.[1] This would confirm that the Inka layout of the city completely transformed the previous settlement. The control of these lands by the Inka people, who were increasingly prominent in the region, laid the foundations for the development of large state operations.

The establishment of Cusco as the capital of Tawantinsuyu was one of those great ventures. Many of the chronicles of the colonial era attribute this tremendously important, singular work to Pachacutic Inka Yupanqui (Betanzos [1551] 1880, 60).[2] The urban restructuring of Cusco and the reorganization of all its groups of inhabitants entailed the complete transformation of the basin environment, as geomorphological studies and archaeological

A reconstructed map of Inka Cusco in the early 1500s shows four roads extending from the Hawkaypata plaza toward each of the empire's *suyus*, or regions.

Map © R. Mar/J. A. Beltrán-Caballero.

The decoration on this *cocha* (ritual vessel) represents division of the Inka empire into four *suyus* (regions) emanating from Cusco. The four lines symbolize the main roads leading out of the city's central plaza, the Hawkaypata, toward the suyus.

Inka *cocha* with four-part division, AD 1500–1600. Tiwanaku, Bolivia. Ceramic, paint. 4.5 × 15.2 cm diam. 20/6341. Photo by Ernest Amoroso, NMAI

documentation confirm. The natural courses of the rivers were channeled or changed in order to control, redirect, and carry away rainwater, thus protecting agricultural soil and urban settlements. At the same time, extensive systems of terraces, intended to increase land surface for agricultural production, were constructed. This massive operation also included the draining of lagoons and residual swamps—which had been created while draining the old Lake Morkill—by channeling the torrents that supplied them with water.

Although the most important changes in the Cusco basin are attributed to the Inka, in reality they represent the continuation of a thousand years of adaption by the pre-Inka

cultures that developed in the valley. Some archaeological indicators provided by documentation from the Killke period have shed light on the sequence of decisions made by the Inka administration that resulted in the city's new urban configuration. For example, the only documented wall, almost thirty meters long and discovered under Calle Triunfo, shows that this street existed before the Inka layout and coincides with the main road, Qhapaq Ñan, which led toward Antisuyu. The network of regional roads may have determined the form of the pre-Inka settlement and been a factor that shaped this new urban project. The roads that preceded those of the Inka, the courses of the rivers, the transformation of the topography

through the construction of great terraces, and the position of the *wakas*, or sacred spots (often natural stone protuberances), helped to establish the main arteries that organized the new city's layout.

In designing and organizing the new Cusco, Pachacutic used an enclosed area as the main unit. This area housed the basic units of Inka spatial organization, which are part of a long Andean tradition: *kanchas*, or courtyards surrounded by structures and perimeter walls. Written sources have established the location of many of the enclosed areas and buildings in the new city: the Temple of the Sun located under the Convent of Santo Domingo, the *acllawasi* (buildings where the empire's "chosen women" lived) in the Convent of Santa Catalina, the Qassana and the Coracora on the north side of the present-day Plaza de Armas, the Amarukancha, occupied by the Jesuits, and the Qolqampata behind the Church of San Cristóbal.

In 1877, Ephraim George Squier drew up a street plan (published by Rowe in 1987), in which some of the above-mentioned complexes were included. Squier's plan differs little from the one published in 2004 by Brian Bauer (2008, 223), which includes data from other research, such as studies conducted by Max Uhle. Most of the layout of the Inka city and the remains of the walls that demarcated its enclosed areas are covered by five centuries of intense urban life. To gain a sense of the original layout we need first to observe the facades of the present-day streets such as Loreto, Triunfo, San Agustín, Hatunrumiyoc, Ladrillos, Siete Culebras, Cabracancha, Awacpinta, and Pantipata. Likewise, the Inka walls embedded in the facades of the Plaza de Armas confirm that their boundaries coincide, for the most part, with those of the ancient Plaza Hawkaypata; only the cathedral and the houses built above the Saphi River are different from their placement in the original layout. This information confirms many of the observations passed on by colonial authors, particularly in the much-commented-upon work of Garcilaso de la Vega, which have informed discussions about the Inka city since the nineteenth century.

An Inka stone wall, including the famous Hatunrumiyoc, or twelve-sided stone (left). Inka stone walls were built without mortar, but the stones were carved so precisely that not even a pin can be pushed between them. Cusco, Peru, 2014. Photos by Doug McMains, NMAI

The puma was a sacred animal associated with the earth. Under the guidance of the ninth Inka ruler, Pachacutic, Cusco took on the shape of a puma, with Saqsaywaman at the head and the confluence of the Tullumayu and Saphi Rivers marking the tail.

Chimú stirrup-spout bottle in the form of a puma, AD 1100–1400. North coast of Peru. Ceramic. 28 × 24.1 × 11.4 cm. 23/190. Photo by R. A. Whiteside

The old city of Killke, in the upper part of the valley, was converted into Tawantinsuyu's great ceremonial center, where the four main roads of the Qhapaq Ñan began. This change required that the rivers flowing down the mountainsides be channeled. Two of them, the Saphi and the Tullumayu, which flowed down the slopes from Saqsaywaman, established the boundaries of the new sacred city. The two rivers demarcate a narrow, elongated triangle that terminates in the confluence of their waters, at the place called Pumachupan (tail of the puma).

For the new urban conglomeration, the land had to be stabilized through the creation of an extensive system of terraces. The first work was completed along the rivers and their ravines. The ravine of the Tullumayu River, much deeper than that of the Saphi, required

much steeper terraces. Moreover, the steep slope that crossed the settlement at an oblique angle was modified through an extensive system of terraces that were supported by zigzagging retention walls. The system begins at the back of the cathedral, flanks Calle Tucumán under the colonial buildings, and continues across the slope of the Almirante. From there it continues, perfectly conserved, behind the buildings of Calle Suecia until it reaches the only important point that is still in public view—the great Inka wall on Calle Teqsecocha—and then continues to the slope of Saqsaywaman near San Cristóbal. The walls that support the present-day Balcón Cusqueño, where there is a difference in height of twenty meters, are part of this system. Near the rocky slope (on Calle Suecia and behind the cathedral) were several springs, which once fed the swampy terrain that existed in this area before the opening of the great Inka plaza (Sherbondy 1982, 15–16). One of the *puquios* (springs) survives. It has been redirected through a subterranean channel beneath the cathedral.

The layout of the zigzagging terraces respected at least three large boulder outcroppings. These were considered to be sacred places and came to play a significant role in the planning of Cusco. The first must have been converted into a platform, of which one corner survives: the angular wall of Calle Teqsecocha. The second is located in the small Plaza del Tricentenario and determines the place where the retaining walls turn at the back of the cathedral and progressively lose height until they disappear on Calle Triunfo, at the level of Calle Herrajes. The third outcropping in the vicinity serves as the large platform for the old Episcopal Palace. Although colonial sources and tradition (Anglés Vargas 1978, 113) locate Inka Roca's "palace" there, more recent studies regard the place as an *ushnu*, or solar observatory.[3] The place, called Hatunrumiyoc (Gran Roca, or great stone), was surrounded by a rectangular platform bordered by the most beautiful green diorite Inka walls in Cusco.

The system of walls and terraces created elevations and depressions in the new Inka city, dividing it into two well-defined topographical units. The upper city—which began above Hawkaypata, the great ceremonial terrace, and became steeper as it rose toward San Cristóbal—connected with the slopes of Saqsaywaman and was organized into several rectangular, terraced platforms. A lower, more horizontal area provided the location for three major ceremonial complexes. The first of these, Hawkaypata, was positioned next to the system of zigzagging terraces. Hatunkancha (Gran Recinto, or large enclosure) was constructed at an intermediate point, bordered by an elevated wall. It was intended to host the new capital's state functions. Finally, on the very lowest level, next to Pumachupan, were the Qorikancha's two houses of the sun. These two units are related to the two areas into which Cusco was divided: *hurin* and *hanan*. Although their boundaries are not known with certainty, they

The remains of Saqsaywaman, Cusco's upper Temple of the Sun. The zigzagging, cyclopean walls can be seen in the center. Cusco, Peru, 2011. Photo by Ramiro Matos Mendieta, NMAI

Many Inka structures in Cusco were used as foundations for colonial structures. Cusco, Peru, 2014. Photo by Doug McMains, NMAI

probably coincided with the line marked inside the city by the two main east-west roads of the Qhapaq Ñan, which extend toward Contisuyu and Antisuyu (Hyslop 1984, 47). To the south of this line, in Hurincusco, is the Qorikancha, or "golden enclosure," the main shrine of the state religion. In the area north of the line, in Hanancusco, on the slope of Saqsaywaman, is a complex with the same name, which occupies the space surrounded by the famous zigzagging cyclopean walls. The first Spaniards described it as a fortress due to the similarity of its "towers" and "ramparts" to those of medieval European castles, even though fortification was clearly not its function. The same colonial sources state that Saqsaywaman was also a house of the sun and the residence of the Shapa

Inka himself, purposes that doubtless were associated with the representative functions of the great capital.

Given the importance of dual organization in Andean traditions, the division into halves of this representative center is not surprising; the houses of the sun of Hurincusco (Qorikancha) would have had their necessary complement in the houses of the sun of Hanancusco (Saqsaywaman). Furthermore, the state character of the solar religion in Tawantinsuyu tied the role of Cusco's two houses of the sun to the seat of government, which would explain the monumental complex of Saqsaywaman and its dominant position above the city. If we take into account the geographic size of Tawantinsuyu, its large population, and the vast range of resources integrated into a centralized administration, we can be fairly confident that there were other government buildings in Cusco. The two houses of the sun and the complex of Hatunkancha, which will be discussed below, are at this time the most likely locations for the Inka seat of government.

Colonial sources cite several other enclosures in addition to the houses of the sun discussed above. Surrounding the Hawkaypata area of the great ceremonial terrace are the enclosures of Amarukancha, Hatunkancha, Kiswarkancha (or Ochullo), and the houses of Huascar, Qora Qora, and Qassana. The remaining space was probably taken up by the seats of the royal *panacas*, the Inka rulers' families.

Colonial sources situate Amarukancha, or Recinto de la Serpiente, on the opposite side of the plaza from the Qassana (Bauer 2008, 243–46). Chronicles indicate that the Jesuit Church was constructed over this complex (Sarmiento de Gamboa [1572] 1963, 113, 151), which was associated with the figure of Huascar, the penultimate Inka before the conquest, although Garcilaso ([1609] 2004, I.7.10 and II.1.32) attributed that status to Huayna Capac.

Set off from the rest of the city, the Hatunkancha, or Gran Recinto, was a center for important state functions. It was made up of several smaller units, or "local enclosures," surrounded by buildings of different types, which coexisted with other structures devoted to worship, such as fountains and wakas. It was here in the Hatunkancha district that the Acllawasi (the House of the Virgins of the Sun), and the Pucamarca (the Red Enclosure) were located, along with two temples, one dedicated to the creator god and the other to the god of thunder.[4] The *coya* herself, the sacred wife of the Shapa Inka, probably played an important role in this area of the city. The Gran Recinto was central to the design and organization of the ceremonial spaces in Pachacutic's new Cusco, as the opening of the main door toward Hawkaypata indicates.

There is no consensus as to the function or intended use of Kiswarkancha, or Ochullo,

The remains of the Qorikancha, Cusco's lower Temple of the Sun, were used by the Spanish in 1534 as a foundation for the Convent of Santo Domingo. Cusco, Peru, 2014. Photo by Doug McMains, NMAI

which is the name that appears on the enclo-sure where the cathedral stands today.[5] Pedro Pizarro ([1571] 1921, 250) notes that there was a great hall, or *kallanka*, in the northern area of the plaza, where Diego de Almagro and other Spaniards were lodged after they entered Cusco. The great hall housed the main church and the primitive Casa del Cabildo, or Council House (Rivera Serna [1534] 1965, 33), which was destroyed in 1559 when construction on the cathedral was begun under the direction of Juan Polo de Ondegardo. Blas Valera ([1585] 1950, 144) notes that the "shed" was the

temple of Tiqzi Wiracocha, a statement that contradicts Garcilaso ([1609] 2004, 439–440), who says that they were the houses of the Inka Viracocha. Bauer (2008, 241) deduces that Valera probably confused the name of the Inka Viracocha with that of the god of the same name. According to Martin de Murúa ([1616] 1992, 108), the Ochullo had in fact served as Huayna Capac's "palace" and "is presently the main church in Cusco."

The Qassana was a monumental enclosure situated to the north of Hawkaypata (Pizarro [1571] 1921, 87–88; Garcilaso [1609] 2004, 335).

It was bordered by the Saphi River and extended to the great retaining walls that frame the ceremonial plaza and face the present-day Calle Suecia. There is scant archaeological data regarding its reconstruction aside from information pertaining to the Inka walls that form the facade of the Plaza de Armas and some documented walls in the interior of the block. Nevertheless, it is possible to postulate a hypothesis about its reconstruction based on indirect sources from the city's historical property records and descriptions gleaned from colonial sources.

In most cases, the location of these complexes has been based on colonial descriptions that list where Spaniards were living in Cusco, in respect to the previous Inka inhabitants. It should be noted that the Spanish Conquest produced a massive expulsion of the old Inka elite and that the new owners still lacked a system of symbolic references for urban spaces. The most effective method was to refer to places where the important Spaniards lived. As plots changed ownership, the system for identifying former Inka structures became less precise, reflecting the transformations that occurred as the colonial city took shape over Inka foundations.[6]

The reestablishment of Cusco was the result of expanding Inka control, which now extended beyond regional boundaries. This integrative project was also aimed at altering the natural environment, thereby facilitating the settlement and reorganization of a large population. The management and distribution of water resources was the main focus for shaping the landscape, which inevitably made Cusco the symbolic and political center of Tawantinsuyu. Channeled rivers, terraces, and a complex network of canals were part of an integrated program aimed at transforming the Cusco basin. This is the only explanation for the massive hydraulic transformation, and the conversion of mountainsides and marshes into terraces and cultivated fields, all of which were created to serve intensive agricultural activity.[7] The intricate hydraulic and road systems were part of a dense network, punctuated by settlements distributed along the length and breadth of the valley, following the configuration of cultivated fields and pastures. This enormous venture was the product and also the consequence of a long architectural tradition that included the use of clay and stone in houses, granaries, temples, tombs, and all the other structures that formed part of Tawantinsuyu's material culture. The diversity of ecological environments (Murra 1975), and the system of ceremonial sites and topographical landmarks (Zuidema 1995), extends far beyond the boundaries of the Cusco Valley. Places such as Chinchero, Pisac, Ollantaytambo, and Machu Picchu were all part of a network that linked Cusco, through the Qhapaq Ñan, with the rest of Tawantinsuyu.

As the reestablishment of Cusco demonstrates, the crowning achievement of one of the most sophisticated pre-Columbian cultures in the Americas was the result of its ability to temporally and spatially organize an enormous variety of complementary but different tasks that were carried out by hundreds, thousands, and even millions of people. Thus, the Inka culture was part of a millennial history of adaptation by Andean societies to a vast, extraordinarily varied, and oftentimes harsh territory.

Mountains and the Sacred Landscape of the Inka

CHRISTIAN VITRY

CHRISTIAN VITRY

THERE ARE PLACES where the landscape and geological formations seem to have had a particular influence on people. Such is the case in the Andes, especially during the fifteenth and sixteenth centuries, when the Inka Empire, or Tawantinsuyu, was at its height.

The policy of expansion in Tawantinsuyu was not solely of a political and economic nature—it was also symbolic and religious. The empire grew in a horizontal fashion, steadily amassing faraway lands, and also vertically, toward the highest peaks of the continent, those that almost touch the sky and were considered to be close to the celestial deities. Indeed, there is archaeological evidence of Inka rituals on approximately two hundred mountains, some reaching heights of more than 6,700 meters, dating several centuries before mountain climbing became a sport.

Mountains represent a break in the homogeneity of the landscape, a vertical projection in a horizontal world, an axis of the relationship between high and low. Mountains, therefore, offer an ideal element for associating the landscape with the almost universal

Sacred peaks are believed to be the homes of *apus,* powerful mountain spirits. Llullaillaco, Argentina, 2011. Photo by Christian Vitry

dual conception of what is earthly and what is celestial. Humanity depends on water for life, and the mountains provide the main reservoir and the place where rivers have their sources. In the Andes it is believed that the mountains take water from the sky and return it to the earth in the form of rivers flowing down their slopes; from both a mystical and a material point of view, mountains are tied to human beings across time and space.

Before the arrival of the Inka, mountains were venerated in the Collasuyu and throughout much of the Andes, but they were never climbed because they were considered to belong to the spirits of ancestors and other divinities and were therefore places where humans could not go. The Inka, who presented themselves to the communities they conquered as the children of the sun, as nearly divine beings and heirs to an ancestral tradition, set themselves the task of climbing the revered mountains (Meyers 2002, 525–35). To the surprise of many ethnic groups, the gods did not punish them and, thus, their symbolic power was reconfirmed, gaining them the respect and fear of the communities annexed to Tawantinsuyu.

Among the important ceremonies related to the mountains was the Capacocha, the official rite of the Inka Empire that defined sacred geography and imperial politics (McEwan and Silva 1989, 163–85). The ritual took place on mountains, islands, and other sanctuaries, or *wakas*, located throughout Tawantinsuyu. From the four corners of the Inka Empire, villages sent one or more children to Cusco so that they could be offered in sacrifice as part of the ceremony, usually on top of a sacred mountain.

Human offerings were made only in the most important places and on special occasions, such as the death of an Inka who was embarking on his journey toward the time of his ancestors. The lives offered up were repaid with health and prosperity. These human offerings were also a way of strengthening the ties between the center of the empire and the outlying areas, as well as between human beings and the Andean gods (McEwan and van de Guchte 1992, 359–71).

Scientists have located twenty-nine bodies offered in Capacocha sacrifice at various latitudes, from Isla de la Plata off the Ecuadorean coast to the snow-covered El Plomo in Santiago, Chile, locations separated by a distance of almost four thousand kilometers. Twenty-seven bodies were removed from fourteen mountains, the heights of which—like those of 96 percent of the mountains in the Collasuyu region, to the south of Cusco—range from 5,000 to 6,739 meters.

The greatest concentration of mountains with evidence of human offerings is around Arequipa, a city 315 kilometers south of Cusco. The volcanoes Misti (5,596 meters), Pichu Pichu (5,634 meters), and Chachani (6,057 meters) are located in this region. To the northwest is Ampato (6,270 meters), and farther away are Coropuna (6,415 meters) and Sara Sara (5,505 meters). On these mountains, between 250 and

Carved offerings such as this llama, which is made from the shell of a *Spondylus* mollusk, are frequently found at high-altitude Capacocha (child sacrifice) sites like those on Argentina's Llullaillaco Volcano. The sites may be thousands of kilometers from the shell's coastal origins.

Inka llama figurine, AD 1450–1532. Trujillo, Peru. *Spondylus* shell. 4.1 × 3.3 × 0.6 cm. 21/2309. Photo by Ernest Amoroso, NMAI

Ruins of a stone structure at the summit of Llullaillaco, near a site where the Inka sacrificed children in ceremonies called Capacochas. Llullaillaco, Argentina, 2011. Photo by Christian Vitry

330 kilometers from Cusco, the Inka are known to have offered up the lives of nineteen children in religious ceremonies.

Another concentration of mountains where human offerings took place is in northeastern Argentina, thirteen hundred kilometers from Cusco, in the desert region of the altiplano, where the volcanoes Llullaillaco (6,739 meters), Quewar (6,130 meters), and Chañi (5,896 meters) are located. Farther south, in the Eastern Cordillera, is Chuscha Mountain (5,420 meters). The Capacocha presently thought to have taken place the farthest from Cusco has been identified in Chile on snow-covered El Plomo (5,425 meters), 2,200 kilometers away as the crow flies (Vitry 2008, 47–65).

Of all the mountains where human offerings were made, one stands out for its height: the volcano Llullaillaco, at 6,739 meters, is among the highest mountains on the continent and home to the highest archaeological site on the planet. It was there that the Inka built a complex system of sites, located at different heights and joined together by ceremonial roads that led to the highest point, where two children around the ages of six and seven were sacrificed together with a girl who was approximately fifteen.

The three bodies were found buried inside a rectangular platform along with a variety of rich grave goods (Reinhard 1983, 27–62; 1999, 36–55; Reinhard and Ceruti 2000).

These grave goods included gold and silver as well as anthropomorphic and zoomorphic statuettes, representing both sexes, made from the shells of bivalve mollusks of the *Spondylus* genus. The human figurines are dressed with textiles, feather headdresses, metal breastplates, shell pendants, chains, bags or purses, and other accessories. Different types of miniature ceramic containers were found, along with wooden cups, combs, whole and crushed mollusk shells, purses containing coca leaves and food, and fine textiles. In the context of the Capacocha, all these items are typical of those most frequently found at other sites.

Among the objects commonly included among grave goods are anthropomorphic statuettes; nearly one hundred of these miniatures have been found in the Andes. The statuettes are made of mineral, animal, and vegetable materials that are found throughout the Andes and the surrounding areas, indicating that these objects probably originated in different regions of Tawantinsuyu.

The Inka expansion led to the diversification of natural resources, which is reflected in the range of sumptuous elements used for offerings, the most original of which were the *Spondylus* shells. The mollusk became a traditional part of offerings on mountain peaks. After a journey of thousands of kilometers on the legendary Qhapaq Ñan—from the depth of the seas almost to the skies—the shells ritually provided a vital element: water.[1]

Miniature figurines of men and women have been found at Capacocha (child sacrifice) sites. In some cases, the figurines have been recovered dressed in elaborate clothing and feathered headdresses, preserved by cold temperatures at the high-altitude sites.

Inka female figurine, AD 1470–1532. Lima, Peru. Silver alloy. 9.5 × 2.5 × 2.9 cm. 19/9106. Photo by Ernest Amoroso, NMAI

Ceramic containers found among grave goods also shed some light on history. The physical and chemical research shows that they originated in Cusco and Lake Titicaca (Bray et al. 2005, 82–100). In the Andes are three pan-Andean worship centers: the Qorikancha temple in Cusco, Pachacamac on the coast, and Lake Titicaca's Isla del Sol (Island of the Sun) and Isla de la Luna (Island of the Moon). (Stanish and Bauer 2011) The children, who were to be sacrificed and thus transformed into divinities, were taken from Cusco and, for the purpose of giving greater symbolic value to the ceremony and the offerings, probably passed by Lake Titicaca on their long pilgrimage toward the south. These state processions, which were of great importance to the Inka, had, among other missions, the aim of creating and legitimizing new spaces for the sacred geography that was being consolidated thousands of kilometers from Cusco.

Llullaillaco is the site of another important recent discovery (Vitry 2014). Five shoes, all without mates, were found in the natural hollow of a rock at the base of the volcano, along with those the Inka used to make their ascents. Called *orco kawkachun* (mountain shoes), they were made with four to eight layers of llama wool. Some of the seams were sewn with human hair while other, more superficial seams were sewn with a thread known as *lloke*,[2] indicating that they were made to resist cold and provide divine

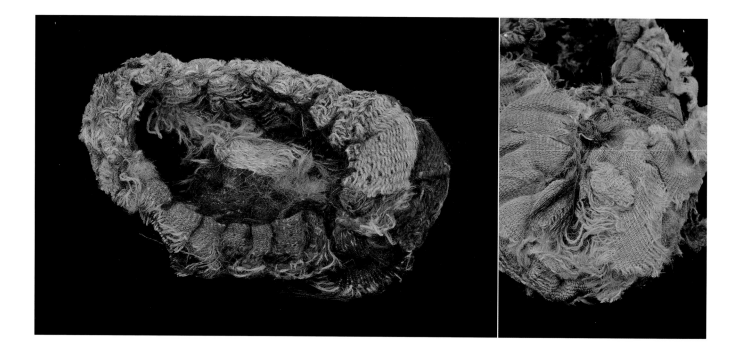

Orco kawkachun (mountain shoes), ca. AD 1400. Llullaillaco, Argentina. Llama fiber, human hair. 27 × 13.7 × 7.5 cm. Museum of High Altitude Archaeology of Salta. Photo reproduced with the permission of Lisardo Francisco Maggipinto

protection for their wearers (López Campeny 2007), who had to traverse a very sacred place. The shoes found at Llullaillaco were a type used especially for climbing high mountains and had not been identified previously.[3] Their discovery was one of great importance for those who study the pre-Hispanic Andean world and for all humanity, since the shoes offer some insight into the way these mystical mountaineers climbed hundreds of mountains in the Andes.

In the pre-Hispanic Andean cultural landscape, the mountains were particularly significant for their role in the social construction of geographic space, both visually and conceptually, and as structural landmarks that contributed to the creation, re-creation, and geo-cultural assimilation of the new order that the Inka established in a vast territory.

facing: This pendant depicts Tiqzi Wiracocha, the ruler of the universe. He was a powerful god to many Andean people, and the Inka reinforced their hegemony by tracing their roots back to Inti, the son of Tiqzi.

Gold pendant with image of creator god Tiqzi Wiracocha, AD 800–1100. Peru. Gold, silver, and copper alloy. 4.75 × 3.25 × .75 cm. 19/907. Photo by Ernest Amoroso, NMAI

CHAPTER TWO

Inka Roads: Engineering and Empire Building

KENNETH R. WRIGHT & RUTH M. WRIGHT

THE INKA TRAILS NEAR MACHU PICCHU

I n an empire that stretched nearly four thousand kilometers from north to south and crossed mountain ranges higher than the Alps, the Inka built a road system that was a wonder of the ancient world. Its superlative design and construction was accomplished without the advantages of a written language, and without the use of the wheel, iron, or steel; the Inka had the design skills, labor forces, and organizational capacity, however, to build trails that were not just routes for travel from one place to the next but also stunning achievements in road development.

Many who know about the marvels of the ancient Inka Trail system have learned about them by hiking from the Kilometer 88 Railroad Stop to Machu Picchu, a four- to five-day trip. Few, however, are aware of the myriad parts and pieces that make up the whole of the Inka Trail. It is important to note that the Inka Trail did not stop at Machu Picchu but continued beyond it and down the east flank to the left bank of the Urubamba River. There, it linked with the trail that took ancient runners, military personnel, and Inka travelers down farther, into the Amazon basin.

The last Inka *tampu* (accommodation for travelers) on the Inka Trail from Cusco is Winaywayna, but it is at the sun gate Intipunku that you get your first breathtaking view of Machu Picchu. Between the Intipunku and the main gate of Machu Picchu, a trail constructed of carefully placed stones descends about two kilometers past some important and interesting places.

A roadway network as grand as the Inka Trail needed supporting infrastructure in the form of terraces and culverts to manage unstable hillsides and provide drainage. The outside walls of these terraces, even the highest ones, are distinctive in that they are often vertical, without the sloping pitch of typical Inka architecture. Stations to house the military guards who controlled trail use can be found at regular intervals along the extensive roadway system.

Ceremonial Rock

After leaving Intipunku, the trail provides a pleasant and scenic route along and down the north slope of Machu Picchu Mountain, with the first stopping point at a religious and ceremonial carved rock that is now known as Huaca #17. This place consists of the carved rock, two *wayrana*-style buildings (structures with open fronts and thatched roofs), and a fine, wide granite stairway leading uphill into

As overgrown vegetation was cleared from the platform at the junction of the main Inka Trail and Trail L, a view of Machu Picchu emerged through the tree branches. Machu Picchu, Peru, 1999. Wright Water Engineers, Inc.

forest, one immediately encounters a narrow stairway leading up to a viewing platform with a spectacular view. Trail L takes a sharp turn to the left at the base of the narrow stairway and continues high up to the mountain ridge between Intipunku and the summit of Machu Picchu Mountain. Hikers should be sure to take time to appreciate the views from the platform; here Inka security personnel monitored the scene and scanned the countryside to insure against unwanted visitors.

Just 250 meters down the trail from Huaca #17, in the forest off to the right, is an isolated building on a large flat rock with a room underneath. As one moves down the trail beyond that building, there are fine examples of trail construction where an in situ granite rock is shaped and carefully integrated into the trail. About five hundred meters farther down, a huge overhanging rock becomes visible on the left side.

Overhanging Rock

This fifteen-meter-high overhanging rock is about 350 meters from the Machu Picchu main gate. It is the site of one of the cemeteries where in 1912 Hiram Bingham found the finest grave in Machu Picchu, which he designated Grave #26. In it was a female skeleton in a fetal position along with the remains of a small dog and exquisite artifacts including a pot. She must have been an important person to be buried in this special way. The pot is a well-known Inka artifact.

Drainage Culvert

Farther downhill, and only a short distance from the main gate of Machu Picchu, lies a little-known dual-purpose highway structure that is both a drainage culvert and an underpass. It was planned, designed, and built so that from inside the culvert, the view of the holy mountain of Putucusi is perfectly framed. A

The outlet of a drainage culvert under the Inka Trail frames a view of the holy mountain of Putucusi. Machu Picchu, Peru, 1999. Wright Water Engineers, Inc.

the forest, to the junction with the little-known trail that we designated as Trail L.

The carved rock is eight meters long and nearly six meters wide with five large, carved rectangular platforms. The stone has a ritual function associated with the Inka Trail, as well as with the important junction. The carved rock and the related structures on both sides of the trail provided a ceremonial environment and a place for making offerings.

Walking up the granite staircase into the

visit to Machu Picchu is not complete without a stop at the culvert, where there is a spectacular view of a mountain that is still revered by the local Quechua people.

The culvert was installed to protect the Inka Trail from being damaged by drainage flow and flooding. The upstream basin contains two hectares of tributary area. To handle the passage of workers under the trail and the expected water flow, the engineers built the culvert to precise dimensions, as shown in Table 1.

The final trail structure one sees before entering Machu Picchu is the beloved and frequently photographed guardhouse that overlooks Machu Picchu. This environmentally situated and aesthetically built three-walled security station was an important facility that served as a military focal point for monitoring and limiting access to the royal estate from

TABLE 1. Inca Trail Highway Culvert

Component	Parameter	Metric Units
Inlet	Height	0.8 m
	Width	0.6 m
	Area	0.5 m^2
Outlet	Height	2.0 m
	Width	0.6 m
	Area	1.2 m^2
Approach Channel	Height	1.9 m
	Width	0.6 m
	Area	1.1 m
Entrance to Outlet	Length	2.1 m
Drainage Basin	Area	2 ha
Coefficient of runoff		0.1
Construction material		Granite Stones

Wright Water Engineers, Inc., 1999

The important guardhouse along the Inka Trail was built to control trail access and use and create an aesthetic setting. Machu Picchu, Peru, 1999. Wright Water Engineers, Inc.

above, from the river below, and from Llacta-pata to the west.

The massive main gate, which is downhill from the guardhouse and has long been considered the end of the Inka Trail, is a tribute to Inka highway builders. The trail and gate are aesthetically joined, and the gate perfectly frames the view of the holy mountain of Huayna Picchu.

East Flank Inka Trail

A long-hidden and impressive portion of the Inka Trail that connects the royal estate of Machu Picchu with the Urubamba River below was revealed by a team of experts during paleohydrological fieldwork from 1997 to 1999. This was a fruitful period of research at Machu Picchu, with Alfredo Valencia Zegarra serving brilliantly as resident archaeologist. Valencia had special knowledge of portions of the east flank because, as a student at the Universidad Nacional de San Antonio Abad del Cusco, he had been sent by his professor onto the steep slope after a forest fire exposed the hillside to inspect the area and to map terraces. His work was later lost at the university.

The east flank trail is connected to the long granite stairway on the east end of Machu Picchu's urban sector. The granite stairway begins

sixty meters north of Intimachay and thirty meters south of the six-building *colcas* (grain storehouses). Taking into account this stairway and other pathway evidence in Machu Picchu, and Valencia's research on terrace systems on the east flank, a field team hypothesized the existence of a major trail there. What they found exceeded their expectations.

The trail they discovered is 1.8 kilometers long, with an elevation drop of 525 meters from the colcas to the river below. Along the trail are several fountains, an Inka building, and impressive staircases, caves, extensive terraces, and a stairway carved into in situ granite. At the bottom of the trail, at the Urubamba River landing, a remarkable Inka wall has somehow withstood nearly five hundred years of river flow and major floods.

The east flank trail was built on a steep and unstable forested mountainside using granite stones well embedded in the thick soil. Over the centuries, as the trail was covered with soil, a vegetative mat, and forest litter it became lost.

To locate and uncover the trail, the team tried to think like Inka trail builders. Eight seasoned Quechua *macheteros* (machete wielders) and two Peruvian archaeologists probed the thick ground cover with their swordlike steel instruments, listening for the clunk of metal

Inka Trail profile view from the Machu Picchu *colcas* (storehouses) to the Urubamba River. Machu Picchu, Peru, 1999. Wright Water Engineers, Inc.

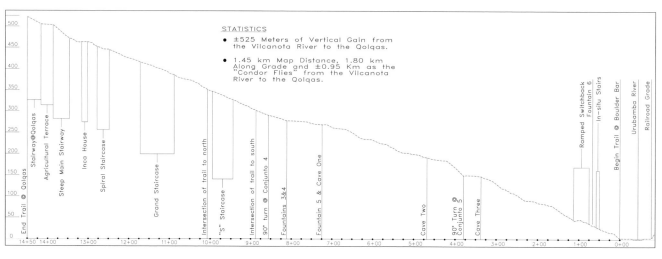

Extensive clearing of 450 years of debris and vegetation along the east flank trail exposed two ceremonial fountains in tandem. Following the clearing, vegetation tried once again to reclaim the area. Machu Picchu, Peru, 1999. Wright Water Engineers, Inc.

on granite. Moving up and down the slope, they located buried stone pavers, uncovered segments, and made connections. Each section of trail and each special curve or stairway told of Inka trail-building genius. The Quechua members of the field team were bursting with pride at their ancestors' work.

Inka Building

Not far from the maintained formal staircase that served as access to the colcas at the edge of Machu Picchu, there are the remains of an Inka building. This building likely served as a security control station to limit entry into Machu Picchu from the Urubamba River. The walls are preserved only to a height of a half-meter.

The wayrana-style building is rectangular with a length of five meters and width of 2.7 meters. The walls are a half-meter wide, while the back wall of the building is a large rock.

Ceremonial Fountains

The field team discovered two ceremonial fountains about halfway down to the river. Although they had been buried for centuries, a telltale carved stone channel was seen poking through the earth, marking the spot where the field team began to clear away the accumulated debris. Further clearing produced the two fine fountains, which are similar to the sixteen above in Machu Picchu but with unique entrance channels shaped like modern Venturi

The sight of Mount Yanatin and the Urubamba River from the ceremonial fountains is one of the most stellar views in the vicinity of Machu Picchu. Mount Yanatin is framed by Putucusi and Huayna Picchu mountains. The horizontal white line is an excavation control string. Machu Picchu, Peru, 1999. Wright Water Engineers, Inc.

tubes. The shapes sped up the water flow for improved water jets into the fountains.

When the water channels were cleaned of almost five hundred years of silt and debris, the fountains suddenly began to flow! In ten minutes, the water ran clear, and the fountains became a convenient water source for the crew. The two fountains were situated at a particular location where the view of the river and Mount Yanantin was framed between two mountain-sides. This perfect view was not a coincidence.

On completing the excavation of the two fountains, one of the Quechua men in the excavation crew, Florencio Almiro Dueñas, called the team together for a traditional Inka thanksgiving prayer. The prayer was made in the Quechua language, the language of the Inka, and translates as follows:

> Today, having finished our excavations at Machu Picchu next to this water fountain, I call to the spirits of the Gods of Machu Picchu, Putucusi, Intipunku and Mandor. Here, Pachamama—Pacha earth, beautiful mother, do not let the fountains go dry; every year water must flow forth so that we can drink.

Only eighty-five meters down the trail from the two ceremonial fountains, the team discovered another, similar fountain, which included a short tunnel into the granite bedrock that served to collect water. This fountain had been destroyed by a large rock that fell from the cliff of Huayna Picchu mountain.

Stairways

Near the fountains were perfectly formed steps of shaped granite stones forming a staircase more than three meters wide. The care taken by the Inka civil engineers to create the trail stairways was extraordinary. The stones were still in place more than four centuries after they were built. Nearby, stairways led off of the main trail to service the terraces that protected the trail from landslides and erosion.

Terraces

The east flank terraces associated with Inka Trail erosion control are extraordinary in terms of their placement, design, and construction. Made to complement the trail and to create stabilization of the steep, landslide-prone mountainside, they have served their purpose well.

During the trail excavation work, other terraces were found and cleared. Associated with these terraces are two utilitarian fountains that are unremarkable in their form. These common fountains would have been used by agricultural workers. All of the terraces on the east flank were found in a good state of preservation, which testifies to the high quality of workmanship of the Inka terrace builders.

Caves

Down the trail from the ceremonial fountains are three caves, two of which Bingham examined in 1912 for burials. The third cave, immediately above the ceremonial fountains, was completely walled with loose-fitting stones. When opened, this cave was found to be partially filled with gravel.

Bedrock In Situ Carved Stairway

Not far from the bottom of the trail, near the Urubamba River's left bank, is a stunning, fourteen-step stairway carved into the granite bedrock. Above the stairway there is a low wall built on top of a rock face that ranges up to four meters high.

River Landing

Eighteen hundred meters down the trail from the Machu Picchu colcas, the east flank Inka Trail exploration team reached the left bank of

From the top of Huayna Picchu mountain, an Inka system of protective terraces can be admired. The sturdy terrace complex protected the Inka Trail from landslides. Machu Picchu, Peru, 1999. Wright Water Engineers, Inc.

the Urubamba River. Here, a natural low-water rock bar of river-deposited stones reveals two remarkable features. One is a clear view to the Machu Picchu guardhouse, which means that the trail landing would have been monitored by the uphill security personnel. The second, at river level, is an intact 1.2-meter-high Inka wall, some six meters long. Most of the wall has been lost to river erosion and displacement, but the remaining portion represents a minor construction miracle; one would expect the river to have destroyed the entire wall over the centuries.

On the left bank and beyond the river landing, no trace of the Inka Trail or a bridge crossing of the Urubamba River can be seen. The beautiful Inka Trail had come to an end.

Inka Perfection

It is clear why so many people are admirers of Inka ingenuity. Few modern highways or trails have as many exquisite features as the stretch of the Inka Trail described here. Without modern tools or even a written language, the Inka exhibited sheer force of will to make many of the things they created functional, beautiful, and enduring. The Inka Trail is a perfect example of the Inka ability to construct magnificent features in harmony with their surroundings.

The wide granite stairway along the Inka Trail tells the story of workmen five centuries ago who measured success by work quality and longevity of function. Machu Picchu, Peru, 1999. Wright Water Engineers, Inc.

A Quechua man walks the Inka Road. Pisac, Peru. The Inka ruins at Pisac may also be those of a royal estate.
Photo by Ramiro Matos Mendieta, NMAI

JOHN OCHSENDORF

SPANNING THE ANDES

History and Technology of Inka Suspension Bridges

In response to the difficult terrain of the Andes Mountains, the Inka civilization constructed numerous suspension bridges to link together the Qhapaq Ñan. These bridges were essential to the expansion and organization of the state and played a crucial role in the social history of the region from the thirteenth through the nineteenth centuries. The bridges solved so well the problem of crossing the gorges of the Andean region that many of them survived for centuries after the fall of the Inka Empire and continued to serve as vital links in the road system until the twentieth century. There is a rich archival record of the bridges, because most written accounts of travel in the Andean region since 1531 describe them. In fact, many of the earliest chronicles from the sixteenth and seventeenth centuries include detailed descriptions of the history and construction of the bridge network. This essay builds upon the pioneering research on Inka roads and bridges by Victor von Hagen (1955), Alberto Regal (1972), Daniel Gade (1981), and John Hyslop (1984).

Inka suspension bridges differ from modern suspension bridges, which have a horizontal roadway suspended from parabolic cables. The Inka bridges may be more accurately referred to as "suspended" bridges or "catenary" bridges, since the main cables serve as the walkway of the bridge. Inka suspension bridges have three primary characteristics: braided cables of natural fiber, which form the floor and handrails; stone abutments that anchor the cables; and vertical ties between the main cables and the handrails.

These elements are clearly seen in a sixteenth-century drawing of an Inka bridge by Felipe de Guaman Poma de Ayala (Guaman Poma de Ayala [1615] 1956). One Inka-period suspension bridge still exists near Huinchiri, Peru, and it is strikingly similar to Guaman Poma's four-hundred-year-old drawing (McIntyre 1973, 729; Bauer 2006, 468–93). The Q'eswachaka, or grass bridge, has survived to the present day via continual replacement during an annual festival in which local villages rebuild the bridge cables from braided grass. This bridge has attracted wider attention in recent years and was featured in a documentary titled *Secrets of Lost Empires* (von Hagen 1996, 180–221).

The construction process for Inka suspension bridges is highlighted in many of the chronicles, most notably those of Juan de Betanzos ([1557] 1996) and Garcilaso de la

Q'eswachaka suspension bridge. Apurímac River, Canas Province, Peru, 2014. Photo by Doug McMains, NMAI

An Inka suspension bridge over the Pampas River. Ephraim George Squier (1821–1888). Wood engraving published in *Peru: Incidents of Travel and Exploration in the Land of the Incas* (1877). Courtesy of Smithsonian Institution Libraries

the rungs of a ladder. Each of the thick osier ropes is twisted round each of these beams so that the bridge will remain taut and not sag with its own weight, which is very considerable. But however much it is stretched, it always sinks in the middle and assumes a curved shape, so that in crossing one first descends and then mounts the other side; if there is a strong breeze at all it rocks. Three of the great ropes are used for the floor of the bridge, and the other two as handrails on either side. (Book Three, Chapter VII)

Illustrations from Ephraim George Squier, a nineteenth-century American traveler, provide two views of the large Inka suspension bridge over the Pampas River, which was capable of supporting horses and hundreds of pedestrians. Though the drawings are based on nineteenth-century photos, as shown by Bauer (2006), the bridges represent Inka technology that was still in daily use some 350 years after the fall of the Inka Empire.

The Inka were the only preindustrial American civilization to develop suspension bridges, though the exact origin of the bridges is unknown. The archival records suggest that the major bridges are linked to the rise of the Inka Empire, and it is therefore likely that they did not exist until the thirteenth or fourteenth century. It is possible that the bridges could have existed prior to the thirteenth century and may even predate the Inka culture, but additional archaeological studies are required to date the roads and the associated bridges. Similar bridges existed in other mountainous regions of the world, most notably in the Himalaya and ancient China, where iron chain suspension bridges existed more than a thousand years earlier (Needham 1971). Civilizations in mountainous regions around the world were faced with the same technical problem, and they independently discovered similar solutions.

Vega ([1609] 1994). The careful description by Garcilaso serves as a good introduction to the materials and geometry of such a bridge:

They make five ropes of the thickest kind; and to get them across the river they swim or use rafts carrying a thin cord to which is attached a cable as thick as the human arm. . . . They mount the cables on two high supports that have been cut out of the living rock in a convenient place, or they make the supports, of masonry, as strong as rock. From side to side of these hollow spaces run five or six beams placed one above another like

The Inka suspension bridge over the Pampas River spanned 135 feet. It was about 30 percent longer than any Spanish bridge at the time. Ephraim George Squier (1821–1888). Wood engraving published in *Peru: Incidents of Travel and Exploration in the Land of the Incas* (1877). Courtesy of Smithsonian Institution Libraries

Inka Expansion via Bridge Construction

In the difficult terrain of the Andes Mountains, rivers and canyons formed natural barriers, which had historically separated different cultural zones. Inka expansion and control of most of the Andean region may have been partly due to their construction of long-span suspension bridges, which united regions that had previously been isolated from one another. The bridges played an important role in the initial expansion of the empire, and their strategic importance in warfare continued for centuries.

The military uses of the bridges can be divided into two distinct activities: for initial conquest of new regions and continued control of land previously conquered.

Numerous chroniclers claim that the Inka constructed suspension bridges to conquer new territories. The most significant early reference to this practice is from Garcilaso de la Vega, who titled one chapter of his history "Many towns are reduced; the Inka [Mayta Cápac] orders the construction of a bridge of osiers." The chapter opens with the following passage:

He [Mayta Cápac] spent three years in these journeys and in reducing the inhabitants and establishing his laws and government among them. Then he returned to Cuzco, where he was welcomed with great festivities and rejoicing. Having rested two or three years, he ordered supplies and men to be brought together for a new conquest, for his spirit could not brook idleness, and he resolved to go to the area west from Cuzco, which they call Cuntisuyu, where there are many great provinces. As he had to pass the great river called Apurímac, he ordered a bridge to be prepared for the passage of his army. He drew the plan for it after consulting the best intelligences among the Indians. (Garcilaso [1609] 1994, 149)

This passage links the early expansion of the Inka Empire with the Inka Mayta Capac, who conquered new lands to the west of Cusco in the thirteenth century. This is the earliest reference to Inka bridge construction and it is specifically linked to the conquest of a new region. In a subsequent chapter, titled "Many tribes are reduced voluntarily to submission by the fame of the bridge," Garcilaso continues:

[The bridge] alone sufficed to cause many provinces of the region to submit to the Inka without any reservations, one being the part called Chumpivillca in the district of Cunti- suyu, which is twenty leagues long and more than ten broad. He was welcomed as their lord with a good will because of his face as a child of the Sun and because of the mar- velous new work that seemed only possible for men come down from heaven. (Garcilaso [1609] 1994, 151)

The practice of conquest through bridge construction continued under later Inkas, and Garcilaso goes on to describe conquests by Capac Yupanqui and Inka Roca, the fifth and sixth Inkas, as well as Pachacutic, the ninth Inka, who came to power in approximately 1438 and led the greatest expansion of the Inka Empire (Rowe 1946, 183–330). Father Bernabé Cobo and Juan de Betanzos both give accounts of Pachacutic's construction of bridges as an act of conquering new lands (Cobo [1653] 1979, 135; Betanzos [1557] 1996). After describing the construction process for the Apurímac Bridge, Betanzos writes:

With all of his men on the other side, he [Pachacutic] went with them to a settlement called Curahuasi, which is three leagues from there. When they went there, the Indians of those regions, the Quichuas, Umasayos, Aymaraes, Yanaguaras, Chumbibilcas, and Chancas, came out to offer them peace, obedience, and vassalage. The Inka did them many great favors and thus won them over with his powerful forces. Thus the Inka went on his way and reached the Abancay River, where he ordered his soldiers and captains to have those who could swim jump into the river and swim across. Then they were to get to work on the supports for two more bridges just like the last ones. They acted on this order right away and made them. Right there many other caciques and lords offered peace. (Part 1, Chapter XVIII)

As these examples relate, the suspension bridges were essential to the expansion of the Inka Empire from the thirteenth to the six- teenth centuries. Clearly, the deep canyons of the Andean region presented natural bound- aries for different regions, and the conquering Inka forces overcame the boundaries through the construction of bridges. The bridges were thus essential to the construction of the Qhapaq Ñan in newly conquered regions.

Control and Maintenance of Bridges

Once constructed, such suspension bridges played important strategic roles in the continued control of land. The bridges were particularly necessary during warfare, and the practice of cutting or burning suspension bridges was common before the Spanish arrived. Betanzos ([1557] 1996, 209) relates several instances of bridges being burned and cut during the Inka civil war of the early sixteenth century to isolate opposing military forces. Betanzos (111) also describes measures to protect bridges from opposing forces and to maintain a stock of repair materials. The strategic importance of suspension bridges continued well into the nineteenth century. Naturally, the bridges played a central role in the Spanish Conquest of 1532, and the Inka destroyed bridges in a failed attempt to prevent the Spanish from reaching Cusco. During an uprising in 1548, Gonzalez Pizarro's men cut the four main suspension bridges that provided access to Cusco (Cieza de León [1553] 1998, 12). As Hemming (1970, 102) has noted, armies would burn bridges with two purposes in mind: to slow the pursuing army and to prevent thoughts of retreat among soldiers of the leading army. Once a bridge was destroyed, creating a new crossing took at least a few days and often required several weeks.

In addition to their important role in the expansion and control of territory in South America, the bridges offer rare insight into the Inka administration of construction and maintenance in large civil projects. In the chronicles describing the role of the individual Inka in the design and construction of the

The annual rebuilding of the Q'eswachaka suspension bridge brings together four communities in a four-day festival, with men, women, and children all participating. Apurímac River, Canas Province, Peru, 2014. Photo by Joseph Dutra

The floor stabilizing sticks of the Q'eswachaka suspension bridge. Apurímac River, Canas Province, Peru, 2014. Photo by Doug McMains, NMAI

the river] on which he put crosspieces of long stones and thick wooden beams. Then he had them make a cable from some twigs that, being quite thin and strong, resemble those of wicker. He had these cables made one and a half times the width of the river. (Betanzos [1557] 1996, 85)

In addition to the role of the individual Inka in construction, the long-term maintenance and repair of suspension bridges offers insight into the organization of public works during the Inka Empire. This maintenance system has proven to be so effective that the Q'eswachaka continues to be replaced each year, though a modern steel truss bridge has existed beside the Inka bridge since the 1960s. The survival of the last remaining Inka bridge can be attributed to the system of shared labor that Garcilaso ([1609] 1994, 149–50) described four hundred years ago. Additional descriptions by Bernabé Cobo illustrate the Inka division of labor in the maintenance of roads and bridges:

> The task of repairing these roads and the bridges that were on them for crossing the rivers was the responsibility of the inhabitants of the provinces and towns that the roads ran through. The people came to these tasks in community groups, according to the number of workers required from each province in the work distribution that the caciques and governors made for this purpose, and the service and work that they rendered for this type of tribute was very hard. (Cobo [1653] 1979, 227)

Beyond the communal system of maintenance, certain bridges may have been guarded and repaired by a *chakacamayuc*, or bridge-keeper. Guaman Poma ([1615] 1956) draws such a figure and claims that the bridge-keeper was responsible for collecting tolls as well as maintaining the bridge. Today, the annual reconstruction of

bridges, it is notable that the Inka took an active role, sometimes contributing his own labor. For example, in his record of building a road through a swamp, Garcilaso ([1609] 1994, 152) gives an account of the Inka Mayta Capac's role in construction.

All of the chronicles make clear that the Inka ruler played an active role in construction and was not an observer in the creation of such large-scale public works. Betanzos describes the construction of a suspension bridge over the Apurímac that Pachacutic directed at each stage.

> With this done and arranged, Pachacuti Inka Yupanque left the city of Cuzco accompanied by one hundred thousand warriors, who always repaired the roads as they went along. Up and down the slopes he had them make stone stairs so that the travelers could walk up and down more easily. When he reached the Apurímac River, which is ten leagues from the city of Cuzco, he had them build bridge pillars or towers [two on each side of

the Q'eswachaka continues to be directed by a chakacamayuc as a remnant of the Inka period (von Hagen 1996).

Suspension Bridges as Technological Exchange

Finally, suspension bridges represent an unusual example of technological exchange between the Spanish and the Inka. Spanish construction technology in the sixteenth century was heavily indebted to Roman construction: stone stacked on stone to create massive structures acting in pure compression. The use of lightweight materials in tension to create long-span structures represented a new technology to the Spanish, and it was the exact opposite of the sixteenth-century European concept of a bridge.

Upon encountering long-span suspension bridges for the first time, the Spanish conquistadors reacted with a mixture of admiration and fear. Cieza ([1553] 1998, 13) gives an account of the Spanish forces crossing over a great suspension bridge "so strong that horses can gallop over it as though they were crossing the bridge of Alcántara, or of Cordoba." Cieza's reference to the great Roman arch bridges illustrates the Spanish perception of a bridge in the Roman tradition of compression bridges, as opposed to the Inka tradition of tension bridges. In part because of their unfamiliarity with suspension bridges, the Spanish were afraid of them. Pedro Sancho recalled how his first crossing terrified him: "To someone unaccustomed to it, the crossing appears dangerous because the bridge sags with its long span . . . so that one is continually going down until the middle is reached and from there one climbs until the far bank; and when the bridge is being crossed it trembles very much; all of which goes to the head of someone unaccustomed to it" (Sancho [1543] 1917, 60). The Inka suspension bridges successfully supported the loads of entire armies in addition to the weight of horses, so it is apparent that

these structures had significant load capacity. Garcilaso ([1609] 1994, 217) describes Inka armies crossing the largest bridges as marching in "triple file."

It is no wonder that the Spanish marveled at the Inka bridges. In fact, sixteenth-century Spanish technology was incapable of spanning the long distances over the raging waters of the Andean rivers. The Inka bridges achieved clear spans of at least 150 feet; some were probably greater (Squier 1877, 548). This was longer than any span in masonry that had

Officials such as *chakacamayucs,* or bridge-keepers, monitored and recorded the movement of people and goods along the road and across its bridges. Felipe Guaman Poma de Ayala (Quechua, 1535–1616). Pen and ink drawing published in *El primer nueva crónica y buen gobierno* (1615). Royal Library, Copenhagen GKS 2232 4°

been achieved by that point in history. The greatest Roman bridge in Spain (at Alcántara) had a maximum span of only ninety-five feet and did not have to be built over a deep gorge (O'Connor 1993, 198). Masonry arch construction requires the building of extensive wooden centering, which was beyond the technical capacity of the Spanish at the time. Efforts to build a masonry arch bridge over the Apurímac River in the late sixteenth century as a replacement for the Inka suspension bridge were unsuccessful, and the bridge construction was abandoned after great loss of life and money (Harth-Terre 1961). A surviving drawing by Diego Guillen from 1619 depicts an arch bridge with the temporary wooden centering to support a stone span of 150 Castilian feet (41.8 meters) over the Apurímac. To construct a timber arch of sufficient strength to support the weight of stone over the rushing river was simply beyond the capacity of colonial Peru—the suspension bridges were superior to Spanish arch bridges for this context. In fact, bridge technology could not offer a superior solution to crossing the deep gorges of the Andean region until the nineteenth century, when the great advances of the Industrial Revolution created long-span iron and steel structures.

Strangely, the origin of the modern suspension bridge owes nothing to the Inka achievements, which went basically unnoticed as a technical concept in Europe at the time, despite the vivid descriptions of the *cronistas* (chroniclers). Long-span suspension bridges were not built in Europe until the late eighteenth century, more than 250 years after the fall of the Inka Empire (Peters 1987). To support wheeled traffic, the development of the level roadway suspension bridge was an essential step, and it would be several centuries before European engineers developed this idea.

Engineering Requirements of the Bridges

A basic engineering analysis can be used to estimate the magnitude of internal forces in Inka suspension bridges. For a small bridge such as the Q'eswachaka, with a span of a hundred feet (30.5 meters), each of the four floor cables must be capable of supporting a maximum tension force of around a thousand pounds. (This calculation assumes a sag of the cable at midspan of eight feet and a total uniform load of twenty-five pounds per linear foot, which accounts for the weight of the bridge plus ten pedestrians.) Load testing of the grass cables has demonstrated that each cable can support up to four thousand pounds without breaking, proving that the existing bridge has a substantial margin of safety (Ochsendorf 1996). Chakacamayuc Victoriano Arispana continues the Andean tradition of repairing and rebuilding the Q'eswachaka each year, representing a living legacy of Inka engineering.

The largest Inka suspension spans, such as the Apurímac Bridge, required significantly stronger cables. Woven from saplings, vines, and vegetal fibers, the cables were described by Garcilaso ([1609] 1994, 149–50) as being "as thick as a man's body." With spans of 150 feet or more and a substantially higher load capacity, these cables needed to safely support at least twenty thousand pounds. As one example, the Apurímac Bridge spanned approximately 150 feet, according to Squier's measurement. Assuming a sag at the center of fifteen feet and a total distributed load of three hundred pounds per foot, the maximum combined force in the bridge cables totaled about sixty thousand pounds. Divided among three main floor cables, each cable would have supported up to twenty thousand pounds. Therefore, to provide a margin of safety, the breaking strength of the larger cables may have been up to fifty thousand pounds or more. The expertise required to build such a large suspension bridge—both in creating cables with this strength and successfully anchoring them to vertical cliffs—represents one of the highest achievements of pre-industrial engineering in the Americas.

Beginning in the thirteenth century, individual Inka rulers designed and constructed suspension bridges as an essential part of their mission to conquer new territories. Thus, the rise of the suspension bridge in the Andean region directly parallels the rise of the Inka Empire and the construction of the Qhapaq Ñan. The long-term survival of such bridges through continual maintenance became the responsibility of adjacent provinces. This method of repair was so effective that many of the bridges lasted until the nineteenth century, and at least one such bridge survives today. The strategic importance of the bridges continued during the Spanish Conquest of South America and for centuries afterward.

The history of the built environment is crucial to our understanding of cultural and social history. The rich archaeological record of the Inka bridge sites is largely untouched, and there is significant future work in the excavation and careful study of the abutment remains. In addition, a map of Inka bridge sites would greatly contribute to our understanding of the chronology of Inka expansion and the relation of the road system to the bridge locations.

The total number of suspension bridges built by the Inka is unknown. Alberto Regal's book on Inka bridges in ancient Peru provides a starting point, but it is far from complete, and some of his claims require a critical reassessment (Regal 1972). According to available sources, up to two hundred significant suspension bridges may have existed at the height of the Inka Empire. To fully understand the accomplishments of the Inka builders as well as the history and technology of the Qhapaq

Inka suspension bridge over the Apurímac River. Ephraim George Squier (1821–1888). Wood engraving published in *Peru: Incidents of Travel and Exploration in the Land of the Incas* (1877). Courtesy of Smithsonian Institution Libraries

Authorities from the four communities involved in the annual rebuilding of the Q'eswachaka suspension bridge cross the new bridge when it is finished. Apurímac River, Canas Province, Peru, 2014. Photo by Joseph Dutra

Ñan, additional interdisciplinary studies of Inka suspension bridges continue to offer a promising path forward.

Acknowledgments

I would like to thank the late Edward M. Franquemont for his guidance and for introducing me to Inka suspension bridges and, more generally, to Inka construction technology. Professors Mary Sansalone and William Streett provided support for me to pursue this research during my undergraduate studies at Cornell University. MIT undergraduate students Antonella Alunni, Celina Balderas Guzman, Linda Seymour, and Mariana Ballina assisted with archival research and Spanish translation as part of the MIT Undergraduate Research Opportunity Program (UROP). Finally, I am grateful to Professors Heather Lechtman and Gary Urton for their encouraging me to research this topic.

GARY URTON

QHAPAQ ÑAN AND THE *KHIPU*

Inka Administration on the Road and along the Cord

t has long been recognized that one of the grandest technological and logistical achievements of the Inka Empire was the development and maintenance of a system of "highways," known collectively as the Qhapaq Ñan. One major route of the highway system passed along the Pacific coastal plain, with its numerous river valleys cutting across what was otherwise a profoundly arid desert. Another major route ran through the heart of the intermontane valleys of the high Andes, from just north of present-day Quito, Ecuador, through the center of present-day Peru, southward through present-day Bolivia and northwest Argentina, and farther south to central Chile (Hyslop 1984). Numerous trunk roads bound together these two grand routes of the coast and highlands, producing a network of roads that allowed for the movement of people, material, and information throughout the territory of what the Inka knew as Tawantinsuyu ("the four parts intimately bound together"), or the Inka Empire.

The term *highways* has been placed in quotes in the above paragraph because the reader who has no experience of walking or otherwise travelling along some forgotten stretch of the Inka road system should understand that this term is used in a loose, generalized sense by students of Inka civilization. For the Inka highway was not a system of wide, smooth roads, like the German *autobahn*, or the interstate highways of the continental United States, nor like the network of highways running around and through Lima and other cities of the Andean region today. In fact, many Inka "highways" are narrow, often no more than two-person-wide footpaths that run up and over mountain passes or that pass along steep mountainsides overlooking deep canyon defiles.

While the characterization of the Inka road system given above is evidenced by remnants of these old, often rock-strewn paths found today here and there across the former territory of Tawantinsuyu, there was another arrangement of roads known to the Inka. This second representation was a radial system rather than the linear (i.e., longitudinal- and latitudinal-like) arrangement described above. In this second representation, the center of the road system was the Inka capital city of Cusco, located in the highlands of present-day southeastern Peru. In this second view, four main roads (and several smaller roads and trails) ran out from the center of Cusco, dividing the empire into its four great *suyus*, or quadrants: Chinchaysuyu,

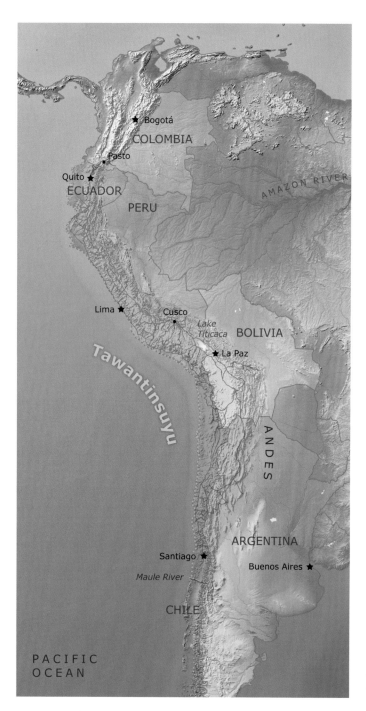

Tawantinsuyu (the Inka Empire) and its road system. Map by Daniel G. Cole, Smithsonian Institution, and Nancy Bratton Design, with core data from ESRI and NaturalEarth. © 2015 Smithsonian Institution

Antisuyu, Collasuyu, and Contisuyu (Hyslop 1984, 312–13; Morris and von Hagen 2011).

One challenge in studying the Inka road system is that of resolving the relationship between what were, in fact, two different perceptions of the organization of the empire via the network of roads. The radial view noted above was primarily related to ritual representations and ceremonial movements within and to and from the capital, whereas the linear system was used for all or most movement and transportation activities relating to the state and its administration (Hyslop 1984; D'Altroy 2002; Jenkins 2001). In general, except when addressing special ritual or ceremonial circumstances, the following discussion of engagements with the Inka roads by the Inka, his state administrators, militia, or other officials refers to the linear/longitudinal-latitudinal system.

The objective here is not to describe all features of the many and diverse roads and pathways that made up Qhapaq Ñan. That task is undertaken elsewhere, specifically in John Hyslop's masterful study *The Inka Road System* (1984). Hyslop's book is the most complete and exhaustive study of the Inka road system produced to date and remains the most authoritative treatment of the topic. Rather, what follows is a survey and discussion of the main organizational principles used by Inka administrators and other officials of the empire to arrange and oversee the movement of people, material, and information along Qhapaq Ñan. A primary tool used by the Inka for this purpose was the *khipu* (knot), the Inka knotted-cord record-keeping device.

The khipu played a vital role in the production, storage, movement, and overall management of goods and services along the Inka highways. New perspectives on the materiality and technology of the khipu may provide us with insights into the conceptions, spatial arrangements, and material qualities that lay behind the structures and organizational strategies that Inka administrators had available to them, and that they manipulated, in their management of the Inka road as well as its facilities and resources.

Three primary contexts within which one can realize the significance of khipus and cord-recording technologies for a study of the Inka road system are: functional, structural, and conceptual, or ontological.

Functional

The first of the three principles is the least complicated to explain, although it was undoubtedly the most important in terms of the day-to-day engagement of people throughout the empire with the infrastructure and economy connected with the road system. The Inka maintained an elaborate system of *tampus* (way stations) for provisioning travelers along the Qhapaq Ñan (e.g., Garcilaso de la Vega [citing Cieza de León] [1609] 1966, 256). Speaking of the principal towns spread throughout the empire, the Jesuit priest Bernabé Cobo noted that:

> In these towns there were royal lodgings and storehouses called tambos, supplied with a great abundance of all the things that could be obtained in these places. Thus the Inca could be accommodated when he passed by there and be served with no less luxury, majesty, and splendor than he would in his court, and everything necessary could be given to the garrison soldiers and the armies when they passed through these towns. Apart from these large towns and many other small ones located on these royal highways or not very far from them, there were well-supplied tambos and storehouses at intervals of a day's journey, which was every four to six leagues, even though it was an uninhabited place and a desert. (Cobo [1653] 1983, 228)

To the extent that the tampus were themselves places for the storage and dispersal of resources for travelers, they formed a part of the complex of storage facilities throughout the empire. Many of the large agglomerations of storehouses, which were generally located near major provincial centers, stood near or next to the Inka roads.[1] These storehouses, called *colcas*, were filled with produce from the Inka's fields, which were worked by local corvée laborers fulfilling their labor tribute obligation to the Inka. As there was, therefore, an intimate connection between the general infrastructure of state storehouses and the small tampus along the Inka highways, the management of resources sent to and redistributed from each was carefully administered by the *khipucamayucs* (cord makers/organizers). Again, citing Cobo:

> There were in these storehouses and warehouses inspectors, overseers, and accountants for the administration of the royal goods; these officials kept careful records of all goods received or consumed and of everything that was sent away. (Cobo [1653] 1983, 221)

In addition to the record keeping that went on at the tampus and colcas, there was another component of what we could term the transportation infrastructure related to the khipus; it involved a system of huts for the stationing of runners, or *chaskis*, who carried messages from place to place along the Inka Road. This system of communication allowed the Inka and his administrators to send messages over great distances with remarkable speed. Cobo recounts that the *chuclla* (chaski huts) were located every half-league (about 2.5 kilometers) along the road and were built in pairs, the two huts facing one another on either side of the road. The structures were said to be just large enough to house two men in each hut. The

DEPOCITODELINGA
COLL CAOCI

topay nga yupanqui

admi nistrador suyo yoc apo poma chaua

depoci tos del ynga

como

QVINTO CALLE

carta

oledad de dies ysocho años

yn de me dio tributo mozeton

enes ra

A *khipucamayuc* (cord maker/organizer) at a set of royal *colcas* (storehouses) displays to an administrator his *khipu* (knotted-cord device) for inspection and review.

A *chaski* (messenger) carrying a *khipu* (knotted-cord device) labeled "*carta*" (letter).

Felipe Guaman Poma de Ayala (Quechua, 1535–1616). Pen and ink drawings published in *El primer nueva crónica y buen gobierno* (1615). Royal Library, Copenhagen GKS 2232 4°

chaskis were charged with carrying messages pertaining to state business, transferring the information in verbal form from the runner from one hut to the runner in the next hut along the road, the message being shouted "in the least number of words" (Cobo [1653] 1983, 229). In addition to transferring information in verbal form, we are told that the runners often carried khipus, whereby more complex information (e.g., censuses, tribute assessments) could be moved over great distances with little or no loss (or confusion) of information.

It is clear, then, that several functions relating to state facilities and personnel along the Qhapaq Ñan were intimately connected to khipu-bearing administrators.

Structural

One characteristic of the Inka khipus was their relative structural simplicity, at least when considered in relation to the great complexity of the information said to have been recorded on them (Ascher and Ascher 1997; Urton 2003; Urton and Brezine 2005). Khipus are composed of a variable number—the average is around eighty-five—of cords, which are made of spun and plied cotton or camelid fiber and suspended from what is termed a primary cord. The suspended cords, often termed pendant strings, are commonly tied in complex arrangements of (usually) tiered clusters of knots. On most samples, the tiered clusters represent a system of numerical registry in a decimal place value system of numeration (Locke 1923). Beginning from the bottom of pendant strings, each higher tier of knots represents a higher power of ten.

Odd as it may sound, the structure of the Qhapaq Ñan was not dissimilar to that of the khipu. The Qhapaq Ñan was composed of linear stretches of road along which were located facilities—tampus, colcas, etc.—in what could be considered a "place value" arrangement strung out along the royal highways.

The Qhapaq Ñan place-value system was (presumably) not ordered in any sort of consistent, incremental, hierarchical arrangement of valued places along any particular stretch of road (e.g., in which each subsequent site was consistently of greater or lesser value than the one adjacent to it); nor do any accounts of the Inka road structure suggest a conscious modeling of either one of these structures on the other. However, this does not deny, nor contradict, recognition of the physical and what one could term "operational" similarities between these two structures, i.e., a linear configuration (road/cord) punctuated by nodes constructed along that structure (tampus/ knots). Nonetheless, one could postulate that tampus located most distant from settled places, such as provincial centers, were likely less charged with place value, in the grand scheme of imperial things/places, than those nearer to larger settlements. This is pure speculation, however, and would require for its confirmation something that does not exist in the written colonial documentation: ethnographic-quality reflections by former Inka administrators on the relative valuation of the assortment of places lining any given stretch of an Inka road.[2]

Conceptual/Ontological
The third context in which one can posit a similarity between Inka roads and the khipus concerns how each were, respectively,

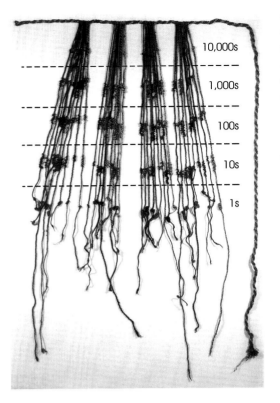

A *khipu* (knotted-cord device) with a diagram showing the decimal organization of the knots, AD 1400–1550. Ica, Peru. Cotton. 67 × 21 cm. Staat-liche Museen zu Berlin, Preußischer Kulturbesitz – Ethnologisches Museum V A 47083. Photo by Gary Urton

conceived of, namely, the roads by the cadres of Inka administrators who carried out state business along the Qhapaq Ñan, and the khipus by the officials and agents who oversaw activities of ritual and ceremonial importance throughout the empire. (It is in the latter context that we will be able to reintroduce the issue of the radial system of roads emanating from the Inka capital, Cusco.) It seems quite possible that there were two paradigmatic expressions and representations in the minds of Inka civil and ecclesiastical administrators as they went about their appointed business, overseeing activities in relation to two vital instruments of communication and coordination within the state: the roads and the khipus.

The two paradigmatic views are outlined below, each related to, or embedded within, Inka ontological views of the way things were, naturally. Each was realized "on the ground" in the road system and in khipu cords.

The Main Line/Branch Hierarchical Paradigm

Looking again at the schematic overview map of the Qhapaq Ñan, one sees an arrangement of two "longitudinal" (although the designation is not strictly correct in the Western understanding of the word) roads running from south of Santiago to north of Quito; one of these roads ran generally along the coast; the other ran through high intermontane valleys. Connecting these two north-south main roads were numerous branch roads. As Jenkins (2001) has shown in his careful study of the placement of major administrative and storage centers throughout the empire, the numerous connecting, trunk roads tended to be located at central places near important regions for the production and eventual redistribution of the staple goods (e.g., tubers, grains, corn) that were stored in bulk in colcas. As Jenkins has argued, the Inka strategy in placing storage facilities and establishing routes was to create a series of regional storage facilities along the branch lines, each controlled from the center (Cusco), thereby denying direct communication and exchange among communities and among regional centers, thus emphasizing vertical ties at the expense of horizontal ones (Jenkins 2001, 661; see Figure 2).

It can be argued that this arrangement and organization of main and branch roads, which articulated the placement and movement of the vital, staple finance goods stored by the Inka state was, conceptually, similar in design to the basic structure of Inka khipu, with its array of pendant strings attached to a main (or primary) cord. It is also likely that the coincidence between the conceptual/ontological characteristics of these two components of state administration—the network of central and branching roads and the cords—provided the foundation for an integrated system of accounting and controls within state administration.

Primary cord-and-pendant structure of a set of Inka *khipus* (knotted-cord devices). Laguna de los Cóndores. Centro Mallqui, Leymebamba, Peru CMA257 series. Photo by Gary Urton

Map showing a stretch of Inka road with *tampus* (inns) near Huánuco Pampa. Map drawing by Julia Meyerson

Center/Periphery Hierarchical Paradigm

The other major organizational context that is key to understanding an important Inka conceptual link between roads and khipus is that of the radial hierarchical system centered in Cusco. As is well known from the work of R. Tom Zuidema (1964), the Inka capital city was organized for ritual and social purposes into an arrangement of forty-one imaginary lines, termed *ceques* (sacred sightlines), along which were located several hundred *wakas* (sacred sites) within the city and throughout the valley of Cusco (Hyslop 1984, 340–41). The symbolic values attributed to these sites indicate that they were part of a hierarchical center/periphery arrangement, with the highest-ranked components standing nearer to the center and the lower-ranked elements located around the periphery, at increasingly greater distances from the center as one moved out along any orientation.

In addition to, or correlated with, the radial system of ritual/ceremonial orientations of the ceques, there was a set of radial pathways emanating from the city center. As noted above, four of these pathways constituted the roads that went to the ends of settled territory in four directions, to establish the boundaries of the four suyus of the Inka Empire. Recent research by Alexei Vranich has resulted in the production of a map of the principal and subsidiary radial pathways centering on Inka Cusco.[3]

As is well known, the khipus were flexible, mobile cord devices that could be arranged in any given configuration when placed on a horizontal surface or suspended on a wall. It is a simple and quite straightforward matter to turn the main cord of a khipu into a circle, thus joining the ends together to form a radial array of cords around a center. The resulting structure, interpreted in relation to the hierarchical arrangement of decimal place values arrayed along the (now) radial array of cords, produces

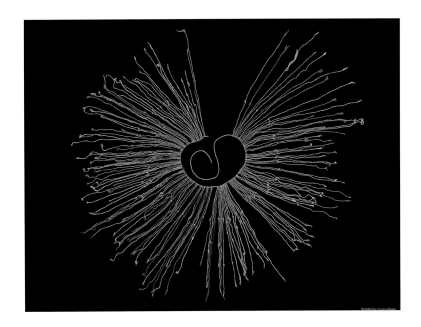

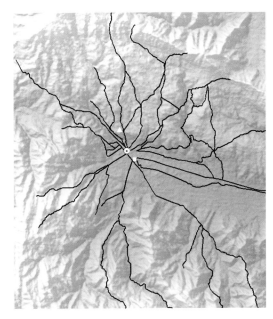

A *khipu* (knotted-cord device) displayed in a radial arrangement, AD 1450–1550. Huacho, Peru. Cotton. 106 × 60 cm. Staatliche Museen zu Berlin, Preußischer Kulturbesitz – Ethnologisches Museum V A 63040. Photo by Claudia Obrocki

Radial roads centering on Inka Cusco (detail). Map by Donato Amado Gonzales, Kevin Floerke, Alexei Vranich, and Ramiro Matos Mendieta. © 2012 Smithsonian Institution

an instantiation of the core/periphery model of the radial roads and ceque system of the city of Cusco. This arrangement of the khipu object was in all cases a possibility and would have served, in conceptual terms, as a representation of the ritually, ceremonially, and politically important radial, center/periphery structure of the organization of the four quarters of the Inka Empire, as seen from the privileged perspective of the capital city, Cusco.

Messages from the Qhapaq Ñan

The *Chaskis* and Their Contribution to Andean Communication

SERGIO MARTÍN

W E MAY BE SURPRISED by the expanse of the Inka Empire, which extended to the most varied spaces and landscapes of the South American Andes, but no one doubts that Inka road systems were the means of realizing the greatest geopolitical achievement of the pre-Columbian world. Beyond their formal function of connecting places so that people could travel, the Andean roads were, in their time, what the social network is for us today: dynamic, efficient channels of communication. All the information used to make important decisions for the functioning of the empire circulated on these roads. In the context of the Andean road system, the feats of the *chaskis* (runners/messengers) stand out. These messengers traveled the roads at maximum speed to orally transmit messages. For help, they used *khipus* (knotted record-keeping devices) (Hyslop 1992, 199; D´Altroy 2003, 291) and sometimes red threads from the tassels of the Inka rulers, or walking sticks that bore certain signs (Baudin 1955, 307).

The chaskis also carried small, lightweight objects between different territories of the empire. Frequently transported items include *cumpis* (fine fabrics), *mullus* (mollusks), tropical fruit, semiprecious stones, and even fresh fish from the Pacific Ocean for the table of the Inka ruler in Cusco. Thanks to atmospheric conditions, it is said that seafood arrived in good condition for consumption (Strube Erdmann 1963, 86). Chaskis were trained from the time they were small and were sometimes subjected to punishment and very severe living conditions as the result of any disobedience. According to the chronicles, "They were raised only on *hamca* (toasted maize), and were not permitted to drink more than once a day; they were also tested to see if they were light-footed and ready for the occasion" (Murúa [1590] 2004, 24).

The *mit'a* (labor-tax service for the Inka state) system was used to select future runners from villages along the

The *chaski* (runner/messenger) carrying the traditional tools of his trade. He blows a conch shell to announce his arrival to the next runner. Felipe Guaman Poma de Ayala (Quechua, 1535–1616). Pen and ink drawing published in *El primer nueva crónica y buen gobierno* (1615). Royal Library, Copenhagen GKS 2232 4°

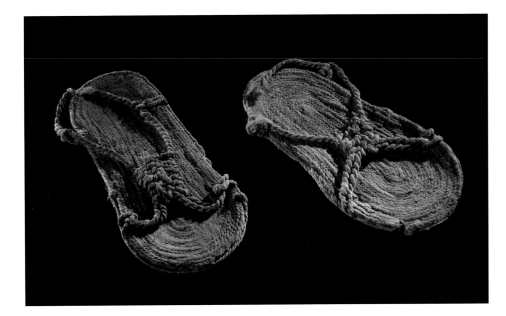

Made of plant fiber, these sandals would have carried a *chaski* (messenger runner) from a half mile to five miles in a single day at top speed.

Inka sandals, AD 1450–1532. Cusco region, Peru. Plant fiber. Left: 21.3 × 9.2 × 3.2 cm; Right: 20.6 × 10.2 × 3.2 cm. 11/363. Photo by Ernest Amoroso, NMAI

Inka Road (Rowe 1946, 232), although sometimes the Inka would choose special messengers from among his own guards (Baudin 1955, 308). Owing to the importance of their task, the chaskis were exempt from farming and mining mit'as. They often had to run on rotating shifts that could last from fifteen days to several weeks (Strube Erdmann 1963, 83; Hyslop 1992, 198).

Chaskiwasis were the posts where the runners lived. The small buildings are mentioned frequently by the chroniclers, and their structural properties are still being debated, along with the distances between them and whether they were built throughout Tawantinsuyu or only on some branches of the Qhapaq Ñan. As with other components of the Inka road system, construction of the chaskiwasis varied locally, depending on available resources, population density, and environmental and topographical conditions (Hyslop 1992). According to historical accounts and archaeological data, the distances covered by chaskis between the posts varied between a sixth of a league (about 500 meters) and a league-and-a-half (some eight kilometers).

Remains of possible chaskiwasis have been detected at archaeological sites in the Collasuyu (Bárcena and Martín 2009; Berenguer et. al. 2005; Martín 2002, 2005; Uribe and Cabello 2005; Vitry 2000). Although the sites are small and fragile, they are beginning to provide important data about the Peruvian segment of the empire. Through these discoveries, the chaskis survive and continue to fulfill their function: transmitting messages from the Andean world of the past.

A *chaski* (messenger runner) carried small personal items such as seeds, amulets, and coca in bags like this one.

Small Quechua bag, 1950–70. Sacana, Bolivia. Camelid hair. 25.4 × 17.8 × 2.54 cm. 14/3355. Photo by Ernest Amoroso, NMAI

Llama Caravans

AXEL E. NIELSEN

THE LLAMA (*Lama glama*) is the only pack animal indigenous to the Americas. Domesticated four to six thousand years ago in the highlands of the central and southern Andes, this animal provided meat, fiber, hides, fuel (dung), and the possibility of transporting a great number of goods over hundreds of kilometers of rough mountains. The average llama can carry approximately thirty-five kilograms a distance of fifteen to twenty-five kilometers per day. During these journeys, llamas can subsist by foraging on natural pastures found along the way. The possibilities for communication, exchange, and integration created by llama caravans were so important in this heterogeneous and hostile landscape that it would be impossible to understand Andean history and society without taking them into account.

The first llama trains accompanied pre-Inka peoples in their journeys and seasonal rounds, consolidating and expanding a pattern of long-distance trade and economic

Herders decorate the llamas' ears with colorful yarn and tassels called *chimpus*, or flowers, before leaving on a journey so that they look beautiful to those who see the caravan pass. Rio Grande de San Juan, Potosí, Bolivia, 1995. Photo by Axel E. Nielsen

diversification that had been initiated by archaic hunters and gatherers. As agriculture and herding developed to form the basis of subsistence, communities became increasingly sedentary, and interregional caravans became a common way of obtaining goods from distant places. Commodities transported ran the entire gamut from basic staples and raw materials such as corn, salt, and obsidian to the most sophisticated valuables: marine shell, precious metals, colored feathers, and psychotropic plants. Caravans achieved new economic and political significance with the development during the first millennium of early states in the central Andes. Studies of complex societies such as the Tiwanaku and the Moche attest to the regular consumption of nonlocal items and the far-reaching distribution of artifacts manufactured in emblematic corporate styles.

Llamas had their heyday during the fifteenth and early sixteenth centuries, at the time of the Inka Empire, or Tawantinsuyu, and of the great Inka Road, or Qhapaq Ñan. Massive llama populations extended from Ecuador to Chile and central Argentina, and from the Pacific coast of Peru to the Ceja de selva, or eastern flank of the Andes. These animals were a necessary complement to the army, providing a moving food supply and an effective way of transporting provisions and equipment over great distances on rugged terrain. They were also crucial for the Inka economy, which operated on the *mit'a*, or labor tribute, system and depended on the redistribution of surplus goods produced in state facilities that were spread throughout the empire. Historical sources mention hundreds or thousands of animals used by the state and by ethnic lords to circulate goods across the multiple regions and ecological zones. The importance of llama caravans is reflected in many characteristics of the Qhapaq Ñan, such as the spacing of way stations (which suggests the daily distances traveled by these animals), the road's proximity to good pastures, and certain design elements, which include corrals and other structures to manage the pack trains.

Inka llama harness bell, AD 1470–1532. Chiu Chiu, Chile. Wood. 10.8 × 5.5 × 7.60 cm. 17/7943. Photo by Ernest Amoroso, NMAI

The llama that leads the caravan wears a decorated necklace with a bell and a *chuspa* (bag) filled with coca leaves as a sign of its high rank. Cerrillos, Sud Lípez, Bolivia, 1995. Photo by Axel E. Nielsen

This thirteenth-to-fifteenth-century rock painting at Cerro Cuevas Pintadas depicts a llama caravan, including the burdens carried by some of the animals. Salta, Argentina, 2013. Photo by Axel E. Nielsen

During the European invasion, a number of Old World animals (sheep, goats, cattle, horses, and donkeys) were introduced to the Andes, often replacing camelid flocks in areas where they had previously thrived. During the sixteenth and seventeenth centuries, however, llama caravans continued to be crucial, not only for the indigenous population but also for the colonial economy, serving as the main beast of burden in Andean mines and in commerce between the Pacific ports and the highlands. Many Andean communities continue to herd llamas (and alpacas), mostly for wool and meat.

From the beginning, llamas also played an important role in Andean religious ceremonies. They were constantly represented in rock art, such as paintings, engravings, and geoglyphs; and in ritual paraphernalia, including snuffing tablets and tubes as well as *illas*, or amulets. They were often placed in the burial tombs of high-ranking people. A white llama, called a *napa*, always walked in front of the Inka and, it is said, sang with him and joined him in his prayers. The Inka believed that llamas served as intermediaries with the gods. Llamas were commonly sacrificed in ceremonies and were even given their own constellations in the night sky.

facing: Inka *khipu* (detail), AD 1400–1600. Nazca region, Peru. Camelid hair, cotton. Primary cord: 105 cm; longest pendant cord: 46 cm. 17/8825. Photo by Ernest Amoroso, NMAI

Llamas and alpacas, cousins of the camel, were the only domesticated livestock in the Andes. They played a critical role in transportation and were a source of wool and meat.

Inka *canopas* (offering jars) in the forms of alpacas and llamas, AD 1250–1532. Peru. Stone. Largest jar: 13.3 × 18.7 × 7.3 cm; smallest jar: 4.6 × 2 × 4.6 cm. 21/6979, 14/5500, 18/2876, 20/1602, 19/501, 9/4839, 24/2422. Photo by R. A. Whiteside, NMAI

JOSÉ LUIS PINO MATOS

THE INKA ROAD TO THE CHINCHAYSUYU

Chinchaysuyu was the name given to the *suyu* (quadrant, or territorial division, of Tawantinsuyu) extending to the west and north of Cusco. According to some sources, the name of this region was adapted from that of the Chincha, the most powerful of the peoples who lived along the coast to the west of the great city. A main road, which originated in the Hawkaypata Plaza in Cusco, left the city and went west toward the Wakapunku area. In some ways, the beginning of that road in Chinchaysuyu marks the beginning of the Inka Empire, since it traces the course of four generations of Inka occupation and expansion.

The Road Begun by Inka Pachacutic

Going west, the road crossed various territories that, before Inka control, were occupied by the Chanka peoples, who had aspired to inhabit Cusco but were mythically repelled and even conquered after the intervention of the Inka Pachacutic. Those events changed the route toward Chinchaysuyu—which goes from the outskirts of Cusco to the regions of Apurímac and Ayacucho—to a commemorative road. Here the Inka embarked on a massive transformation of the landscape. They built ceremonial centers, farming platforms, and terraces to prevent erosion on almost all the slopes that descended into the valleys.

From the plain of Anta to the Curahuasi area, the slopes of some mountains have complex systems of farming platforms, creating contours that emphasize cut rocks and rocky formations. The settlement of Tambocancha and the vast platforms of Zurite on the plain of Anta are among the most important places on this road. These structures were built along terraces at the foot of a monumental hill renamed Wanakauri, which also refers to one of the *wakas*—important, sacred places in the Inka Empire. Similar platform complexes, constructed with canal systems, are found in Limatambo at a site along the road called Tarahuasi, which features a ceremonial platform cut from stone. Along this stretch of road, the Inka desire to leave an imprint on the landscape is quite palpable. The Inka presence is monumental and harmonizes with nature, highlighting the most striking aspects of the landscape, such as the unevenness of the topography and, above all, the use of rocks and

Inka *a'qa* (also known as *chicha*, or maize beer) jar with human face and corn feet, AD 1450–1532. Río Casma Valley, Peru. Silver alloy. 23.5 × 15.2 × 16.5 cm. 17/8935. Photo by Ernest Amoroso, NMAI

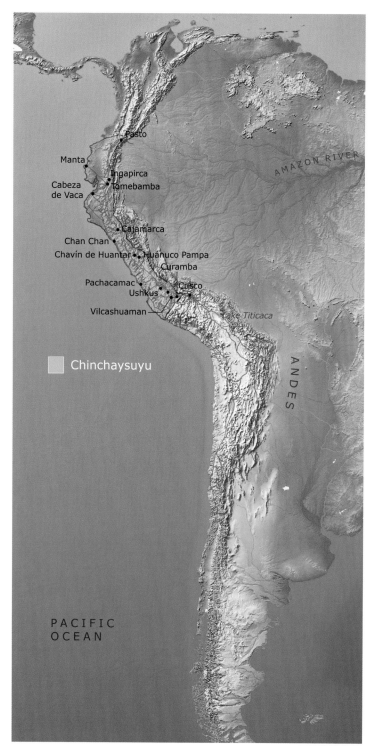

Chinchaysuyu was characterized by its open river valley, ideal for growing a variety of crops. It boasts the best-preserved roads and structures in what was the Inka Empire.

Map by Daniel G. Cole, Smithsonian Institution, and Nancy Bratton Design with core data from ESRI and NaturalEarth. © 2015 Smithsonian Institution

boulders, which have sacred meaning. In some cases, these rocks were carved to emphasize their profusion in the landscape.

This stretch leads to Curahuasi, an extremely important region. From there, the road extends north as far as the canyon of Apurímac, on the way to Choquequirao, a settlement associated with an Andean oracle that takes its name from the Apurímac River. Over this river is one of the most significant examples of Inka road technology: the hanging bridge called the Q'eswachaka.

Along the Chinchaysuyu Road, aquatic symbolism strongly influenced the design of roads and settlements. An excellent example is the Saywiti architectural complex, a settlement located next to a spring. It is a group of engineering and architectural structures intended to highlight the circulation of water. Saywiti is particularly striking because of the numerous rocks carved in the form of platforms, channels, felines, and abstract geometric shapes. One of the most prominent interventions is on a hill, the entire east side of which is covered with descending terraces, which are magnificently constructed with carved stones that form an artificial complex of consecutive cascades with stone receptacles and gutters. On the road from Saywiti, one frequently sees *ushnus*, or ceremonial platforms dedicated to various offerings and sacrifices, primarily those involving liquid and ritual libations, which had to be carried out at each important point on this road every time a significant date on the Inka calendar was commemorated. A fermented beverage, or *a'qa* (called *chicha* by the Spanish), was used in the ceremonial libations. A'qa toasts were shared by the main authorities and the *enqa*, objects that represented the major imperial deities that traveled with the Inka on this road, including the sun god known as Punchao, who was depicted as a child made of solid gold.

These ushnu platforms were also considered wakas and always included a stone receptacle in which to place offerings. The ushnus not only served as symbolic milestones marking the process of Inka expansion but also were points where directions and transit roads converged on pilgrimages. As such, the ushnus were constructed in strategic places that could visually connect the platforms with the mountains and the most prominent aspects of local geography. After Saywiti, Tamburco is the next place on the road with this type of construction. Tamburco is in the valley of Abancay, where there is a platform with terraces facing the snow-covered peaks of Ampay.

The next stretch of the road toward Chinchaysuyu—from Tamburco in Abancay to the hanging bridge on the Pampas River—is characterized by settlements with less elaborate finishes but with more complex urban designs and more monumental ushnus, which were always strongly linked to the surrounding landscape. Upon crossing the Pachachaca River, the road climbs from Abancay to the foothills of the Ccorawire Mountains, where the road leads to another ushnu at the edge of a lake known as Cochacajas. From there, continuing west, the road reaches a peak where the tops of the Ampay and Ccorawire Mountains divide. On this site, called Curamba, is an Inka settlement where a strikingly monumental, terraced-platform ushnu can be seen beside a broad plaza surrounded by administrative structures and an area for metalworking. From Curamba, the road goes toward Lake Pacucha, where the site known as Sondor is located. This site is made up of Inka ceremonial structures at the foot of a large, rocky hill surrounded by rounded terraces that give the impression of a superimposed complex of terraced platforms at the top of an enormous rock. The site and lake served as the major local wakas. The symbiotic relationship between structures and landscape is quite palpable along this stretch, despite the presence of more mundane structures used for

Inka political and administrative activities, as well as artisanal workshops and some storage buildings for processed products.

The Chinchaysuyu road continues west and crosses the Pampas River, then climbs until it reaches a stretch of landscapes linked together to commemorate the family events of Inka leaders through an emphasis on nature and direct association with their places of origin. These links to the Inka rulers are reflected in the orientation of the architecture and in the renaming of places on the road after the main wakas of Cusco. In fact, after crossing the Inkachaka, the hanging bridge over the Pampas River, the road enters a region marked

This large *arybalo* was used to store *a'qa* (also known as *chicha*, or maize beer). The sharing of chicha was a symbolic component of religious ceremonies and state festivals.

Inka *arybalo*, AD 1450–1532. Peru. Ceramic, paint. 109.2 × 86.4 × 73.7 cm. 14/5679. Photo by Ernest Amoroso, NMAI

by architecture of finely worked stone, easily on the level of Cusco itself. Indeed, when a major settlement was constructed along the road, it was called "new Cusco," in a tribute to the central capital of Tawantinsuyu. The major settlements in this area feature not only the most prominent architectural elements of Inka craftsmanship but also the names of the wakas of Cusco.

Such is the case in Vilcashuaman, a settlement featuring a trapezoidal plaza with a monumental platform (ushnu) on its west side and a temple dedicated to the sun toward the southeast. All of these buildings were constructed with finely worked stone, and in the center of the plaza is even a carved stone with incised, zigzagging forms. The Temple of the Sun rises above superimposed platforms, decorated with double-jamb, blind porticoes. The ushnu seems to have been an architectural

complex of several superimposed rectangular platforms, with a terrace facing the rising sun during the equinox. The association with the solar deity at this site is quite evident. Another settlement near Vilcashuaman on this same road was Pomacocha, located in an area surrounding a lake with the same name. The site included platform complexes, canals, fountains, and enclosures with finely worked stone intended to commemorate the birth of the first son of the Inka Pachacutic, named Amaru Tupac Inka.

From Vilcashuaman, the main road turns to the northeast, while a second road veers to the west and passes through several major settlements before reaching the coast and the territories of the Chincha. One indication that the Inka used this route is the road that goes through the valley of Pisco from sites near the headspring of the basin—such as Inkahuasi

An Inka *ushnu* (platform) dedicated to Inti (the sun) and Pachamama (Mother Earth). Curamba, Peru, 2006. Photo by Megan Son and Laurent Granier

de Huaytara, built with cut stone—to Tambo Colorado, which is a settlement built completely with mud bricks and exquisitely painted in red and yellow. This road continues onward to a village whose inhabitants were Inka allies. They were reputed to be great seafarers who were highly esteemed by the Inka rulers.

A Road Ruled Jointly by Father and Son—Pachacutic and Tupac Inka Yupanqui

Returning from Vilcashuaman to the northwest, the main road continues toward Lake Chinchaycocha and then drastically changes direction, entering regions where the Inka employed new architectural strategies. From Vilcashuaman to the region of Cajamarca, it is possible that the Inka expansion was carried out by Pachacutic in conjunction with his son Tupac Inka Yupanqui, who had demonstrated skills necessary for becoming the next leader. Moreover, both Inkas chose several high plateaus on which to design settlements that became increasingly more elaborate. The most prominent of these are Hatun Xauxa, Tarmatambo, Chakamarca, Pumpu, and Huánuco Pampa. All these sites were developed with increasingly more administrative infrastructure and with more *colcas*, or storehouses, where food such as dried maize and tubers were kept along with highly prized manufactured products, such as fabrics, weapons, sandals, and vessels. In addition to the traditional ushnu platforms, another type of private construction can be seen adjacent to the plazas of these settlements. Simple in design but of great functional importance, these structures have been referred to as *kallankas* (large halls) by many researchers. Although their original name is not known, they were composed of large elongated enclosures with multiple accesses for entering from the plaza. They were used to lodge travelers and for festive celebrations where magnificent banquets

were served with great quantities of food and drink, often to secure alliances or to forge agreements.

Along this stretch of road were some large planned settlements, including, most importantly, Pumpu and Huánuco Pampa, both located on vast, frigid plateaus. Both featured ushnu platforms at the center of broad plazas that were bordered by various kallankas and *kanchas*, characteristic structures in Inka architecture. Moreover, these settlements were located close to hills on which hundreds of colcas were constructed. It should be noted that this route from Chinchaysuyu runs along the entire western shore of Lake Chinchaycocha, which is the second-largest and second-highest lake in the Andes, after Lake Titicaca.

After Pumpu the road continues on to Huánuco Pampa, a settlement that was perhaps the most elaborately designed in all Tawantinsuyu. It was considered a new Cusco, not only for its numerous structures, which reflected refined, imperial Inka architecture, but also for its urban design, which followed a radial layout, with the ushnu platform as its central axis. The

Some parts of the Inka road were paths worn into the ground, while others were paved. Here the road has been paved to prevent erosion as travelers move up the hillside. Molleturo, Ecuador, 2005. Photo by Tamara L. Bray

half-kilometer-wide plaza of this settlement may
have been the largest Inka plaza in the Andes,
and its ushnu possibly the largest and most
monumental in the empire, although the ushnu
at Vilcashuaman was the highest. Both Pumpu
and Huánuco Pampa have canal systems and
water fountains of carved stone in their internal
layouts, especially Huánuco Pampa, which had
a series of troughs or pools representing the
lakes seen in other settlements such as Pumpu,
Hatun Xauxa, Ñawinpuquio, Pomacocha,
Sondor, and Cochacajas. These stretches are
also characterized by wide, paved roads, despite
rugged terrain marked by steep slopes, streams,
and swampy areas. The region was traversed via
long, stone roads with well-designed drainage
systems. Among the best examples are the

passes over the Huarautambo River and along
one section of Lake Lauricocha.

From Huánuco Pampa north to Huamachuco, the landscape is dotted with settlements made up of enclosures that are mostly
rustic, yet some are built of finely hewn stone.
Although these structures are not as frequent
as those found in the Vilcashuaman area, their
presence indicates the importance of these settlements while also emphasizing sacred aspects
of a local nature, as evidenced by Inkajamanan
and Soledad de Tambo in the area near Wam-
anin Mountain in Ancash. From the region of
Huamachuco, where Catequil, an important
deity-oracle for the Inka, was greatly revered,
the road reaches Cajamarca. Just as on the
preceding stretches, springs are of particular

importance here, especially hot springs. In addition to being a settlement constructed with volcanic stone, Cajamarca features structures that the Inka used near the local hot springs.

North from Cajamarca, the road connects sites such as Mitupampa, Caxas, and Aypate, the latter with constructions representative of the Inka administration, which in some cases included temples and monumental platforms, such as those at Mitupampa and Aypate. This stretch of road is characterized by extremely varied landscape, which ranges from valleys and plateaus to high plateaus and even areas with lush vegetation. Aypate is a magnificent example of a planned settlement considerably far from Cusco. The site was constructed from stone and is close to areas that are increasingly more wooded. Tupac Inka Yupanqui's route of expansion possibly reached as far as Quito, but, at least as far as Aypate one can see a certain style and uniformity in the treatment of landscapes and the design of settlements.

The Road That Huayna Capac Followed
From Aypate the Chinchaysuyu Road would later extend as far as Quito, in Ecuador, and into Pasto territory in Colombia. This road is more associated with the government and expansion of Huayna Capac, the son of Tupac Inka Yupanqui and the grandson of Pachacutic.

The Inka site of Ingapirca, Ecuador, 2008. Photo by Ramiro Matos Mendieta, NMAI

According to sixteenth-century sources, Huayna Capac was an extremely popular ruler of Tawantinsuyu.

The most representative settlements of this period are Tomebamba, Ingapirca, Callo, and Quito. The architecture of Ingapirca, despite being largely built from stone, features rounded forms and an oval platform, indicating reverence for the sun. Likewise in Callo, at the hacienda of San Agustín, there are enclosures that represent one of the finest kanchas of the northern territories of the Inka Empire. This stretch of the Qhapaq Ñan travels through landscapes dominated by massive volcanoes. According to some sources, this region was

very difficult for the Inka to conquer, yet it was highly prized by Huayna Capac and by Atahualpa, one of his sons. Quito was so important, that a new Cusco was constructed there; it was considered a second Inka capital before the fall of the empire after the arrival of the Spanish conquistadors. The extreme northern part of the empire was of great significance to the Inka because of the access it afforded to the tropical coastline where the *mullu*, or *Spondylus* (a genus of mollusks) was found in abundance. The mullu shell was extremely important in offerings and is found among ceremonial grave goods. The equatorial region was also important; it was there that the sun passed through the zenith of

The Spanish fight the Inka.

The Spanish execute the last Shapa Inka, Atahualpa.

Felipe Guaman Poma de Ayala (Quechua, 1535–1616). Pen and ink drawings published in *El primer nueva crónica y buen gobierno* (1615). Royal Library, Copenhagen GKS 2232 4

the sky during the equinox, a phenomenon that was considered central to Inka society, particularly in terms of the Inka calendar and religion. Some research relates that stones from Cusco were taken to Ecuador for the construction of ceremonial enclosures.

The Inka Huayna Capac managed to expand the empire as far as the extreme north of Tawantinsuyu, meaning that during the Inka period the Chinchaysuyu Road likely reached as far as the Pasto regions, the inhabitants of which were sent for religious purposes to Copacabana, on the shores of Lake Titicaca, at the southern edge of Collasuyu.

The Chinchaysuyu Road as the Beginning of the End of the Empire

In some ways the death of Huayna Capac, who was attacked by an unknown illness that probably came from the north, marked the beginning of the end of the empire. Chinchaysuyu was the scene of battles for imperial power, in which the two sons of Huayna Capac, Huascar and Atahualpa, played leading roles. These internal rivalries would never be resolved, however, due to the arrival of the Spaniards from across the sea. As a result, the road of Inka expansion was soon transformed into the road of the Spanish

Conquest. From Tumbes, Francisco Pizarro ascended the Andes and arrived in Cajamarca, where he captured and executed Atahualpa, who, in turn, had ordered his brother Huascar to be killed. This allowed the Spanish contingent to plan their conquest of the Andes. But that is another chapter in history, one that is not marked by reverence for the landscape or offerings to the earth but of exploitation and repression, a clash of cultures that left other tracks in its course along these Andean roads.

Carved and natural *mullu (Spondylus* shells), n.d. Lima, Peru. *Spondylus princeps* shells. From left: 8.5 × 9 × 2.6 cm; 8 × 10 × 3 cm; 8.1 × 8.6 × 2.5 cm. Large shell: 14/3861; small shells: 17/5217. Photo by Ernest Amoroso, NMAI

Ceques, Roads, and Astronomy in Cusco and the Inka Empire

R. T. ZUIDEMA

THE BEST INFORMATION from a Spanish chronicler about the organization of the Inka Empire was written by Juan Polo de Ondegardo, a prominent lawyer in colonial Peru. During the 1560s, with local experts as his sources, he told about the *ceque*, or sacred sightline, system of Cusco, the capital of the Inka Empire. This system of forty-one ceques, each extending in its direction from the central Qorikancha, or Temple of the Sun, toward the whole horizon, recorded 328 sacred places, or *wakas*. Thus it provided extensive information about social organization (families and groups of families), the politics of both local and regional groups, agriculture and water management, family and state rituals, and the Inka religion. Moreover, this system was worked out according to a precise annual calendar of days, weeks, months, seasons, and half-years. To use the calendar, one counted the wakas on the ceques from the inner- to the outermost, following the ceques according to the hands of a clock. Although the number of wakas on individual ceques could vary appreciably from an average of eight (41 × 8 = 328), the numbers of days in months revealed not only a greater calendrical logic but also a practical adaptation to geographic, demographic, and temporal realities.

To a certain extent, the ceque system functioned like a wind rose (a graphic tool that shows wind speed and direction) in Western geography and also like the moving hand of a Western clock. Nonetheless there were important differences in those functions, because the distances between ceques were not equal. Moreover, ceques of different lengths could end either before or beyond the horizon. However, for the sake of the connection with the horizon and the sky, they were regarded as straight lines. This fact was suggested not only by the very name *ceque*, or "straight line," but also the word as it is understood by present-day Quechua speakers.

The difference between the concept of a ceque and its actual use was well understood in Inka culture. I shall demonstrate this by means of some important examples. But before doing so, allow me to explain some of its inherent problems by drawing on my own experience. I made a first attempt at making a map of the ceques. Brian Bauer, with a team of collaborators, later worked out a more detailed map (Zuidema 1986, 2011; Bauer 1998). We approached the subject from two different but compatible angles and concepts. My first questions had to do with how ceques were conceived of and used. For ritual and calendrical reasons, ceques were used to proceed from an inner place to a place close to or beyond the horizon, as seen from the Qorikancha. It was therefore

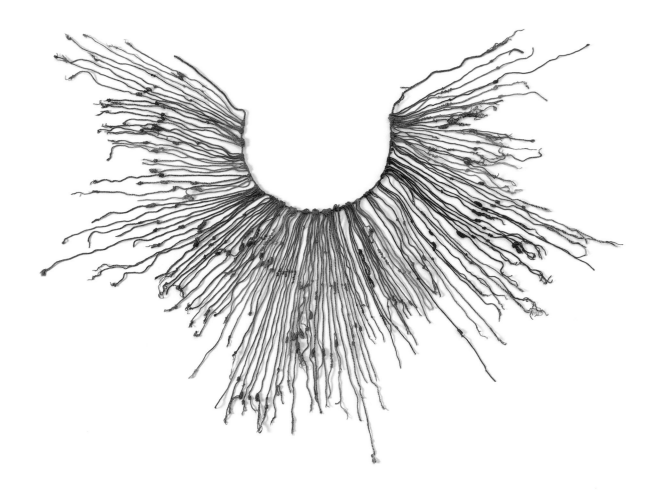

more practical to situate the more distant place first and from there devise a straight line, oftentimes with an impressive view, toward the Qorikancha. In this way it would also be possible to plan the actual road for ascending from the Qorikancha, following the wakas on a practical road. I took advantage of my experience with informants walking through the mountains. They would point out the direction that one needed to go, which would have to be kept in mind, but how one actually went about it was one's own affair. I made my map based on ceques as straight lines-of-sight. Bauer, as an archaeologist, was more interested in locating the wakas on a ceque first, and then establishing their connections. One always has to use a combination of the two concepts. I will give examples of Inka rituals that show this distinction and others showing how the combination was used in roadbuilding and astronomical observations. I will do so first with Cusco and its surroundings and later in relationship with other parts of the empire. This framework allows me to come to some conclusions about the relationship between ceques and actual roads.

Perhaps the most important ritual use of the ceque system occurred at the beginning of September, the Inka month of sowing. At that time, four groups of a hundred

The *ceque* (sacred sightline) system is mirrored in the organization of *khipus* (knotted-cord devices). Individual strands radiate from a primary cord, just as the forty-one ceque lines extend outward from the Qorikancha temple in Cusco to *wakas* (sacred places) throughout the Inka Empire.

Inka *khipu*, AD 1400–1600. Nazca region, Peru. Camelid hair, cotton. Primary cord: 105 cm; longest pendant cord: 46 cm. 17/8825. Photo by Ernest Amoroso, NMAI

Miguel Araoz Cartagena (b. 1977). *El Sistema de seques del Cusco*, 2005. Oil on canvas, 250 × 500 cm. Convento de Santo Domingo del Cusco. Photo by Doug McMains, reproduced with the permission of the artist.

warriors each would run to the rivers, which formed the borders of the four parts (*suyus*) of the province of Cusco, and cast away "the trials and tribulations of daily life," which would then flow into the sea. We have a good description of the places they passed through but, oddly enough, these routes do not agree with any routes within the suyus, but rather with the borders between them! Later all the families of Cusco, each from its own waka, would perform the same rite, going to the place where their ceques came to a stream flowing away from Cusco, where they could discard their tribulations in a ritual act of expiation. We do not know if they were following actual paths. But we can theoretically understand some of this problem through descriptions of four customs, three of them Inka and one modern.

The chronicler Cristóbal de Molina ([1575] 1988), who gave us the best account of the calendrical rites of Cusco, also tells us how a person to be offered in sacrifice, e.g., a child, would travel to his or her final destination. While those accompanying the child would follow an actual road, the person to be sacrificed had to follow a straight path through the countryside. If this was difficult or impossible in some places, then a pot of blood was thrown to the difficult terrain on a rope. The Inka ritual confirms the distinction that was made between a straight pathway and a normal road, and combines them in a procession from Cusco to a great sacred place and back.

Around the time of the June solstice, priests from Cusco would celebrate the event in the temple of Vilcanota, a place some 160 kilometers southeast of Cusco, which today is called La Raya. The Vilcanota River, which flows through the Sacred Valley near Cusco, originates there. To reach the temple, the priests first walked from Cusco in a straight line for ten days through the countryside, resting at night in designated places that are still well known. On the return trip, however, they followed the same river on a more comfortable route and arrived at a place close to Cusco. From there, they would follow another route through the countryside. However, on the last part of this journey, already in the valley of Cusco, they would follow a straight actual road. The same procession was repeated in November for another astronomical reason, but apparently in the opposite direction, first going up the river and then returning in a straight line through the countryside. It is interesting that the same distinction between a straight

The gray stone wall in the center of the photo is one of the few structures from the original Qorikancha (Cusco's lower Temple of the Sun) that remain intact. Cusco, Peru, 2014. Photo by Doug McMains, NMAI

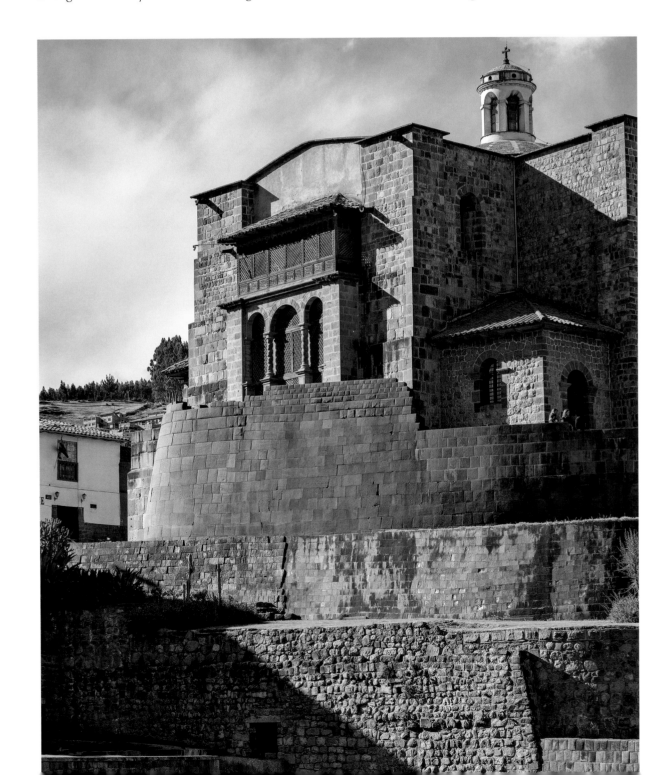

path and a comfortable path is still applied in ritual visits to sacred places (Bastien 1978; personal information).

Visits to or from Cusco, or to sacred places in the Inka Empire, were highly significant to the political and ritual organization of the Inka state. I should mention two descriptions of interest in the chronicles. These descriptions do not deal with straight pathways, but we can assume that in these cases, imperial ceques (from Cusco to the ends of the empire) played a role, although actual roads were used.

The first example is given by Fernando de Santillán ([1563] 1968, 111), in which he also confirms that Polo de Ondegardo discovered the ceque system in Cusco and wrote an "account" of it. In mythological fashion, he describes for us how Topa Inka (the Inka ruler Tupac Yupanqui) founded the great waka, the Shrine of Pachacamac, dedicated to the god Pacha Camac (or Pachacamac), who had four sons. To the first, the god gave a "house," that is, a temple, in the valley of Mala; to the second, he gave one in the valley of Chincha; to the third, one in Andahuaylas "near Cusco"; but, "he wanted to give to Topa [Inka] as the fourth son a house in Cusco itself." Several myths explain how the god Viracocha traveled (in a straight line?) from Lake Titicaca to different places on the coast. A myth from Huarochirí tells a story in which the god Cuniraya Viracocha traveled (in a straight line?) from Pachacamac to Lake Titicaca, where he met Huayna Capac, who later, as a god (of the sun?) ascends to the heavens, leaving as his representative the king of Cusco under the same name (Taylor 1999). Apparently, Santillán was describing an actual road from Pachacamac to Cusco but thinking of the straight direction as a more theoretical concept.

The following example, which is a summary of information gleaned from several authors, pertains to the main waka of Aysavillca, near the coast in the Inka province of Cajatambo in Chinchaysuyu, the imperial suyu to the north of Cusco. Apparently, we are dealing with the same waka that played a leading role in the account of idolatries written by Rodrigo Hernández Príncipe ([1621] 1986). Here he relates a story that tells of the sacrifice of the daughter of a provincial *curaca* (chief) after she had participated with the Inka ruler in the Feast of the Sun, probably during the December solstice. Tanta Carhua returned to her village of Ocros with tributes that the Inka granted to her father. Pilgrims traveling toward the coast from Aysavillca would worship the sea there when they saw it for the first time and pray for a safe return. We have good descriptions indicating that the beginning of the same road from Cusco, which the warriors used in the ritual of expiation, was also used by the travelers descending to the coast through the regions of Pachacamac and Aysavillca. We can suggest that the ritual return journey of Tanta Carhua followed the same road, probably in its straighter form (Zuidema 1989, ch. 4).

When the priests of Cusco returned from the temple of Vilcanota in June, their first view of the valley of Cusco was from the top of the hill at Quispikancha. From there, the final part of the journey coincided with the line-of-sight from Cusco toward the rising sun on the two days when it passed through its zenith in the sky. Using the same line in reverse, as the priests did when they returned walking from Vilcanota, the setting sun can be seen going through its nadir at the end of April and in August—two of the most important dates for agriculture. Once, the Inka Huayna Capac used this return route to Cusco as part of his coronation ceremonies. We know a good deal about the last part of this journey from two other detailed accounts. The first describes the conquest of Cusco by Mama Huaco, one of the sisters of the first Inka, Manco Capac (Zuidema 1993, 2011). Bartolomé de Segovia gives us the second (Molina [1553] 1968) description. One year after the Spanish entered Cusco, he witnessed at the end of the state harvest rituals a great procession in which the Inka ruler himself participated. For this event the nobles of Cusco formed an avenue with their tents for the journey toward the city. At that time, this avenue followed the same road between the old suyus of Antisuyu and Collasuyu. It was used by warriors traveling toward Collasuyu in the rituals of expiation, and it still coincides with the modern road extending in that same direction. It is also very close to the last ceque of Antisuyu and thus provides the best example of the relationship between a ceque and an actual road.

The old harvest festival was replaced by the Christian Feast of Corpus Christi, which is popular in Cusco. Using the modern road that replaced the old avenue used by the Inka and the Inka nobility, the communities of San Jerónimo and San Sebastián now carry the images of their saints when they participate in the city festival of Corpus Christi, which is celebrated at around the same time of the year.

Tampus

Tampus, also known as tambos, formed an integral part of the Inka road system, as can be seen along the Qhapaq Ñan itself. These structures also constitute much of the Inka Empire's archaeological remains. One frequently finds descriptions of them in early colonial literature, and their omnipresence and usefulness makes them worthy of attention. Similarly, all subsequent studies of the Inka Empire mention this widespread state institution. John Hyslop, one of the most prominent scholars of the Inka civilization, has noted that different sources agree on a series of characteristics: "The tampu [sic] were located at a distance of one day from each other and cared for by the *mitayuq* (a person performing labor tax service) from a nearby community; they sheltered individual travelers as well as groups on official missions; they had storage places where food, forage, firewood and other products were stored (clothing, weapons, etc.)" (Hyslop 1992, 137).

Historical sources suggest that the tampus were more or less the same everywhere. The latest archaeological research, however, indicates that they were not at all similar to one another. On the contrary, they show a great diversity, suggesting a very complex, versatile system that was adapted to the empire's vast territorial expanse and varying environmental and cultural circumstances (Chacaltana-Cortez 2010; Jenkins 2001).

In fact, aside from serving as inns or outposts for lodging people and animals, the tampus represented the most revealing and tangible of the political strategies for Inka expansion and Andean integration (Rowe 1946). Moreover, they continued to be used throughout much of the colonial period, were recognized by the Hispanic administration, and remained popular among the entire population, although they eventually lost some of their original connotations, especially their links with the state and with Native communities (Guaman Pomo de Ayala [1614] 1944; Vaca de Castro [1543] 1908).

It is quite possible that the origin of the tampus predates the Inka, as is suggested by underlying roads and facilities spread across the Andes that

The archaeological record suggests that *tampus* (inns) were diverse, with each one adapted to the particular environmental and cultural circumstances in which it was constructed. Raqchi, Peru, 2014. Photo by Doug McMains, NMAI

are distinct from the Cusco system. Nevertheless, the Inka tampus are clearly recognizable, with immediately identifiable elements. Their orthogonal layout aligned with the Qhapaq Ñan and almost always included a group of *kanchas*, or courtyards with interior enclosures, as well as *colcas*, structures for storage. In all of them, a rectangular plan tends to dominate, along with the use of special types of stone, the construction of double walls with filler, trapezoidal windows and doors, and low roofs.

On occasion, and in accordance with its importance or proximity to population centers, a tampu might have included a *kallanka*, or large shed, which served important political and religious functions. In general, while situated at some distance from local groups, the tampus were located close to rivers, grazing areas, and forest resources, and they were

The remains of a *tampu* (inn), 2011. Catarpe, San Pedro de Atacama, Chile. Photo by Ramiro Matos Mendieta, NMAI

Tampus (inns) are easily recognized by their orthogonal layout to the road. Remains of a tampu above Tauli, Peru, 2006. Photo by Megan Son and Laurent Granier

The daily care of *tampus* (inns) was undertaken by *mitayucs*, workers fulfilling their *mit'a* (labor-tax service). The *arybalo* jug on this figure's back is often associated with mit'a.

Inka jar in the form of a male worker carrying an *arybalo*, AD 1500–1600. North coast of Peru. Ceramic, paint. 22.2 × 12.7 × 21.6 cm. 20/6477. Photo by Ernest Amoroso, NMAI

facing: The Inka adopted many ideas from other Andean cultures to develop their world view. Before the Inka conquest, the puma was an important symbol of the earth to the Tiwanaku people.

Ceremonial incense burner in the form of a puma, AD 600–900. Tiwanaku, Bolivia. Ceramic, paint. 26 × 34.5 × 21.7 cm 20/6313. Photo by Ernest Amoroso, NMAI

separated from one another by a distance that could be covered in one day. Their characteristics have allowed colonial observers and archaeologists to differentiate between royal tambos and more modest *tambillos* as well as smaller installations such as the *chaskiwasis* (way stations for message runners). They all had functions linked to the road, were administered by state personnel, and were managed by local inhabitants. In some cases they even became state administrative centers.

At the height of the Inka Empire, at least a thousand tampus stood along the almost forty thousand kilometers of roads that carried people, materials, resources, and the enormous wealth of the imperial Andean state.

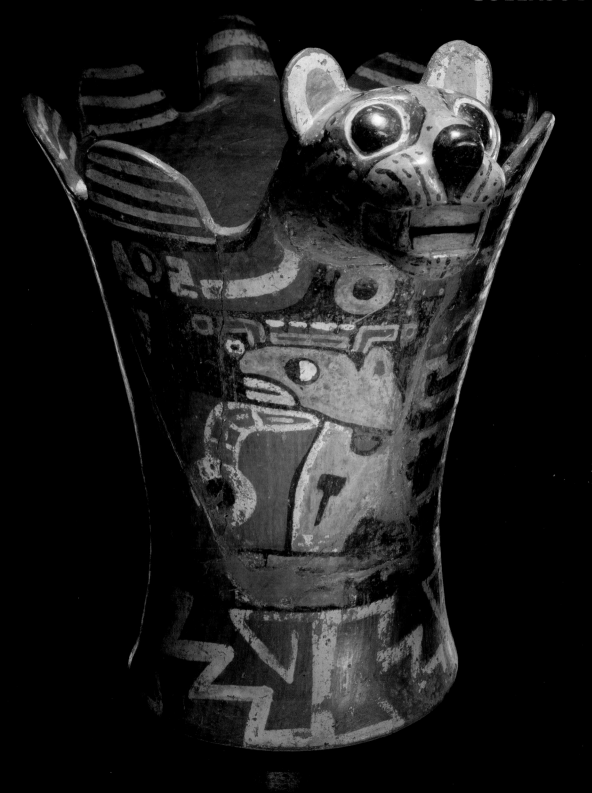

JOSÉ BERENGUER

THE INKA IN CHILE

Most chroniclers agree that the Inka conquest of Chile was begun by Tupac Inka Yupanqui (also known as Topa Inka) around 1470. Only a few sources attribute some role to his father, Pachacutic Inka, or to his father's predecessor, Viracocha. This last attribution is consistent with most radiocarbon dating, which places the earliest Inka traces in Chile at the end of the fourteenth and beginning of the fifteenth centuries.

The Inka expansion into Chile stretched some eighteen hundred kilometers, almost half of the Tawantinsuyu territory. From east to west, dominant topographical features include the Andes, in the foothills of which lie the greatest copper-ore reserves in the world; the Western Cordillera; a central valley lying between the two mountain ranges; and a narrow strip of coastline lapped by one of earth's richest oceans. This area can be divided into three broad regions: the Norte Grande (the Great North), which stretches from the border with Peru to Taltal and is crisscrossed by valleys but mostly covered by the Atacama Desert; the Norte Chico (the Small North), extending from Taltal to the Aconcagua Valley,

a semiarid region also traversed by valleys; and the Zona Central (the Central Region), which extends from the Aconcagua Valley to the Bío Bío River, includes the fertile Llano Central (Central Valley), and is known for its Mediterranean climate. The Inka's effective control extended to the area around the present-day city of Rancagua, although sporadic incursions by Cusco's army reached as far as the Maule River.

In Chile, the Inka usually forged alliances with the populations they conquered, granting them some degree of political and religious autonomy, provided they upheld their loyalty to the empire [state] and continued to pay a high tribute, especially in forced labor (mit'a). In the Norte Grande region nearest Peru, however, the Inka governed indirectly through alliances with the powerful Andean altiplano kingdoms of Pacajes and Carangas. These kingdoms had long maintained colonies in the highlands, although they lived in a constant state of tension with the mountain and coastal populations. With the arrival of the Inka, the Pacaje and the Caranga consolidated their hold on the mountains; they reorganized agricultural activities for the state and pushed Cusco's hegemony toward the coast, relying on "inkanized"

The road system allowed metals mined in Collasuyu to be transported throughout the empire. This *tumi* (ritual knife) was likely made from Collasuyu copper near Cusco or along the northern coast by Chimú metallurgists.

Chimú-Inka *tumi* (ritual knife), AD 1300–1500. Chan Chan, Peru. Copper. 25.1 × 12.7 × 1.6 cm. 15/7200. Photo by Ernest Amoroso, NMAI

Paving often was unnecessary in the dry, flat terrain of the Atacama Desert. Many roads were simply delineated with stones. The modern metal poles (left) mark the Tropic of Capricorn. Region III, Atacama Desert, Chile, 2011. Photo by Ramiro Matos Mendieta, NMAI

officials who oversaw land cultivation and the exploitation of the sea by the local people. The Inka center Zapahuira, in the foothills of Arica, managed work in villages such as Mollepampa in the Lluta Valley and Pampa Alto Ramírez in the Azapa Valley. The administrative center Saguara, in the headlands of the Camarones Valley, probably played a similar role. Farther south, the Inkaguano center—located along the border between the altiplano and the desert—appears to have neutralized previous conflicts between the Carangas and Tarapacá groups, with the latter, from the village of Tarapacá Viejo, controlling agricultural production in the ravines and forests of the Pampas of Tamarugal and along the routes toward the Pacific coast.

As was true elsewhere in the Andes, the Qhapaq Ñan functioned as a fundamental integrating thread in the process of expansion. This network of roads provided the empire with an infrastructure for controlling the provinces. Its layout, *tampus* (inns), *tambillos* (hostels), and administrative centers facilitated the quick and efficient movement of troops and workers, the rapid circulation of information, the transport of goods and supplies, and the activities of the state bureaucracy. In Chile, this road system was laid out primarily over preexisting paths that were upgraded to roads. Known as the Camino Real de los Llanos (Royal Valley Road) or the Camino de la Costa (Royal Coast Road), the Qhapaq Ñan began in Peru, entering Chile

A copper and lead mining area. Region III, Atacama Desert, Chile, 2011. Photo by Ramiro Matos Mendieta, NMAI

by way of the lower courses of the Lluta and Azapa Rivers. After crossing the valleys to the south of Arica, the road turned east away from the desert, running along the foothills and passing through Tarapacá Viejo and the oasis of Pica toward the Loa River and the oasis of San Pedro de Atacama. From there it headed to Copiapó, crossing more than five hundred kilometers of the Atacama Desert, dubbed the Despoblado de Atacama (Deserted Land of Atacama), the driest and most desolate part of the Norte Grande. In the Norte Chico, the Qhapaq Ñan split: one fork hugged the Andes; the other ran closer to the coast, cutting across seven lateral valleys before merging into a single road at the Aconcagua River. After traversing the Chacabuco Mountains, the artery entered the Llano Central, passing through what is now Santiago and crossing the Maipo River in the direction of the Angostura (de Paine), where it apparently ended. Many branch roads connected this Camino de los Llanos with its parallel artery, the Camino Real de la Sierra, which ran through Bolivia and Argentina. Other branches also split off toward various points along the coast.

The Inka carefully assessed the resources of their conquered territories, using them according to their own needs. Because the Inka initially gave precedence to constructing the road network over developing the economic resources of the annexed territory, it is evident

Portrait of Tupac Inka Yupanqui, the tenth Shapa Inka (r. 1471–93). Felipe Guaman Poma de Ayala (Quechua, 1535–1616). Pen and ink drawing published in *El primer nueva crónica y buen gobierno* (1615). Royal Library, Copenhagen GKS 2232 4°

that the fundamental objective of their expansion in Chile was to exploit the new territory's mineral resources. The sole exception was in the extreme north, where the state seems to have placed greater value on the simultaneous development of livestock, agricultural, and marine resources. The main road and its feeders passed through the leading gold, silver, and, especially, copper deposits; in fact, more than half of Inka sites are associated with copper resources. Clearly, the Inka were interested in producing metals and semiprecious stones, including a variety of oxides, silicates, and carbonates of copper, native copper, and turquoise.

To exploit these riches, the Inka organized agro-mining complexes in almost every region, from Camarones south. With the harvests from local agricultural settlements, it was possible to feed the workers who mined the minerals on a grand scale. For example, in areas with abundant water, such as Paniri and Toconce in the Loa Superior (Upper Loa), and Socaire in the Atacama Salt Flat, many new terraces and irrigation channels were constructed, converting these places into true state farms for the production of potatoes, corn, quinoa, and other crops, which were stored in *colcas* (state warehouses). In this way, the regional harvest remained available to supply mining camps such as those at Chuquicamata, Cerro Verde, and San Bartolo, the deposits of which had been exploited for centuries by the Atacama inhabitants.

The Inka state reorganized mining in Chile, intensifying the extraction of semiprecious stones for lapidary work—as was done in the mines at El Abra along the Loa River, and in La Turquesa in the Atacama Desert—or copper smelting at Collahuasi in the altiplano south of Tarapacá, and at Viña del Cerro in Copiapó. This enterprise seems to have been purely extractive metallurgy, since most of the cast metal left the area in bars and ingots for trans-Andean metallurgy centers, where it was smelted again with tin to manufacture bronze axes, *tumis* (ceremonial knives with semicircular blades), maces, and other objects according to Inka designs. In short, the occupation of Chile by the Inka probably led to the first economic, social, and political organization of the territory, even though it is not possible to identify *wamanis* (administrative divisions of the empire), as can be done in Argentina. But it also brought about an interregional division of labor that led to the integration of mining and metallurgical activities on both sides of the Andes.

Administrative centers such as Zapahuira and Saguara in the extreme north, Tarapacá Viejo in the ravine of Tarapacá, Turi on the Loa Superior, Catarpe in San Pedro de Atacama, La Puerta in the Copiapó Valley, Quillota near Viña del Mar, and Santiago on the banks of the Mapocho were established to control the strategic resources of their respective regions. The highest priority for the Inka was controlling water resources, croplands, grazing land, livestock, mines, gold-panning sites, quarries, marine products, and traffic routes. As crucial, however, was securing the labor force that was needed to exploit these resources. To this end, almost all the centers with standing architecture—some of which may have functioned as provincial administrative centers—have several of the basic components of the Inka "architecture of power," such as *kanchas* (courtyards surrounded by groups of houses), *kallankas* (large, niched halls), and plazas. It was here that feasts cementing the ties between the rulers and the ruled were celebrated, creating the conditions for the system of forced labor called mit'a, an arrangement that became the basis of the state's wealth. The presence of imperial cooking vessels in many of these places—including the *makas* (*arybalo* jug) used to store *a'qa* (also called *chicha*, a maize

beer), the *manca* (pedestal pot), and the *chúa*, or serving dish—is evidence that reciprocity feasts were celebrated between the state and the *mitayucs* (forced laborers).

The quality of masonry in the public buildings in Chile decreases toward the southern reaches of the Inka strongholds, perhaps because construction was carried out primarily by local people, and the architectural traditions of the southern societies were less developed than those in the north. Nevertheless, all the major centers in Chile were built at carefully planned sites. In several cases, the site features transcend the practical criteria usually considered when locating settlements of this nature, and include the introduction of symbolic concepts related to Inka "sacred geography," such as springs, rocky outcroppings, and guardian mountains.

The Inka domain in Chile also manifests itself in what has been dubbed the

The heat and aridity of the desert required shorter periods of travel. Travelers frequently stopped to leave stones or other tokens at *apachetas* (offering places) to give thanks for a safe journey. Region III, Atacama Desert, Chile, 2011. Photo by Ramiro Matos Mendieta, NMAI

facing: Colla means "high plain," and Collasuyu was given its name due to its extensive high-altitude grasslands, which were ideal for llama and alpaca herding. The region is also a source of salt, potatoes, gold, silver, copper, and other metals. Access to these resources was one of the driving forces behind Inka expansion into the region.

Map by Daniel G. Cole, Smithsonian Institution, and Nancy Bratton Design with core data from ESRI and NaturalEarth. © 2015 Smithsonian Institution

"inkanization" of the landscape—the deliberate attempt to symbolically project the Inka's political power through public architecture, the Qhapaq Ñan, and *sayhuas*, or route markers (*mojones del Inka*). Some sources suggest that the approximately forty highland sanctuaries (*santuarios de altura*) found in Chile are part of this "inkanization" process. Many of these sites have only modest low walls and platforms, some also have offerings of fine objects, and only a few contain the remains of Capacochas, ceremonies in which individuals were buried with lavish grave goods. The most important sites of this kind include the Cerro de Esmeralda in Iquique; the Llullaillaco Volcano, on the border of present-day Chile and Argentina; Mount Aconcagua; and Cerro El Plomo, near present-day Santiago.

There is little evidence that the local population put up any resistance to the invaders. The *pukaras*, or fortresses, which had previously functioned as the main line of defense, were largely abandoned by the time the Pax Inkaica was established. In fact, the Diaguita of the Norte Chico served as agents for the conquest and Inka occupation of the Zona Central,

where the people archaeologically known as the Aconcagua were located. The situation at the edge of the empire differed greatly, however; there, fortifications such as Chena and La Compañía show that the Inka faced threats from hostile indigenous groups. To the south of La Compañía, beyond the Cachapoal River, lay a wide, unstable stretch of border where Inka penetration consisted only of simple forays.

The Inka obsession with metals, and Chile's early fate as a country rich in mining resources, are clearly seen in Huayllullo's encounter with the troops of Diego de Almagro in Tupiza, in October 1535. The Inka official was coming from Chile, bearing the customary gift of gold that this faraway kingdom offered the universal king of Peru. The load, transported on several gold-embellished litters, was borne on the shoulders of prominent indigenous figures. It consisted of fine gold rods and ingots as well as two large nuggets of the same metal. The pieces were stamped with the visage of the Inka ruler and had probably been cast near the banks of the Marga Marga, a stream in the Zona Central near Quillota, whose alluring wealth was renowned in Collasuyu.

SOUTH AMERICA

AMAZON RIVER

Cusco
Wanakauri
Raqchi
Lake Titicaca
Q'eswachaka
Tiwanaku
Arica
Paria
Salar de Uyuni
Potosí
Collasuyu
Catarpe
Tilcara
San Pedro de Atacama
Jujuy
Copiapó
Shinkal
Catamarca

ANDES

Maule River
Talca

PACIFIC
OCEAN

ATLANTIC
OCEAN

J. ROBERTO BÁRCENA

QHAPAQ ÑAN

Andean Road System through the Collasuyu to the End of the Tawantinsuyu

Colonial documents record that when Francisco Pizarro was exploring the Pacific coast south of Panama in order to reach Tumbes and areas farther south, he encountered a tall ship on the sea carrying indigenous people with raw materials and manufactured items for trade. These Native seafarers apparently knew the routes to the north very well.

At that time, the Andean region was over-populated. Its people had been expanding and integrating their territory, at first mainly along the Andean axis. The empire they established would inevitably encompass a vast area. This expansion was undertaken with the aid of those upon whom they imposed their state organization, which was based on an economy that complemented the diverse ecological zones they shared. These zones extended from the sea to the mountains, and from there to the altiplano and, later, to a strip of jungle and tropical forest to the east.

The Inka, as they were called generically, were continually subjugating kingdoms and preexisting ethnic groups. They established a state organization that used *mitimaes, mitayucs,* and *yanacona* (politically relocated laborers,

those engaged in labor-tax service, and selected servers of the elite) as a way of structuring state service to manage its population and vast possessions. The official religion was centered on Inti (the sun god) and extended to the provinces.

After securing control of the sea routes of the period, at least those that extended from Peru to the northern sectors, the Inka needed a corresponding land route, since no sustainable social and economic organization and expansion would be possible on a state scale without intraterritorial communication. There were state roads such as the Qhapaq Ñan and secondary roads for human traffic and llama caravans.

A similar mobilization, seemingly imperialistic (to use a more European concept of the same period), involved peoples organized as chiefdoms or kingdoms, each with its own history and customs and many with advanced social, political, economic structures. Two such groups under Inka control were the Chimú along the coast and the Colla in the altiplano. The Quechua made use of these peoples' accomplishments and, although their communication channels were less advanced, they likely preceded those that eventually would

Former leaders of subjugated groups could be pacified with gifts like this finial head, which would have adorned a staff used during Inka rituals.

Inka staff finial head, AD 1400–1500. Ica region, Peru. Gold. 8.7 × 4.1 × 3.8 cm. 14/3680. Photo by Ernest Amoroso, NMAI

structure Inka organization. These foundations also aided the Inka in their technological development, specifically in developing sustainable road engineering that was suited to the means, requirements, and characteristics of the surfaces to be traversed. Using this technology, Inka engineers wound up adapting or building forty thousand kilometers of state roads (the Qhapaq Ñan) and other roads that followed the Andes and the coast along a north-south axis, with many interconnections from east to west.

What, then, is the significance of the Qhapaq Ñan, the main Andean road and cultural route of the Andean peoples? This road, and secondary ones, united the region and continue to unite its people, as though the superimposed layers of this traveling palimpsest had always prefigured an Andean America. The network symbolizes integration, and with it, the concept of a more united hemisphere, integrating both peoples and ecologies.

This essay explores the impressive reality of thousands of kilometers of roadway as well as its corresponding architectural infrastructure and social structures—all built, maintained, and administered by provincial authorities, eventually under the organization of the Inka of Collasuyu. The Qhapaq Ñan not only was a physical road but also was associated with other structures such as *tampus* (inns).

We have been asked to accompany you through Collasuyu, specifically through that part of the road system that is located, according to available historical and archaeological information, within present-day Argentina. Many of the early Spanish colonial chronicles and documents reveal the limitations faced by their writers and the conditions under which they were written. Subsequent historical criticism and anthropological examination, as well as other scholarship, have enabled us to decode much of the documentation and thereby gain greater scientific veracity.

Our narrative begins with the accounts of a Spaniard named Cristóbal de Molina, from the armies of Francisco Pizarro and Diego de Almagro. Wounded as a result of a disciplinary measure, Molina traveled on his own and, between 1532 and 1536, reached what is now a central area of present-day Chile, where he encountered Almagro and his forces arriving from Cusco. Using logistics of scale, this army of Spaniards, supported by local indigenous rebel groups such as the Cañari, first crossed the regional border into the present-day Bolivia, reaching northwest Argentina. From there, going through the high Andes, they reached the indigenous Copayapo (the present-day Copiapó), who were situated in what would be the extreme north of the Chilean Norte Chico (Small North) at the edge of the Atacama Desert.[1]

This campaign, directed by Pizarro, highlights the dramatic excesses of Spanish domination, the strength of the position of the Native peoples, and the epic ways in which they resisted the foreigners' attacks. However, the most immediate point of interest in this campaign was the participation of the Paullu Inka, a member of the *panaca* (royal family)—the brother of Manco Inka Yupanqui and the bearer of the *mascaypacha* (imperial ribbon).

The Paullu Inka and the *villac umu* (the high-status priest of the Inka church), along with other officials and indigenous peoples, accompanied the expedition, preceding it in its entire first part through the Collao, together with three Spaniards on horseback sent by Almagro. They advanced over the Inka Road, thereby facilitating the Spanish expedition, carrying the prestige of high-ranking officials and the authority of the state organization. It was most probably in the territory of northern Argentina that they met the greatest opposition.

Just at the point of entry into northern Argentina, something happened that highlights

one characteristic of Inka domination: Almagro's expedition intercepted and appropriated a shipment of gold ingots bearing the official Inka insignia, which was part of the payment to the state by the indigenous Chileans (Diaguita).[2]

Another crucial documented event concerns the villac umu, who apparently traveled with Manco Inka Yupanqui to return to Cusco and participate in the indigenous uprising in 1536–37 against the Spaniards who held the city. The villac umu had just managed to escape a relentless pursuit by Almagro from the Chilean valley of Aconcagua, or Mapocho, in 1536, driven by news of the uprising in Cusco. Although this uprising was eventually quelled, it marked the beginning of a period of Inka resistance, first from Ollantaytambo and then from a new capital, Vilcabamba, where the struggle against Spanish domination lasted until 1572.[3]

Almagro's journey can be contrasted in part with another that took place some years later under the command of Diego de Rojas, which followed in Almagro's steps along the Inka Road. This new expedition by Rojas into northern Argentina—and a later one made by his companions Heredia and Gutiérrez—left Cusco in 1535 with an army of one hundred men and, like Almagro, the expedition passed through Collasuyu on the Inka Road, skirting Lake Titicaca and continuing in the direction of the city of La Plata, which had been founded a few years earlier. From there, they passed through Tupiza and reached Chicoana in the present-day province of Salta, in northern

Road through the desert in Jujuy Province, Argentina, near the Bolivian border, 2006. Photo by Megan Son and Laurent Granier

Argentina. Rojas then turned to the southeast toward the Río de La Plata—whereas Amalgro probably went around Lake Poopó, reaching Uyuni and the crossroads, where one road would have taken him toward Copiapó through present-day Calama and the desert of Atacama. Amalgro opted, however, for the Tupiza Road to Chicoana, which he entered at the beginning of 1536, and, according to some sources, continued from there to Quire-Quire and the Andes on Inka paths and roads. This dramatic expedition is amply documented by chroniclers.

These expeditions, especially the one carried out by Rojas, were described by Juan de Matienzo in January 1566, in his "Carta A.S.M. del Oidor de los Charcas, Licenciado Juan de Matienzo" (Letter to the King from the First Judge of the Real Audiencia de Charcas), in which he provides details of the Spanish advances along the Inka mountain road and the coastal road in Chile, and describes all the difficulties involved in crossing the Atacama Desert. He also mentions the inns, or tampus, along the route from Cusco to Collao, detailing how the expedition proceeded along the road that skirts the western shore of Lake Titicaca and extends to Sucre/La Plata, avoiding some of the difficult environmental conditions in the area of Lake Aullagas and Poopó (although, strictly speaking, Almagro had used the route through this area), and continued on to Salar de Uyuni (Uyuni Salt Flat), crossing the Azanaque Cordillera to reach Tupiza, as Rojas did through Potosí.

Almagro's journey was not easy, because following the Inka Road—which took them to Chicoana from Tupiza—involved traveling some two hundred leagues from Cusco through a land that was "under Inka control," and continuing "to a border town of the Inga [sic], where they killed six Spaniards on horseback" (ibid., 85). This account places them, in all probability, at the edge of northern Argentina, which they had to enter through Calahoyo, near La Quiaca, where there is a road with a tampu. This tampu is shared by Bolivia and Argentina, so the construction is on both sides of the present-day border.[4]

After Tolombón, in southern Salta, Almagro tried to follow the main Inka road toward the southwest, through the tampu of La Ciénaga, reaching the notable site of El Shinkal de Quimivil, in Londres, without doubt a "new Cusco," in Catamarca province. From there, he took a more easterly direction along Inka roads and paths in search of the mountain pass that would allow him to descend from the Andes toward Copayapo, or Copiapó.

The last part of that journey is the most difficult to retrace, and really pertains to the final stretch that reaches into the province of La Rioja, in the central and western expanses of which exist more than one thousand kilometers of known Inka road. Our research, therefore, has extended to roads and excavations of associated tampus to the west of Laguna Brava, and requires going over each possible step between La Ollita and Pircas Negras, passing through Peñas Negras and Comecaballos, among other areas.

In all these places, we found traces of the Inka presence and, as was to be expected, vestiges of coexisting local and regional populations as well as evidence of settlements that preceded the Inka domination. We have not, however, been able to record material evidence of Almagro's expedition with his army, although at one of the archaeological sites of a pre-Inka culture with subsequent Inka influence we have found ceramics that were made using a technology introduced early in the colonial period.

For this reason, we do not agree with colleagues who are certain that the Paso de Comecaballos was the one used by Almagro. We suggest that even if Almagro did use it, our research in that ravine and pass has not yielded evidence of his passage. This is why, based on

Stepped platform and *ushnu* at Shinkal, the site of an Inka administrative center. El Shinkal de Quimivil, Argentina, 2011.
Photo by Ramiro Matos Mendieta, NMAI

documentary verifications and geographical realities, we consider it likely that the passage was between La Ollita and Pircas Negras, with the expedition, given its magnitude, using some of those passes as well as what are called their "side paths."

La Rioja constitutes a sort of cultural axis between northern and west-central Argentina, where the chiefdoms of the Period of Regional Development—which supported Inka domination all the way up to the first Spanish incursions—give way toward the south, in San Juan and Mendoza, to ethnic groups that probably did not have the same social, political, or economic systems but who nonetheless were ruled by the Inka.

The road system extends through the south of La Rioja and then through the western parts of the present-day provinces of San Juan and Mendoza, in Argentina, bringing roads and architecture linked to structures with distinct functions, where tampus predominate, to the valley of Uspallata in Mendoza. This is where the Collao's north-south road reaches its southeastern-most point, and then extends to the west, near the tampu of Ranchillos, toward the present-day mountain pass of Las Cuevas. It then passes over the so-called Puente del Inca onto a variant of the Inka route that continues to the Horcones River, as far as the small tampu of Confluencia, and from there possibly ascending the southeastern slope of Mount Aconcagua, known as La Pirámide (the Pyramid).

During the Inka period, this route reached a height of 5,300 meters above sea level, leaving as evidence the remnants of a Capacocha, the funerary bundle of a young boy, whose grave goods indicate that he was placed there as an offering and who probably hailed from Chinchaysuyu. The site was bounded by a simple wall, almost a *wayrana*, or three-walled structure, serving as a religious symbol of water, giver of life to the fertile fields of the land oases below.

Engineering the Inka Road

CLIFFORD SCHEXNAYDER, CHRISTINE M. FIORI,
& GERARDO CHANG RECAVARREN

T HE ENGINEERS OF THE INKA EMPIRE had a unique consciousness of nature. The foundation of their construction skills grew from careful observation of the powerful forces of nature. These lessons were first applied in creating level land and channeling water on steep Andean peaks to grow crops. As a result, the Inka by the early 1500s were so well developed agriculturally that they were cultivating almost as many plant species as the civilizations of Asia and Europe combined (National Research Council 1989). The Inka Road demonstrates the superior skills of those who built it.

Agricultural terraces on the side of steep Andean peaks. Pisac, Peru, 2005. Photo by Clifford Schexnayder

Grass-surfaced Inka road south of Banos, Peru, 2012. Photo by Clifford Schexnayder

Single steps used on a 10 percent grade north of Huacahirca Pass, Peru, 2010. Photo by Clifford Schexnayder

An engineering masterpiece, the road is the result of careful attention to three major components: the power of water, the energy expended by users (human and llama) of the road, and the energy required to construct it.

Using skills honed in creating farmland, Inka engineers proceeded to build a twenty-five thousand mile road network (Hyslop 1984, 277). Success ensued because they respected the powerful forces of nature. Examination and reverse engineering of their accomplishments can lead to solutions to current engineering challenges (Schexnayder et al. 2011).

Energy of Nature—Water

The structure of the road is dictated by the power of flowing water. If the slope of the road is not steep, water will flow over or down it without causing damage. In such locations the road is very wide and the surface is grass, with the sides marked by walls or rocks. Where the slope of the road is steeper but not greater than fifteen degrees, the energy of water flowing rapidly down the grade could destroy the road. At such locations Inka engineers built steps—one, two, or three steps, in series—into the roadway. A human or llama can easily climb the road slope at such locations. Therefore it is clear that these steps were not built to aid in climbing the grade, for the energy expended by the builders to construct even a single step across the road required a greater construction effort. The purpose of such steps was to protect the road from erosion by dissipating the energy of water running down and over the road. Without these energy-dissipating steps, erosion caused by swiftly flowing water would have destroyed the travelway surface. Hyslop (1984) reported observing single, double, and triple steps used when the road grade was less than fifteen degrees.

Paved Inka Road section, looking south to Huacahirca Pass, Peru, 2010. Photo by Clifford Schexnayder

Inka engineers understood the power of flowing water and engineered the road to control that energy. Considerable effort was exerted to protect the road from water. Through the grasslands at elevations above where agriculture is feasible and for slopes steeper than fifteen degrees, the road was often paved with readily available local stones to withstand rains and snowmelt that were, and still are, the major effects of nature at higher altitudes.

When the Inka built walls, either to support a road embankment or to retain the earth above a cut, the walls were not solid. Following practices perfected in building walls to create terraced farm fields, road walls were built with local stones and had open joints so that water could drain. Open-joint walls allowed water pressure to dissipate, so that excessive flows would not overturn the walls and destroy the structure.

Energy of the User

The shortest distance between two points is a straight line. Understanding this, the Inka engineers, whenever possible, built a straight road to join critical locations such as mountain passes and river crossings. They always employed

In profile a uniform grade

A straight road with a uniform grade. Quebrada Shilqui Valley, Peru, 2010. Photo by Clifford Schexnayder

A series of steps along
an Inka road. North of
Huacahirca Pass, Peru,
2010. Photo by Clifford
Schexnayder

directional straightness, meaning that between two points the road ran unerringly straight and had a uniform grade. They would often surmount obstacles rather than avoid them (von Hagen 1955). Adhering to their practice of direct routes, the engineers would sometimes excavate mountain rock using human energy, but this was done to conserve the energy of the traveler.

Energy to Construct

When possible the road follows the grade of the natural ground. To construct such a road the walkway was smoothed to the desired road width. Only when forced by the terrain would the Inka expend human construction energy to build multiple steps. The road was designed for two types of travelers: men wearing sandals made of fibers from the cabuya plant (the sisal hemp) and llamas. Steps were not difficult for either of these users. A camelid, the llama has feet with two toes and a soft footpad. As a result it does not destroy the stone pavement or steps of the road. In fact, chroniclers describe llama caravans of tens of thousands traveling the road (Zárate [1555] 1862).

Inka in Tiwanaku

ALEXEI VRANICH

T HE INKA JUSTIFICATION for conquering and ruling was based on the claim that they were the firstborn and favored sons of the gods. However, when the Inka arrived in the Titicaca basin, they were confronted with a millenarian sacred landscape and the impressive ruins of Tiwanaku, a civilization that was clearly far older than they. Rather than ignore the obvious, the Inka promoted the sacred history of the lake and lavished attention on the ruins of Tiwanaku. The ethnohistorical data clearly show that the Inka considered Tiwanaku to be a significant ritual place, the birthplace or creation place of the first Inka (Betanzos [1557] 1987; Garcilaso de la Vega [1609] 1987; Molina [1575] 1988; Sarmiento de Gamboa [1572] 1907). There is even a reference to the birth of a boy child in Tiwanaku while the Inka court toured the provinces. He was said to be the son of Huayna Capac, the last uncontested Inka emperor (Betanzos [1557] 1996, 176).

The sun gate at Tiwanaku. A relief of the Andean creator god, Tiqzi Wiracocha, can be seen in the center of the gate. The figure holds a thunderbolt in each hand. Tiwanaku, Bolivia, 2009. Photo by Wayne Smith, NMAI

This pendant depicts Tiqzi Wiracocha, the ruler of the universe. He was a powerful god to many Andean people, and the Inka reinforced their hegemony by tracing their roots back to Inti, the son of Tiqzi.

Gold pendant with image of creator god Tiqzi Wiracocha, AD 800–1100. Peru. Gold, silver, and copper alloy. 4.75 × 3.25 × .75 cm. 19/907. Photo by Ernest Amoroso, NMAI

Inka reinterpretation of the sacred nature of the Titicaca region served as part of an imperial strategy to establish control over the important Colla region. Lake Titicaca and its islands, as well as the archaeological sites scattered along its shores, formed an important part of the mythologies, especially the creation myths, of the local inhabitants. The substantial modifications to the sacred installations on the Island of the Sun established the ritual hegemony of the Inka over this critical region (Bauer and Stanish 2001). Control of the Titicaca region had additional imperial benefits for the Inka. Lake Titicaca was considered the source of all water, and the Inka control over this sacred resource gave them blanket rights to all other forms of water in the Andes, especially the springs, which along with the lake served as the origin points of diverse ethnic groups across the Andes.

In case this point was lost on their subjects, Inka reoccupation and reinterpretation of the ruins of Tiwanaku asserted that the deity Viracocha had created all the peoples of the Andes but, most important, the original Inka royal couples, who then traveled to Cusco, where they established their birthright to rule. Inka rule was based on being firstborn and having brought civilization and reason to the previously barbarous inhabitants of the Colla and other conquered regions. The ruins of Tiwanaku served as evidence of this absolute truth. Recent excavations at the Pumapunku temple complex, which is thought to have been a spiritual and ritual center for the Tiwanaku, uncovered the remains of an impressive Inka settlement, complete with sizable buildings, plaza areas, and large amounts of refuse associated with festivals. On the prominent stone platform of the Pumapunku, the Inka built three doorways, perhaps to create in stone their origin myth of the three caves where the original Inka were born.

With a minor degree of historical and mythological revisionism as well as a great deal of construction, the Inka were able to transform the Titicaca basin and its sacred sites from a potential ritual liability into a powerful source of religious capital.

Salt Routes from Uyuni and Atacama

KARINA A. YAGER

I N COLLASUYU, the largest and southernmost quarter of Tawantinsuyu, the Inka roads and caravan routes lead to some of the most extreme places on earth—the Atacama Desert and the Uyuni Salt Flat, or Salar de Uyuni. The Atacama Desert is located on the Pacific coast of South America, west of the Andes and southwest of Lake Titicaca, on the high Andean plateau at an altitude of twelve thousand feet, or 3,660 meters. Considered the world's driest desert, the Atacama covers an area of 105,000 square kilometers, or forty-one thousand square miles. The Pacific Ocean's cold Humboldt Current creates a temperature inversion that inhibits rainfall along the coast, making the Atacama the driest desert in the world. It receives an average of fifteen millimeters of precipitation per year, with several locations receiving nothing over multiple years. Geologic records indicate that the Atacama has had severe aridity for several million years. The dry Atacama Desert transforms into salt puna and expansive salt lakes, and extends to the region of the world's largest salt flat—the Salar de Uyuni.

The Thunupa Volcano rises from the Uyuni Salt Flat, Bolivia, 2014. Photo by Gabriel Zeballos Castellón

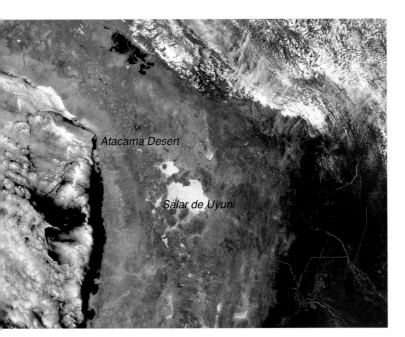

Atacama Desert

Salar de Uyuni

A satellite image of the Atacama Desert and the Uyuni Salt Flat, taken from the Terra Spacecraft, February 5, 2001. NASA

Salt production, Uyuni Salt Flat, Bolivia, 2005. Photo by Gabriel Zeballos Castellón

facing: Paracas feather fan, 100 BC–AD 100. Paracas, Peru. Seabird feathers, plant fiber. 32 × 37 × 2 cm. 19/5791. Photo by Ernest Amoroso, NMAI

The extremely arid area is not ideal for human settlement and has supported only sparse populations. In pre-Columbian times, the region was controlled by Aymara-speaking Atacameño tribes. During the Inka Empire, the Inka established the settlements of Lasana, Chuichui, and Turi in the Atacama region—a feat that exemplifies their ability to occupy, fortify, and establish control in extreme and outlier environments. Following the Spanish Conquest, the Atacama was extensively mined, and mining there continues today.

The Salar de Uyuni (Uyuni Salt Flat) is located on Bolivia's altiplano at an altitude of 3,656 meters. Between thirty thousand and forty-two thousand years ago, the Uyuni was a large, prehistoric lake called Lake Minchin. The enormous salt flat covers an area of 10,582 square kilometers, or 4,086 square miles. Below the accumulation of salt, which can be as thick as a few meters, is a layer of lacustrine mud and rich brine containing large mineral deposits. The Uyuni contains approximately 40 percent of the world's lithium reserves. Islands created by ancient volcanoes, with unusual flora and ancient geology, are found in the center of the salt flat. Considered one of the flattest places on earth, the Uyuni has been used to study satellite calibration and surface reflectivity, given its high albedo and clear visibility from space.

Harvesting salt from the Uyuni has occurred since human occupation. Extensive salt production was well established during the Inka Empire, and roads leading to the area were likely used for this purpose. Salt was needed for culinary and nutritional purposes, including preparing *charki* (sun-dried alpaca meat) and preventing endemic goiter and cretinism due to iodine deficiency. Salt from this region was harvested and packed on camelid caravans for long-distance trade with communities across the Inka Empire's highland areas and beyond. Today, some Andean communities continue to support themselves by cutting and selling large blocks of salt from the Salar de Uyuni.

CHAPTER FIVE

CONTISUYU

EDMUNDO DE LA VEGA MACHICAO

THE CONTISUYU ROAD

Contisuyu was the smallest region of Tawantinsuyu. Located to the southwest of the city of Cusco and covering an area between Chinchaysuyu, to the north, and Collasuyu, to the south, it played an important ancestral and geopolitical role of coordination between the central and southern Andes. Its territorial range extended from Cusco to the valleys and shores of the Pacific and the coasts of Arequipa, comprising diverse, productive places with surrounding areas that facilitated the rapid movement of populations and officials as well as the exchange of resources, products, and ideologies.

The main characteristic of Contisuyu was its function as a region that joined the Andes and the Pacific coast, a distance of only three hundred kilometers. The highest altitude of the mountains, however, exceeds six thousand meters above sea level, making for a complex geography with rapid changes in altitude and a continuous series of ecosystems and productive spaces. Andean societies took advantage of this rich and varied terrain in their complementary economic activities—from harvesting and fishing on the seacoast to agriculture in the valleys to raising livestock and mining in the mountains.

This region was also a sacred space. To the south of Cusco was the mythical cave of Tamputocco, considered to be a *pacarina*, or place from which the Inka dynasty originated. In the Arequipa highlands are the snowcapped peaks of Solimana, Coropuna, Hualca Hualca, Sabancaya, and Ampato as well as the great volcanoes Misti and Chachani, all of which were considered pacarinas by the various peoples of the region and thus were objects of reverence, offerings, and rituals which, on special occasions, included the sacrifice of children in ceremonies called Capacochas.

Contisuyu played an important role in the organization of ritual and sacred space in the city of Cusco. The forty-two *ceques,* or imaginary sacred sightlines that radiated outward from the Qorikancha (Temple of the Sun), divided Cusco and the area around it into four *suyus,* or regions. Contisuyu, the sector "between the south and the west," contained fourteen ceques, the most of any suyu, while the others had a total of nine. The ceques of Contisuyu interconnected eighty *wakas,* or sanctuaries, and they also served as pilgrimage routes. The course of the Qhapaq Ñan through Contisuyu follows the path of the tenth ceque, which also marked the boundary between the

Ocean resources from the coast were transported throughout the empire along the Inka Road. Pueblo Nuevo, Peru, 2014. Photo by Doug McMains, NMAI

119

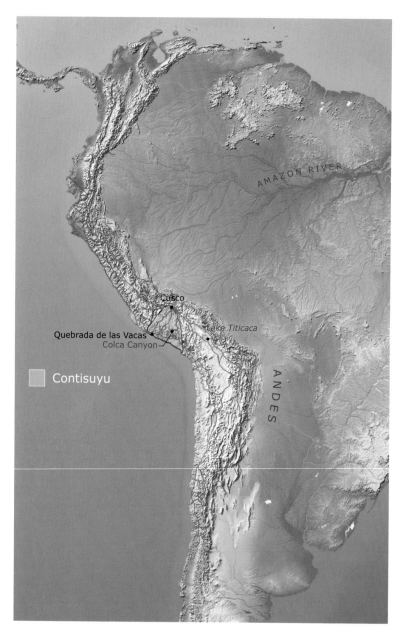

Contisuyu provided ocean resources directly to the *chawpi,* or center, of the empire at Cusco. The dramatic landscape of the coast—high peaks, volcanoes, deep gorges, and coastal deserts—presented complex problems for Inka road engineers.

Map by Daniel G. Cole, Smithsonian Institution, and Nancy Bratton Design with core data from ESRI and NaturalEarth. © 2015 Smithsonian Institution

two sectors—*hanan* (upper) and *hurin* (lower)—in the dualistic division of Cusco. The second waka on this ceque was Pukikancha, one of Cusco's most important sanctuaries, which was dedicated as a temple to the sun, the moon, and lightning, but which was also a sort of art gallery that housed literary *khipus*—painted wood and cloth panels that showed the history of the Inka.

The pre-Inka settlements in this region extend back to the presence of groups of hunter-gatherers (8000 BC), who were the first to establish trade routes for transporting highly prized raw materials such as obsidian from the quarries of Alca and Chivay. These materials were distributed to regions as far away as Ayacucho, Cusco, the Titicaca basin, the Chilean altiplano, and northeastern Argentina. Rupestrian cave paintings have also been found at sites such as Toro Muerto and La Calera, which later were way stations on the trade routes of caravans traversing the region. This group of interregional roads, a direct anteced-ent of the Qhapaq Ñan, may have been part of the Wari state. After the collapse of the Wari and Tiwanaku cultures, various independent and ethnically differentiated groups appeared, such as the Chilque, Masca, Chumbivilca, Aruni, Cunti, Cabana, and Collagua. The Inka were primarily aware of the Cunti, and so they named the region Cuntisuyu, or "province of the Cunti." This ethnic group, which consid-ered the snowcapped Hualca Hualca (6,025 meters) their divine guardian, had settlements scattered throughout the region, primarily in the inter-Andean valleys of Cotahuasi, Caravelí, Chuquibamba, Cabanaconde, and the warm valleys of Acari, Ocoña, Majes, Siguas, and Tambo.

According to legend, the Inka conquest of the Cunti region was begun by Capac Yupanqui (the fifth Inka). During the administration of Yahuar Huaca (the seventh Inka), however, the Cunti rose up, attacked Cusco, and even killed the Inka himself. Later, Pachacutic (the ninth Inka), through a persistent military campaign, permanently conquered the entire region to convert it into one of the four suyus of Tawantinsuyu. Pachacutic not only began a process of territorial expansion but also consolidated and strengthened the state through social, political, economic, and ideological integration, the expression of which is reflected in the Qhapaq Ñan, a road system that interconnected all parts of Tawantinsuyu.

Contisuyu had two lengthwise routes, which were organized and formed part of the Qhapaq Ñan. One was the coastal route. The other was the mountain route, which left Cusco, went through Contisuyu, and continued through Collasuyu. Between these two lengthwise routes were transverse routes that interconnected, crossing the continental watershed between the slopes of the Atlantic and the Pacific and following natural routes marked by the rivers that formed the basins of Ocoña, Camaná, Quilca, and Ilo. There was a great diversity of routes, from narrow paths less than a meter wide to broad, paved roads and side roads, some of which were more than ten meters wide.

One of the characteristics of this region is the steep, furrowed topography, with the many rivers and streams that run through narrow ravines and deep canyons creating serious challenges for road builders. Andean engineering nevertheless overcame such difficulties with the construction of a great variety of bridges, ranging from those made of stone and wood for crossing narrow streams to the famous hanging bridges made with thick ropes of braided plant fibers that crossed the fast-flowing Apurímac River. The latter created such admiration and surprise that some villages of Contisuyu yielded voluntarily to Mayta Capac (the fourth Inka) when they saw them built.

Like all roads of the empire, those of the Contisuyu began at Hawkaypata, the central plaza in Cusco (3,399 meters above sea level). Two main routes began there. One went in a southeasterly direction, passed by the Pukikancha waka, and headed toward Ccorca (3,650 meters), where it turned to the south and crossed Chanca (3,780 meters) and Cusimarca (3,330 meters). It crossed the Apurímac River (2,300 meters), via the famous Huacachaka, which, according to Garcilaso de la Vega, had been built by Capac Yupanqui during the conquest of the region. From there it climbed to Ccapi (3,200 meters) and continued toward

The eight-point star is an Inka motif reserved for persons of high rank. The design was particularly prevalent in Contisuyu.

Folded Inka cloth fragment with eight-point star decoration, AD 1470–1532. Chuquibamba, Arequipa, Peru. Camelid hair. 97.8 × 45.1 cm. 24/5628. Photo by Ernest Amoroso, NMAI

Capacmarca (3,550 meters) and Colquemarca (3,590 meters). Here the road forked, with one section crossing to the southeast toward Velille (3,750 meters), while the main road continued south, crossing Santo Tomas (3,670 meters) and Huarajo (4,120 meters) to reach Iñapata (4,400 meters), an area with many lakes and swamps, which makes it quite likely that this was the place where the Inka Mayta Capac ordered that a great stone roadway, almost five meters wide and a meter and a half high, be built to cross "three leagues of terrible swamp."

From Iñapata began the descent to the sea, where the Inka obtained seaweed, fish, and shellfish which, according to Bernabé Cobo, arrived fresh in Cusco because the *chaskis* ran

a little "more than seventy leagues" (about 450 kilometers) in less than two days. From the coast also came sea sand which, according to Juan Polo de Ondegardo, covered Hawkaypata, Cusco's central plaza, "two and a half hand-spans" deep.

From this point, the most direct route to the sea was along the highest section of the Cotahuasi Canyon, whose abyss of 3,535 meters makes it one of the deepest on the planet. From the town of Cotahuasi (2,670 meters) there were two roads: one that followed the river to its mouth in the valley of Ocoña, and another that crossed the canyon and ran west, along the north slope of snowcapped Sara Sara (5,350 meters) to the lagoon of Parinacochas. From

The coastal desert of Peru, with the Andean highlands visible in the distance. Near Camana, Peru, 2014. Photo by Doug McMains, NMAI

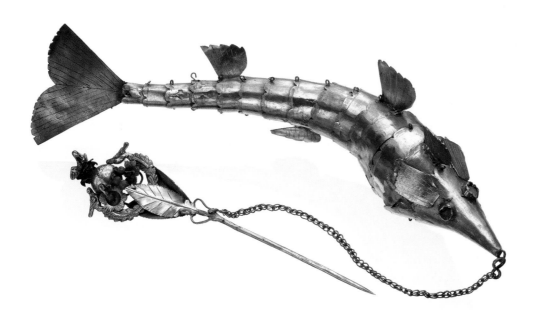

The articulated fish pendant on this shawl pin may have served as a protective charm.

Quechua shawl pin, 1880–1920. Bolivia. Silver, glass. Fish: 24.8 × 6.4 cm; pin length: 14.4 cm. 13/3401. Photo by Ernest Amoroso, NMAI

there, the second road went toward Puerto Inka, a town on the seashore where various marine products were obtained, processed, and stored.

From Iñapata there were also two roads that skirted snowcapped Huajrahuire (5,438 meters), converging at the base of Antapuna (4,938 meters) and then continuing toward the towns of Orcopampa and Andagua (3,550 meters). From there it went around the eastern slope of snowcapped Coropuna (6,305 meters) and crossed the settlements of Viraco and Pampacolca (2,915 meters) to reach Chuquibamba (2,730 meters), a wide valley the strategic location of which made it a regional center, since various intervalley roads started there. In the north and west these roads connected with the Cotahuasi-Ocoña basin and in the south and east with the Colca-Majes-Camaná basin.

The other road that extended outward from Cusco proceeded in a parallel direction, crossing Yaurisque (3,330 meters) and ascending to Ranraccasa (3,790 meters), where a branch road went to Tamputocco, in the old town of Pacariqtampu, while the road itself went to Paruro (3,080 meters) and from there descended to the Apurímac River. After crossing the river, the road climbed to Accha (3,600 meters) to arrive finally in the town of Velille, which was an important point where the roads that united Cusco with Contisuyu and Collasuyu met and diverged.

From Velille, one section of the road extended toward Iñapata and followed one of the routes already described, but the main section went in a southeasterly direction, crossing Coporaque (3,950 meters) as far as the town of Yauri (3,915 meters), where other roads that were headed toward Collasuyu converged. From Yauri there were two routes. One continued southeast to the source of the Colca River, where it descended to the towns of Sibayo and Callalli (3,880 meters). The other path to the southeast passed through Suykutambo, continuing onward to Caylloma

Two figures sit in a *balsa* (reed boat). Waves, fish, and seabirds are modeled into the body of the vessel beneath them.

Chimú-Inka vessel with balsa, AD 1400–1532. Chan Chan, Peru. Ceramic. 21.3 × 12.7 × 7.8 cm. 24/3474. Photo by R. A. Whiteside, NMAI

(4,340 meters), from where one section went to Callalli and another crossed the Cordillera de Chila, the most distant source of the Amazon River, continuing to Chivay (3,640 meters) and entering the Colca Canyon, which is deeper than the Grand Canyon and has one of the most beautiful landscapes in the Andes. From Chivay, following the left rim of the canyon, the path crossed various towns to reach Cabanaconde (3,300 meters), where one stretch of the road continued to Andagua and another changed direction, heading south along the western side of the snowcapped peaks of Hualca Hualca and

Ampato (6,310 meters) to converge with the course of the Siguas River and continue into the Quilca valley.

From Callalli and Chivay two roads extended outward and converged at the *tampu* at Caña-huas, where they met the road to Collasuyu. From here, they continued south and, after skirting the Chachani Volcano (6,057 meters), they reached the valley of Arequipa (2,350 meters), one of the most important in the region. Under the name Camino de Calderas (Road of the Hot Springs), it continued through the valleys of Vitor and Siguas, passing by tampus and areas

Colca Canyon's name comes from the idea that the canyon forms an immense *colca* (storehouse). Colca Canyon, Peru, 2014. Photo by Doug McMains, NMAI

Seabirds fly back to Macabi Island on the northern coast of Peru. Near Trujillo, Peru, 2009. Photo by Ernesto Benavides del Solar

facing: This *paqcha* (ritual vessel) is painted with plants and animals of the Antisuyu region.

Carved *paqcha* (detail), 1700–1800. Cusco, Peru. Wood, resin, pigment. 77.8 × 16.8 × 20.3 cm. 15/2410. Photo by Ernest Amoroso, NMAI

with petroglyphs that marked the route to the sea. At the ocean, it met the coastal road.

The coastal road, called Camino de los Llanos (Road of the Flatlands), ran along the coast and linked the region of Collasuyu to the south with that of Chinchaysuyu to the north. All along its trajectory, it connected mild valley towns of fishermen and farmers, crossing great valleys, such as the Quilca, Camaná, Ocoña, and Ilo as well as small coves, beaches, hillocks, and ravines such as Islay, Atico, and Chala.

All these roads communicated with main routes, the construction, maintenance, and sup-ply infrastructure of which were linked directly to the state. However, the road network was far more extensive and complex, because it also included countless interconnecting minor roads, thereby enabling multidirectional mobility, the linking of valleys, and fluid movement within one of the most intricate of Andean landscapes. In this way, the Qhapaq Ñan gradually grew in magnitude and complexity and, most import-ant, was transformed into a powerful means of communication and a symbol of political power. It continues to serve as a symbol of identity and integration for all Andean peoples.

MARIO A. RIVERA

ANTISUYU

Antisuyu is one of the four quarters (*suyus*) of the Inka organization. Originally it comprised all the lands to the north and east of Cusco, including the upper drainages and headwaters of the Amazonian tributaries, as well as the eastern slopes of the south-central Andes. According to Brian Bauer (1992, 19), Antisuyu, or the northeastern quarter, "appears to have contained the northern bank of the Huatanay River near Cusco and parts of the Vilcanota/Urubamba River from Caycay to Lamay, extending into the Paucartambo region." Michael Moseley defines Antisuyu as "the eastern quarter of Tahuantinsuyu, stretched into the rugged Montaña forest overlooking the Amazon" (1992, 32). John Hyslop (1984) emphasizes that roads to the eastern forests were important as routes to zones where wood, coca, wax, honey, feathers, and medicinal plants were secured. It is difficult to determine how far Antisuyu extended, but the core area, from Chaco in Bolivia to eastern Ecuador, included the sierra and puna uplands. Extreme, varied landscapes dominate narrow and stratified areas where vertical agriculture was practiced. It is possible that, at its furthest reaches, Antisuyu took the

Inka Empire into the flat areas of the rainforest and the *yungas* (montane forests), towards the headwaters of the Amazon.

The Path of Inka Expansion into Antisuyu

In 1992, Martti Pärssinen advanced the hypothesis that the Inka had penetrated deeply into the Amazon basin, especially along the present-day border between Bolivia and Argentina (1992, 120–36). Here, a line of fortresses was built to protect the Inka Empire against "barbarians," indigenous people from the tropical forest. During Tupac Inka Yupanqui's reign, according to Pärssinen and Siiriäinen (2003, 72), the empire extended its dominion toward the eastern Andes, from Ecuador to northern Argentina. They suggest that the expansion can be broken into three main regions. In the northern area it included the Urubamba Valley, where Tupac Inka Yupanqui (also known as Topa Inka) penetrated down to the confluence of the Urubamba and Tambo Rivers, and farther still, along the Ucayali River as far as Pucallpa. A second area encompassed the Madre de Dios and Beni Rivers. The third section included the Chaco region, where Topa Inka extended his expansion to the headwaters of the Mamore

The upper Amazon, near Loromayo, Peru, 2014. Photo by Doug McMains, NMAI

Antisuyu

PACIFIC
OCEAN

Chachapoyas

Machu Picchu
Ollantaytambo
Cusco

Lake Titicaca

Inkallacta
Samaipata

ANDES

AMAZON RIVER

Extending through the upper Amazon, Antisuyu was characterized by
heavy rainfall, high humidity, and lush vegetation—all unfamiliar conditions to the Inka. The *suyu* was populated by small groups who fiercely
resisted conquest. While the Inka never expanded far into Amazonia, they
controlled many of its prized resources, including coca, medicinal plants,
gold, and exotic bird feathers.

Map by Daniel G. Cole, Smithsonian Institution, and Nancy Bratton Design
with core data from ESRI and NaturalEarth. © 2015 Smithsonian Institution

River. It is possible that Topa Inka's son, Huayna
Capac, consolidated expansion into this region.
The archaeological evidence shows that in the
first region, the Inka had a permanent settlement near Pongo de Mainique. They formed an
alliance with the Piro group, which was crucial
for Inka expansion, since this group controlled
all the traffic along the Urubamba and probably
had good contacts with other groups. Following this pact, the fortress of Mainique was
built by the Piro and Inka together. From this
stronghold, Topa Inka went into Manaresu
and Opatari provinces in the middle and upper
Urubamba and upper Madre de Dios regions,
respectively.

Pärssinen (1992) uses ethnohistorical
sources to document contacts that the Inka
maintained farther north, in the Huallaga
region, with the local groups around Tingo
Maria, especially the Panatahua and Carapacho.
Both tribes served as allies during the Inka
incursion into the Chachapoyas region of the
Amazon, where strong Inka settlements were
established.

Both Hyslop (1998) and Idrovo (1998) have
emphasized that a series of fortresses, built
earlier by local tribes in Ecuadorian lands to
the north, were reutilized by the Inka to fortify
the frontier. In fact, from Gualaceo to Chorde-
leg and Sigsig, the Inka reinforced their posts
against the Shuars and other tropical forest
groups.

The Bolivian floodplain to the east of the
Andes presents an entirely different ecosystem
and topography than that found in the northern
region. Here the Mamore, Beni, and Madre de
Dios Rivers flow more directly eastward into
the Amazon basin. Of particular importance
to the Inka was the Mamore River, which
crosses the highly colonized region of Mojos,
where people once practiced furrow agriculture
(Denevan 1966; Erickson 2000). This area has
been identified as Paitite, where, according to

several written sources, there was a temple dedicated to the sun and the moon.

To further explore Pärssinen's theory that the Inka occupied the Madre de Dios and Beni regions, Ari Siiriäinen (2003) traveled to Riberalta in northern Bolivia in 2003. Specifically, he explored a site known as Las Piedras on the western flank of the Beni River. This appears to be a defensive post consisting of a wall about 650 meters long and several buildings. Findings at the site reinforce the hypothesis that it was a military fortress established by the Inka in an area originally settled by other tribes. The design and architecture of this fortified site, along with the presence of Inka ceramics, particularly sherds of *arybalos* (pointed-bottom bottles), corroborate this hypothesis.

The northern part of the Gran Chaco region, the largest dry forest in South America, was home to the Chiriguanos, a fierce tribe who were a constant menace to the Inka. Here the empire was obliged to fortify and defend its boundaries in an aggressive way. This led to the establishment of two prominent fortresses: Samaipata, the origin of which is pre-Inka, and Inkawasi. To the south, Pachacutic and Topa Inka took over the fortress of Oroncota, located on the Pilcomayo River.

Samaipata

Samaipata, in the far eastern reaches of the Inka Empire, probably represents the outermost limit of Inka control. It sits in a valley dominated by the Piray River, a tributary of

This *paqcha* (ritual vessel) is painted with plants and animals of the Antisuyu region.

Carved *paqcha*, 1700–1800. Cusco, Peru. Wood, resin, pigment. 77.8 × 16.8 × 20.3 cm. 15/2410. Photo by Ernest Amoroso, NMAI

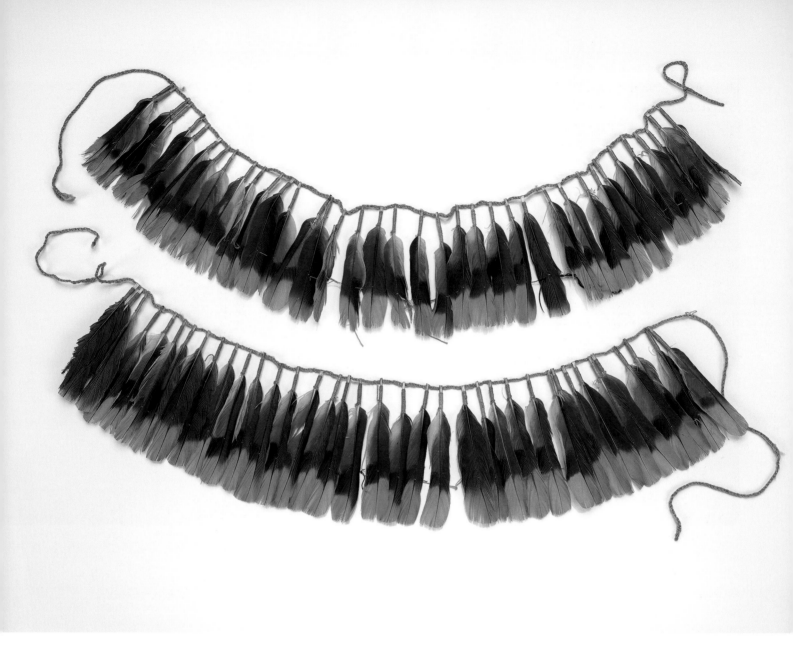

the Amazon at the edge of the jungle in eastern
Bolivia. H. Trimborn (1967) defined the site as
an Inka ceremonial center and border garrison,
although he also considered the possibility that
the site could have been occupied in earlier
times. This hypothesis was also considered by
both O. Rivera (1979) and C. Ponce Sanginés
(1957). E. Nordenskiöld called attention to
the strategic location of the site at the border
with the lowlands, especially between the
humid Llanos de Mojos region to the north
and the drier Chaco region to the south (1924).

A. Meyers, who has done extensive fieldwork in
the area, concludes that Samaipata represented
a meeting point and a travelway for different
waves of people from both the jungle and the
highlands. He theorizes that it was a junction
connecting inhabitants to the more developed
Cochabamba valley. Meyers recognized several
typical Inka architectonic structures, such as
an elaborate complex strongly suggestive of an
acllawasi (a compound where *aclla*, or "chosen
women," lived and worked), with many remains
of spindle whorls and textiles in pots. He and

his team also identified a great hall, or *kallanka* (comparable to the one found in Cochabamba at Inkallacta), a plaza complex, a ceremonial rock area, and terraces and storage complexes (*colcas*). With an extensive canal system, cisterns, stairways, a small fortress with concentric walls, and traces of the old Inka road, Samaipata "clearly suggest[s] an imperial complex similar to those found in the Cusco area or in other provincial Inka centers" (Meyers and Ulbert 1997, 81).

Samaipata was very probably an important ceremonial, administrative, and defensive center, perhaps on the rank of a provincial capital. It is interesting that in many buildings, mostly wooden foundations were found underneath the stone structures, which are considered to be Inka and appear to be associated with imperial Inka ceramics (Meyers and Ulbert 1997, 82). Samaipata continued to be occupied by the Spanish in early colonial times as an effective bulwark against incursions by the Guarani-Chiriguano people.

Another important site some fifty kilometers east of Samaipata, known as La Fortaleza, could represent the easternmost point of Inka expansion. It consists of a valuable defensive post that dominates the plains between the Piray River to the north and the Rio Grande to the south and may well have controlled the route into the mountains. Meyers has definitively identified the site as Inka because it includes a rectangular kallanka-like stone building, a central platform that seems to have been a ceremonial *ushnu*, and surface finds of sherds of Inka arybalos as well as local lowland types. Additionally, Meyers notes that the location of La Fortaleza further suggests that it served as a defense system for important Inka centers such as Inkallacta to the north and Inkawasi to the south.

Further south, Pachacutic and Topa Inka conquered the fortress of Oroncota, a garrison

A paved stretch of Inka road extending through the upper Amazon from Chachapoyas to Moyobamba. Near Chachapoyas, Peru, 2014. Photo by Inge Schjellerup

located along the Pilcomayo River that had been established earlier by local tribes. Another important fortress south of Samaipata is Cuscotoro, which some authors have identified with Inkallacta, Ingapirca, Inkawasi, and Oroncota.

The Road System in Antisuyu

As one can see from the information gathered on numerous expeditions into the farthest reaches of the Inka Empire, the Antisuyu region represents an extremely fractured topography that could not have accommodated large populations except in the core area near Cusco. The Inka incorporated into their empire much

of the Montaña, but their penetration of the Amazon forest was negligible. The borders were unstable and difficult to maintain against tropical forest peoples. Thus, not surprisingly, the road system in Antisuyu is complex and poorly studied because it covered a diffuse area with no clear borders. The difference between the roads near Cusco and the travelways identified in less developed areas further east is pronounced. Clearly the best known segment of the system in the Antisuyu core area is the road from Cusco and Machu Picchu, also known as the Inka Trail, which was discovered by Hiram Bingham (1930) and described by Paul Fejos (1944). Hyslop (1984) mentions that the width of the main Antisuyu road was observed to be three to five meters at several points near Cusco. Roadbuilding on the more isolated eastern slopes would have been difficult, mainly because of the dense forests and forbidding terrain. For this reason, it is assumed that rivers played an important role in Antisuyu, as a means of both travel and communication.

The Inka used roads as a way of navigating cultural geography—to identify and locate people as well as places. Roads also signaled the empire's power and presence, its omnipresence as order and rule, and linked the authority of the state to commoners. Complementarity also played a crucial role, as the Inka clearly understood that foreign areas were integral to the empire. Perhaps the best documented route to the eastern jungle, specifically to the Madre de Dios–Beni area, is that covered by the Spanish army in 1539 under the command of Captain Peranzures. This road, which the Spanish commanders recognized as part of the Qhapaq Ñan, went all the way to the Omapalcas River, entering territory occupied by the Marquires tribe and connecting with Paitite. There were at least two alternate routes to Paitite, one by

land from Cochabamba, and the other, mostly fluvial, from Santa Cruz.

In addition, the roads led to border regions such as the tropical forest, where they played a crucial military role. Along the jungle frontier, lines of fortresses were established to protect the empire. These fortresses were either old fortifications from pre-Inka times that were reoccupied by the Inka, or new fortifications built by the Inka with local labor. *Mitmaq* (groups of people relocated for state purposes) were settled in some areas to maintain the posts.

The Eastern Frontier and the Inka Empire
The occupation of the eastern frontier had a twofold function. First, it provided a defensive zone against the tropical forest groups. In establishing a presence on the frontier, the Inka were able to integrate more peaceful local tribes into the empire by offering them security and protection from aggressive neighbors. In this way, the state obtained local labor for the building and upkeep of fortresses and, using mitmaq, it developed a subsistence economy far from the core area. Second, their presence on the frontier allowed the Inka to explore the eastern region more extensively, solidifying control, accessing valuable natural resources, and pacifying rebellious groups if circumstances dictated.

In general the Inka built up and maintained an effective line of fortresses, where Inka warriors and local and foreign mercenaries interacted. Several authors have suggested that the Inka occupation inside the fortress line can be considered a control zone, while the territory outside can be seen as an influence area. Within this latter zone, the real Inka occupation was probably limited to sporadic incursions that nevertheless created more security.

The upper Amazon, near Loromayo, Peru, 2014. Photo by Doug McMains, NMAI

The Coca Route

SAMANTHA PARY GHAYOUR MCKNEW

Coca (*Erythroxylaceae*) is a venerated pan-Andean medicinal plant that grows principally in the upper lowlands and the coastal valleys of northwestern South America. Considered sacred, it is deeply ingrained in Andean society. Coca is imbued with a profound spiritual significance and plays an important role in the Andean universe as well as in day-to-day community life. Coca provides comfort, energy, and vitality to laborers, diminishing the pain caused by hunger and providing strength and endurance for the long hours worked at high altitudes and low temperatures.

During rituals, coca is the leaf favored by Pachamama (Mother Earth) and the *apus* (mountain spirits). Coca also serves as the main element of socialization, expressing indigenous identity, kinship, and the Andean philosophy of reciprocity (Allen 2002).

The consumption of coca is as old as Andean civilization. At the height of the Inka Empire, coca was well established in the Andes and increasingly in demand. After its conquests, the Inka state assumed control over the production, distribution, and consumption of the plant, and it transported coca from native growth areas via the Qhapaq Ñan (Murra 1992). This is evidenced today by coca material found at way stations such as Huanco Pampa (Morris 1967), Pumpu (Matos Mendieta, 1992a), and Xauxa (Hastorf 1987).

Harvested coca leaves. Kosñipata Valley, upper Amazon, Peru, 2013. Photo by Samantha Pary Ghayour McKnew

facing: Aymara model of coca plant, 1850–1950. Bolivia. Silver alloy. 14 × 15.2 × 8.3 cm. 22/5020. Photo by Ernest Amoroso, NMAI

There were several varieties of coca, with the highest quality reserved for offerings to the gods, nobility, and elite. The rest was shared with the communities and those who were engaged in *mit'a* (labor-tax service for the state). Other notable coca chewers were the *chaski*, or Inka couriers, who carried bags of coca on their travels to alleviate the strain of long-distance running.

Ethnohistorical data reports that many routes were used to transport coca leaves, including one through the *yungas* (mountain forests) in Bolivia (Stothert 1967). The best documented route, however, is from Paucartambo in southern Peru through Cusco and the Aymara territory to the city of Potosí in Bolivia, where the famous silver mines are located.

After the Spanish conquistadors arrived in 1532, they continued to use the same Paucartambo–Potosí route (Glave 1989). The use of coca became more widespread

The leaf of the coca plant, when chewed or brewed into tea, relieves fatigue and altitude sickness. Workers laboring in the Andes often carried a ready supply in small bags.

Pair of coca bags, 1850–1950. Peru. Camelid hair, cotton, plant material. Left: 15.2 × 8.9 × 3.2 cm; right: 23 × 12 × 2.5 cm. 23/8467, 23/8449. Photo by Ernest Amoroso, NMAI

as a result of Spanish exploitation of the Inka mit'a system. Spanish chroniclers such as Cieza de Leon documented the coca trade, describing how the plant would be transported to the mines of Potosí, where thousands of laborers would routinely chew coca leaves, a ritual that persists into the twentieth century (Cieza de León [1553] 1984).

It is important to understand that the Andean coca leaf continues to have tremendous cultural significance for present-day Quechua and Aymara people. It is still used extensively in Peru, Bolivia, the Jujuy region of Argentina, and southern Colombia. Unfortunately, many present-day routes for the coca trade are also being used by drug cartels for trafficking cocaine, which can be derived from large quantities of coca leaves through a complex chemical process (Léons and Sanabria 1997). This overlap of trade routes has intensified misperceptions about coca and perpetuates a disregard for the cultural importance of the coca plant to contemporary Andean society. Bolivian president Evo Morales has been an advocate for the importance and continued use of coca leaves, citing his policy as "zero cocaine and zero drug trafficking, but not zero coca or zero *cocaleros*" (Associated Press 2005).

facing: Included in this sculpture are animals and plants native to the Andes (llamas, guinea pigs, potatoes) and from around the world.

Vergilio Oré (Quechua). *Noah's Ark*, 1900–1930. Ceramic, paint. 45.1 × 36.5 × 26.7 cm. 26/7958. Photo by Ernest Amoroso, NMAI

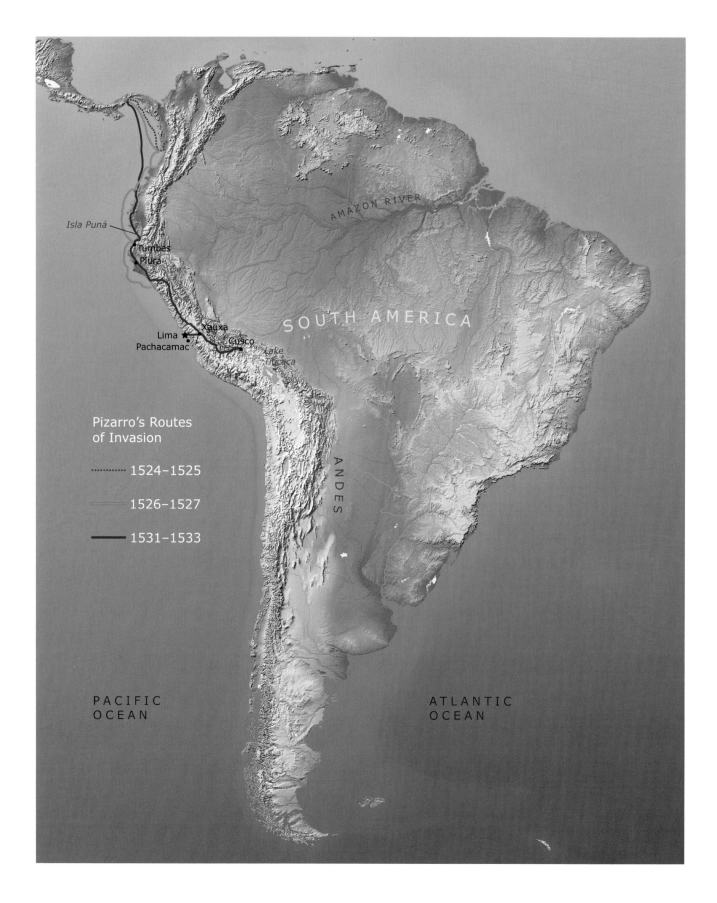

Isla Puná

Tumbes
Piura

Xauxa
Lima
Pachacamac
Cusco

Lake
Titicaca

SOUTH AMERICA

AMAZON RIVER

A N D E S

Pizarro's Routes
of Invasion

············ 1524–1525

———— 1526–1527

———— 1531–1533

PACIFIC
OCEAN

ATLANTIC
OCEAN

CARMEN ARELLANO

FROM INKA ROAD TO ROYAL ROAD

The Inka Road in Colonial Times

When the Spanish arrived on the Pacific coast of South America in 1532, they quickly realized they had discovered the edges of a great civilization. They were astounded to encounter a massive road system the likes of which "could be found nowhere in Christendom" according to an early chronicle (Hemming 1970, 101). Known as the Qhapaq Ñan, the road enabled the movement of goods, people, and armies through all kinds of climate and topography. It made possible the social, political, economic, and religious integration of disparate cultures and nations across an entire continent. Sadly, the same road all but guaranteed European conquest of the Inka Empire, resulting ultimately in the establishment of a new Spanish administration, the introduction of the market system, and the ruthless exploitation of indigenous labor.

Once the Spanish had consolidated their occupation, the intricate road system was thrown into disarray. Originally divided into main and secondary branches, it no longer connected indigenous communities and the state. While many main roads continued to be used in colonial times, secondary roads grew more important because suddenly they were connecting Spanish cities, towns, and indigenous villages that were settled or relocated along the roads. Much of the main road had consisted of administrative and storage centers for the Inka state and held no economic interest for the Spanish. By contrast, it was by traveling the secondary roads that the Spanish could access the economic wealth of the empire, notably gold and silver mines, black and white salt, coca, and other valuable crops. Many of these secondary roads were developed and expanded by the Spanish and christened the Camino Real, or Royal Road.

Transporting Commercial Goods

Under Spanish rule, use of the Inka road system was adapted to suit the needs of a new government. The roads served as a major means of transport for commercial goods and also for the movement of *mitayucs* (indigenous workers, also known as *mitayos*) in service to the Spanish Crown and in forced labor at mines, farms, and manufacturing facilities. Transportation through the mountainous regions of the Andes and through the sands of the coastal desert was particularly challenging and expensive because the movement of goods had to be accomplished

The Spanish used Inka roads to gain access to the empire. They established new cities and founded Lima as their colonial capital. Cusco, stripped of its power and riches, was rebuilt with cathedrals, public halls, and houses in the Spanish style.

Map by Daniel G. Cole, Smithsonian Institution, and Nancy Bratton Design with core data from ESRI and NaturalEarth. © 2015 Smithsonian Institution

Inka roads were built for foot and llama traffic. The iron-shod hooves of Spanish horses accelerated the roads' deterioration.

Quechua figure of a horse and rider, 1910–40. Peru. Ceramic, paint. Left: 8.9 × 9.5 × 3.2 cm; right: 9.5 × 3 × 8.5 cm. 22/1890, 21/8619. Photo by R. A. Whiteside, NMAI

facing: Quechua mule head ornament, 1880–1920. Lake Titicaca, Peru. Sheep's wool, camelid hair. 48.3 × 30.5 × 20.3 cm. 15/8322. Photo by Ernest Amoroso, NMAI

on foot, either by mitayucs or herds of llamas, mules, and donkeys serving as pack animals. Commercial goods were loaded on the backs of indigenous Andeans or carried by animals, which meant that water and food had to be factored into the cost of transportation, thus increasing the final price of the product.

The Spanish introduced wagons, carriages, and carts pulled by horse or oxen, but their use was restricted to flat terrain such as that in Chile and Argentina. In areas where carts could be used, a single load of goods might weigh in at 250 kilograms. While llamas had been the primary beast of burden for the Inka, as well as a major source of clothing, food, and fuel, they were not as practical a pack animal as the mule. A llama could not carry more than thirty-five kilograms, while a mule could be loaded with up to fifty kilograms. As a result, the mule began to supplant the llama and was in great

demand in the new Spanish colony. Following conquest, Tucumán in northwestern Argentina became a leading center for the production and distribution of mules throughout the Andes.

Many indigenous groups followed the Spanish lead and began to use draft animals to bring products to market. Wealthier Native communities in particular had large herds of mules and developed a robust long-distance trade in agricultural goods. In the less affluent indigenous communities, however, the nimble llama continued to be used to carry resources over often treacherous terrain.

From *Chaski* to Dispatcher

During the Inka Empire, the roads were used by *chaskis* (runners) who worked via a relay system to convey messages and small goods. Information was delivered by spoken word or by *khipus* (knotted-string recording devices) over great

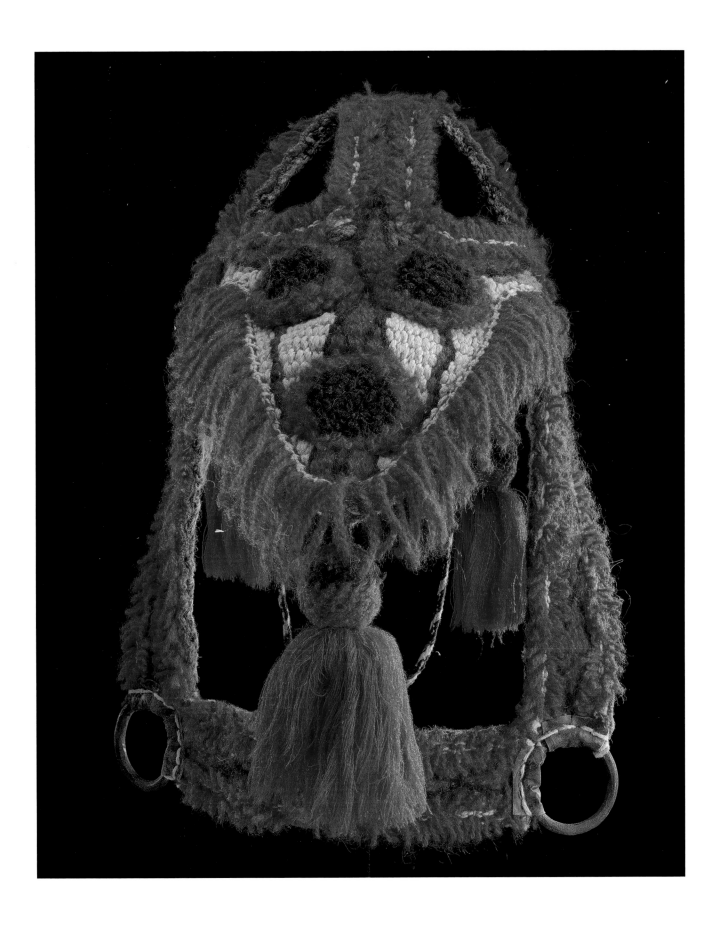

distances and with remarkable swiftness. Most of the *chaskiwasis* (huts that housed chaskis) were located along barren secondary roads on the high plateaus of the Andean cordillera, where there were few settlements. Chaskiwasis were provided by the ethnic groups to which the individual chaski belonged. It was a great honor to be chosen as a chaski, and training was rigorous. Only the strongest young boys who had great athletic ability and stamina were selected.

The Inka did not use a monetary system, so the messengers were not paid. Rather, as with all subjects of the empire, the chaski offered his service as a form of *mit'a* (tribute or tax) and was paid in land, food, and/or clothing. These principles of reciprocity and redistribution were the cornerstone of all relations between the community and the Inka state. After the Spanish Conquest, the system of reciprocity

was officially abandoned. The Spanish administration continued to use the roads to convey important messages, but the chaski system no longer functioned as it had during Inka times. New Spanish laws insisted that postal carriers be paid. Further, messengers were no longer young men but more often dispatchers or European officials who walked the road carrying mail from one Spanish settlement to another.

Roads to the Mines

The emphasis that the Spanish Crown placed on the extractive economy, particularly gold and silver mining, made the roads to the mines extremely important during the colonial era. Evidence of this can be seen in what is now Bolivia, where major mining centers and the cities of Oruro and Potosí were founded along what had been secondary Inka roads. When the Spanish arrived in the area, Inka silver mining was already a huge industry, and the roads leading to these mineral-rich regions were the chief economic routes linking valuable resources to Inka centers and to the capital itself. Some of the roads also bore a religious significance and were dotted with shrines or sacred places, and with *apachetas,* piles of stones or cairns erected at specific points, possibly as a way of giving thanks for nature's bounty. Apachetas tended to be located at high points along the road, marking the juncture of two landscapes, or community or city limits. Acutely aware of the economic and spiritual importance of the Bolivian highlands, the Inka nobility of Cusco managed to conceal the economic importance of these roads for ten years following the Spanish Conquest.

Ultimately, however, the colonists discovered the region's riches and set about exploiting them. Potosí became Spain's primary source of silver in the New World. The city lay at an altitude of more than four thousand meters, and everything needed for operating the mines

The metallurgical resources of the Andes were perhaps the territory's greatest asset in the eyes of the invaders. The Spanish exploited the same mines the Inka had, but to a greater and far more destructive extent.

Map by Daniel G. Cole, Smithsonian Institution, and Nancy Bratton Design with core data from ESRI and NaturalEarth. © 2015 Smithsonian Institution

—including food, firewood, and clothing—had to be transported to the mining sites. Further, only native Andeans had the physiology to work effectively at such altitudes. Again, the side roads provided a crucial link. Secondary roadways were used to connect this vital industry to new Spanish haciendas, indigenous communities with ample supplies of labor, and manufacturing facilities that processed the silver ore.

Roads to Coca

The coca plant was highly revered and widely used by the Inka. It did not grow well within the original boundaries of the empire, but as the Inka expanded eastward they annexed valuable territory for mass cultivation. Expansive coca plantations were established on the eastern flank of the Andes in the upper Amazon. As the Spanish began exploring the region after the conquest, it didn't take long for them to realize that coca held immense commercial value. It was found to be especially effective as a stimulant for the indigenous laborers who were forced to work under dreadful conditions for long hours in the mines. Coca production increased significantly after the arrival of the Spanish, and the coca trade became one of the most lucrative businesses in their new territories. As a result, roads to the coca fields in the Amazon were developed and expanded. Two centuries later other highly prized goods from the Amazon, such as quinine, cacao, and wood, would be discovered and would begin enriching the range of exports to Europe.

Tampus

A *tampu* (*tambo* in Spanish) in Inka times was an imperial outpost comprising buildings used primarily for administrative and military purposes. Tampus varied greatly in size, from very small sites to extensive installations covering hundreds of meters. Each reflected the varying needs of the Inka state at a particular location. Usually located about a day's walk apart, tampus were built along the main roads and provided lodging for travelers, storage facilities, and depositories for khipu-based accounting records. The functional size of a settlement probably corresponded to its importance within the Inka political and administrative hierarchy. With the demise of the Inka Empire, many tampus were abandoned, while others served as the foundation of new Spanish towns and Indian villages. More often, however, the Spanish colonial authorities established entirely new tampus along the secondary roads, which increasingly were connecting the most productive and populated areas of the New World. Many chaski way stations were reconditioned as tampus, and small settlements that had been of little importance during Inka times were repurposed as supply centers, leading to the formation of major commercial centers. This is the case with the city of Huancayo, the modern-day capital of the department of Junín, in Peru.

During the colonial era, the meaning of the tampu changed. Tampus ceased functioning as administrative or military centers and came to signify simply roadside inns, which provided overnight lodging and welcome places to rest and recover after a hard day of travel. They also operated as supply centers, stocking the goods and services required on a long journey as well as pens and feed for purveyors of fresh pack animals.

Depiction of the treatment of Native people who worked in colonial-era *tampus* (inns).

The *alcalde mayor* was an indigenous authority who oversaw the maintenance of roads and *tampus* (inns). In this drawing, the alcalde wears shoes and European pants, but the upper part of his body is covered with traditional indigenous clothes.

Felipe Guaman Poma de Ayala (Quechua, 1535–1616). Pen and ink drawing published in *El primer nueva crónica y buen gobierno* (1615). Royal Library, Copenhagen GKS 2232 4°

Maintenance of Roads and Tampus

Under the Inka state, the widely dispersed tampus had been serviced and provisioned by the ethnic groups in a given territory as a form of mit'a. Likewise, local populations were responsible for maintaining the roads that ran through their land. In return for these services, the state allocated property and provided security, food, clothing, and the occasional feast. The roads connected extended families or kinship groups known as *ayllus*, who collectively possessed specific, although often disconnected, expanses of territory; it was thus in their interest to keep the roads, bridges, and buildings in good working order. Post-conquest, as the system of reciprocity and redistribution deteriorated, the upkeep of roads and tampus became erratic. In highly traveled areas and economic centers where new Spanish settlements were established, public works continued to be maintained. The main difference was that colonial authorities compelled the indigenous communities to provide supplies and labor without compensation. In other areas, however, the Spaniards either dug up the roads completely or allowed them to decay under the iron-shod hooves of horses or the metal wheels of ox carts.

Many indigenous communities were abandoned or uprooted, and the roads fell into ruin. In newly settled areas, as the local populations diminished, the Spanish were forced to seek workers from ever more distant communities. The far-flung Native communities would refuse to provide service, alleging that they were only obliged to attend to the tampus and roads in their territory. It became a source of ongoing conflict. Many coastal roads, in particular, disappeared following the conquest. The fertile coastal valleys were separated by vast stretches of desert, and without a centralized state, the Native communities in these areas quickly declined. Moreover, the Spanish found that

they could transport goods along the coast by ship much more cheaply, with less manpower and fewer pack animals than were required for overland travel.

In the 1560s, Spanish authorities began exploring ways in which they could harness Native administrative ability. They designated indigenous *alcaldes*, local authorities who were tasked with managing civil and judicial affairs. Among an alcalde's duties was the maintenance of roads, bridges, and buildings such as tampus. Perhaps this is one reason that many roads and structures associated with the Qhapaq Ñan are in good condition to this day.

The Inka Road was a monumental feat of engineering and an undeniable symbol of the power and authority of the Inka state. For more than three hundred years, it was essential to

Aymara model of a ship, 1880–1920. Bolivia. Silver alloy. 9.5 × 8.9 × 3.5 cm. 22/5025. Photo by Ernest Amoroso, NMAI

Inka stepped platform with a Catholic church built over it. Vilcashuaman, Peru, 2006. Photo by Megan Son and Laurent Granier

the development and expansion of the Inka Empire. For Francisco Pizarro and his comrades, it was a pathway to a world of unimaginable wealth and opportunity. By shrewdly navigating the road, he conquered the largest empire in the Western Hemisphere and established a Spanish foothold in South America that would last for centuries.

Qeros and Long-Distance Exchange

EMILY KAPLAN

FOR MILLENNIA ANDEAN PEOPLE made *qeros*—ceremonial vessels for ritual consumption of *a'qa* (also known as *chicha*, or maize beer)—of wood, gold, silver, or pottery.[1] Examples of qeros have been excavated from Inka and pre-Inka sites, and colonial chronicles describe their importance to the Inka.[2] Following the 1532 arrival of the Spanish, who restricted the use of gold and silver, qero artists continued their work in wood using *Escallonia* spp. (in the Quechua language, *chachacomo*), perhaps along with other woods.[3]

Inka qeros were typically decorated with incised geometric designs. During the colonial period, qero motifs included flora, fauna, *tucapu* (small geometric design blocks), and human figures, often in complex colored designs. Little is known about the artists but, over time, production varied based on material choices, manufacture, and iconography. Qeros were likely produced around Cusco, Lake Titicaca, and Chuquisaca; most were probably made after 1570 in the Southern Sierras, where many indigenous people were sent to work in silver mines (Cummins 2002).

Two workers toast each other, the Inka state, and Inti (the sun) with *qeros* (drinking cups) of *a'qa* (also known as *chicha*, or maize beer).

Inka carving of two workers toasting, AD 1450–1532. Trujillo, Peru. Wood. 4.5 × 3.2 × 0.6 cm. 14/9747. Photo by Ernest Amoroso, NMAI

Scientific investigations are critical in identifying the raw materials used for colonial-period qeros' intricate polychrome decoration.[4] Artists used resin from *Elaeagia* spp. mixed with colorants as fine, often layered inlays in shallow carved grooves, with plain wood providing contrast. Resin from the species *Elaeagia pastoensis* is still used in Colombia's Pasto region in a technique called *barniz de Pasto* (Newman et al., forthcoming). Chemical analyses of the resin can distinguish *Elaeagia* species, which may enhance understandings of production and origins of raw materials (Newman and Derrick 2002).

Colonial-period qero artists used a broad range of mineral pigments and natural dyes, including copper-based minerals such as azurite, verdigris, and brochantite (green shades); orpiment (golden yellows and browns); and cinnabar (reds). (Cooke et al. 2008) Cinnabar was used by Andean civilizations from Chavín to Inka, and mercury isotope studies have identified Huancavelica in central Peru as the source for the cinnabar used on some colonial qero (Newman and Derrick 2002). Dyestuffs commonly known from textiles were also used: cochineal yielded reds and browns, and indigo provided blues or was mixed with orpiment for greens (Frantz et al., n.d.).

Colonial-period artists introduced distinct white mineral pigments that correlate with early, middle, and late colonial qero styles. Analyses show that early colonial qeros exhibit an unusual, naturally occurring white pigment composed of the mineral cristobalite, a natural form of silica, containing small to moderate amounts of titanium dioxide in the form of anatase.[5] The only known source of the mineral is an ore deposit near Tacna in Peru's Tarata province, part of the Inka Empire's Collasuyu region, which was exploited for its rich minerals.[6] Two other white pigments—varieties of white lead or lead carbonate—have been identified iconographically on qeros as originating during the middle and late colonial periods (after Viceroy Toledo's campaign in the 1570s to extirpate Native "idolatries") (Cummins 2002). Despite familiarity with lead and its ores, Andean artists do not appear to have used it to produce lead-based pigments before the arrival of the Spanish (Howe and Petersen 1992; Schultze et al. 2009; Cooke et al. 2008). Lead isotope analyses identify the source of the lead white used on middle colonial-period qeros as European, which is corroborated by late sixteenth- and early seventeenth-century documents that describe the importation of painting materials from Europe to the Andes as early as 1545 (Iñañez 2010; Siracusano and Barnett 2011). In contrast, late colonial qero artists used lead white from Andean sources, likely associated with mining (Iñañez 2010; Siracusano and Barnett 2011).

Pairs of *qeros* (cups) were used in Inka toasting rituals to reflect the Andean concept of duality, the union of opposite yet complementary halves.

Pair of Inka *qeros* (cups), AD 1470–1532. Cusco, Peru. Wood. 14.6 × 11.4 diam. at top. 16/9707. Photo by Ernest Amoroso, NMAI

This *qero* is decorated with flora and fauna typical of Amazonia, including macaws, butterflies, and snakes.

Colonial Inka *qero*, AD 1550–1800. Cusco region, Peru. Wood, resin, pigment. 24.1 × 19.1 cm diam. at top. 15/2412. Photo by Ernest Amoroso, NMAI

RAMIRO MATOS MENDIETA

THE LIVING ROAD

The history of the Inka Road is integral to the evolution of Andean civilization. The road system's beginnings are unknown, and little has been determined about its development during the first high cultures. Its history during the Inka period, however, has been more thoroughly documented. Under the Inka Empire, or Tawantinsuyu, it was officially known as Qhapaq Ñan—Camino del Señor or Camino del Shapa Inka (Road of the Mighty Inka)—and represented an important political tool for regional unification.

Even though the Inka Road may have lost its political importance after the Spanish invasion, its unifying purpose and spiritual significance have endured. The road also has continued to serve the various communities living in the Andean region: for modern-day Quechua and Aymara communities, for example, the Qhapaq Ñan represents an intrinsic part of their universe, Inka heritage, and day-to-day lives. Metaphorically, it is part of the fabric that links and binds together the towns and *ayllu* (extended-family) communities.

The Qhapaq Ñan is the largest archaeological site in the Americas, an extraordinary ethnographic legacy for the Andean region and the thread that links the present to the past. The powerful Qhapaq Ñan is known today as Inka Ñan, Ñawpa Ñan, or Chaki Ñan, with certain regional variants such as Ingañan in Ecuador and Chakinaani in Peru's northern sierra. Still others know it as the Camino Real (the Royal Road) or the Camino del Inka (the Inka Road), names that distinguish it from non-Inka roads.

The worship of Pachamama (Mother Earth) and the evocation of Inti (the sun god), both examples of Andean cultural continuity, still prevail nearly everywhere in the former Tawantinsuyu territory: in the Peruvian and Ecuadorean highlands as well as in Bolivia, northern Chile, and some of the northeastern provinces of Argentina, even in Putumayo in Colombia. The *wakas* (also known as *huacas*, or sacred places), *apachetas* (stone offerings), *sayhuas* (route markers), and cave paintings associated with the Qhapaq Ñan, despite the overlay of the Christian crucifix, continue to tacitly preserve indigenous belief systems and, in so doing, jointly express traditional and Christian customs. These sacred spaces and route markers serve as altars where travelers continue to make offerings. While the traveler

Christian cross on top of an *apacheta.* Wanakauri, Peru. 2010. Photo by Ramiro Matos Mendieta, NMAI

A modern *tampu* (inn). Ayaviri, Puno, Peru, 2009. Photo by Ramiro Matos Mendieta, NMAI

prays before the Christian cross, he also makes an offering, or *pago* (Quechua), *camarini* (Aymara), or *ch'alla* (liquid offering) to the Andean divinity. The offering is usually a stone decorated with coca leaves, flowers, and, sometimes, an *illa*, or amulet. Where modern roads intersect the Inka Road, truck drivers also stop to pray and make offerings.

The ongoing evolution of the Inka *tampu* (or *tambo*, way station) is an interesting phenomenon. Today these sites preserve their traditional names, but they have been adapted to new conditions in communities or cities. Most of the original Inka tampus have been abandoned and stand in ruins, but the tampu's concept and function persist in many Tawantinsuyu provinces. Tampus still provide lodging and services for travelers and their animals, but they are now called *tampuy-pata* or *tampuy-wasi*; there are municipal tampus and also tampus within private residences. The user pays for services with a present, generally a product from the traveler's place of origin such as *charki* (meat jerky), potatoes, *chuñu* (dried potato), or textiles. It is a form of *ayni* (reciprocal exchange). As the present is given, the giver says, "*Huaqcha cayllayta chayquiyquway*" (Please accept my poverty).

For contemporary Andean communities, the Inka Ñan, or Camino Real, is a "living road" or a "road with life," a route that is imbued with spiritual energy. Users understand the spirit of the road, and even recount having heard voices emanating from its very stones. The spirit may also appear to them in a dream to warn them about possible dangers on the journey.

For the Quechua of Cusco, the road itself is the traveler's guide: "it is what takes the traveler to the right place." In Peru's central mountain range, the country people say that the Inka Road shortens distances. In many places in Peru, Bolivia, and northeastern Argentina,

people tell of their personal experiences, for example, "You don't get tired walking the Inka Road." The healers of Cañar in Ecuador, Oruro and Kallawaya in Bolivia, and Tilcara in northeastern Argentina say, "The spirit of the Inka walks at night, especially in the month of June" (n.d., personal communications).

There is no ethnographic map of Andean roads but, by relying on users' experience, the Inka Road can be identified primarily through toponymy that repeats the word "Inka" and pairs it with a second word describing a specific place—for example, *Inka-tiana* or *Inka-samana* (in Peru); *Inka-arana* (in Bolivia); *Inka-paskana*,

Made in Quechua communities, offering cloths like these are used as part of celebrations and rituals involving *ayni* (reciprocity).

Quechua offering cloth, ca. 1965–70. Cusco region, Peru. Cotton thread, dye. 29.2 × 33.7 × 0.3 cm. 26/7069. Photo by Ernest Amoroso, NMAI

AN DAS DELINGA

topa ynga yupanqui — mama bello coya

Cleuan al ynga los y[n]s callaua
ya - espauio
apasear se

pascase el ynga   como

Demetrio Roca Wallparimachi at the Rumi Colca, the Inka entrance to Cusco on the Collasuyu road. Cusco Valley, Peru, 2014. Photo by Doug McMains, NMAI

The Shapa Inka traveling with his wife on the Qhapaq Ñan. Felipe Guaman Poma de Ayala (Quechua, 1535–1616). Pen and ink drawing published in *El primer nueva crónica y buen gobierno* (1615). Royal Library, Copenhagen GKS 2232 4°

which means a "resting place" (in Chile); and *Inka-pata, Inka-chaka, Inka-qawarina,* and *Ñusta-wayqo.* Moreover, because it is the only road that extends over great distances and holds deep geographical and cultural significance, local elders also refer to it with great respect, using the terms *Inkanshis* or *Inkanshispa* ("from our Inka"). For the Kallawaya (traditional healers from Bolivia), for example, the Inka Ñan is a repository of energy—to regain energy, folk healers will often travel along the road.

Crossroads and/or the division of roads into two or three branches have implications for health and treatment.

The introduction of mules by Europeans dramatically changed the Andean landscape. Although the Spaniards used the Inka Road intensely, they did not maintain it. The settlement of colonial cities and the establishment of a new economic market system sparked the construction of new roads for horse, mule, and, in some places, carriage traffic. Many Inka Road segments were converted to bridle paths for shod animals; others were made suitable for carriage traffic. Given the proliferation of new roads, the Qhapaq Ñan became a pedestrian road but remains the "Camino del Inka." The Yumbo ethnic group of Ecuador, for example, differentiates between the local *coluncos* (pre-Inka road systems) and the "Camino Real."

The Andean barter system, which worked well without any money changing hands, was replaced by trade in coin. This market system and itinerant trade converted the Andean *hatu* (market) into annual or semiannual fairs. The fairs coincide with religious celebrations of colonial origin that indigenous societies continue to observe and participate in. Community members come to the fairs to sell their products for cash or to trade them for other goods. For example, shepherds from the high plateau descend to the valleys with products such as charki, chuñu, wool, or cloth to trade them for corn, beans, and other crops that are cultivated in the valleys. In recent decades, traders in goods such as rice, sugar, clothing, and tools, who move about in motorized vehicles, have taken over the fairs, while indigenous people continue to travel via the "Chaki Ñan," with their caravans of llamas and donkeys.

Along with the trade of consumer goods, there has been an increase in the distribution and consumption of coca and wine and the acquisition of transport animals. Before the highway existed, mules, horses, and donkeys were the beasts of burden, and the sale of livestock was an important and viable enterprise. For example, mules from Tucumán and Salta, famed as the best for transport, were highly prized. Muleteers devoted to moving animals traveled between Tucumán and Salta in Argentina and Ayacucho, Cajamarca, and Arequipa

A muleteer. Maras, Cusco, Peru, 2010. Photo by Ramiro Matos Mendieta, NMAI

A llama-crossing sign on Highway 38. Near Santa Lucia, Peru, 2014. Photo by Doug McMains, NMAI

facing: Alpacas grazing. Marcapata, Peru, 2014. Photo by Doug McMains, NMAI

in Peru, passing through Oruro and La Paz in Bolivia, and through Cusco. The Acuchimay de Huamanga fair was famous for the sale and trade of livestock. Many indigenous peoples specialized in mule driving, some dedicated to moving animals and others to the transport of goods. Cipolletti (1984) has gathered the oral histories of muleteers from Puno who drove packs of mules over great distances between 1915 and 1940.

Field researchers have found muleteers who to this day travel with their mules on the Inka Ñan. In Jujuy and Huamahuaca, for example, researchers interviewed people who went to the Ayacucho fair when they were young in the 1950s, bringing mules from Salta. The mule drivers remember that the journey took between ten and eleven days and required walking between eight and nine hours each day. In Paria (Oruro), the researchers also interviewed a man who was about seventy years old, a member of a family of muleteers. He reported having brought livestock to Cusco, Arequipa, and Arica. On the road from Andahuaylas,

halfway to Cusco and traveling on the Qhapaq Ñan, the researchers encountered muleteers bringing donkeys and horses to Cusco. The muleteers said that the journey between Andahuaylas and Cusco takes between three and four days, while the trip between Andahuaylas and Ayacucho takes between two and three days (author's field notes, 2011).

According to ethnographic and ethnohistorical data, until the mid-twentieth century the Qhapaq Ñan was the main artery through the Andes for pack-animal trade and traffic, followed by the transverse roads that descend to the Peruvian valleys of Lima, Ica, Arequipa, and Moquegua, and to the valleys of northern Chile, and by the roads that go into the high-altitude jungle (*selva alta*) in Bolivia, Peru, and Ecuador. Extensive sections of these roads continue to be used today; in fact, mule driving was a common activity until the 1970s. Much of the traditional transport by mule continues today along the Inka Road, in keeping with Andean customs.

Transport by llama is now an exotic activity, and only a few communities of herders in Peru's southern mountain range and in Bolivia's altiplano continue to practice it. The journeys coincide with the harvest and the dry season. Until the mid-twentieth century, it was common to see caravans of llamas everywhere in the highlands of Peru and Bolivia, as well as in Jujuy, in Argentina. Even between 1980 and 1990 it was still possible to see herders in the altiplano of Canta and Huarochirí and in the mountains outside Lima, as they made their way to the coastal valleys of Cañete, Huacho, and Chancay to work during the corn harvest, transporting the product to storage places with their llamas. As compensation, they would receive corn, pumpkin, beans, and other goods. They were called "the mountain swallows" because they appeared once a year, during the harvest. The llama herders stayed to work in

Panpipe music often accompanies ceremonies, processions, and llama caravans.

Fernando Hugo Barragán Sandi (Quechua). Double row panpipe flute, 2005–7. Buenos Aires province, Argentina. Bamboo, yarn. 61.6 × 25.4 × 3.5 cm. 26/6552. Photo by Ernest Amoroso, NMAI

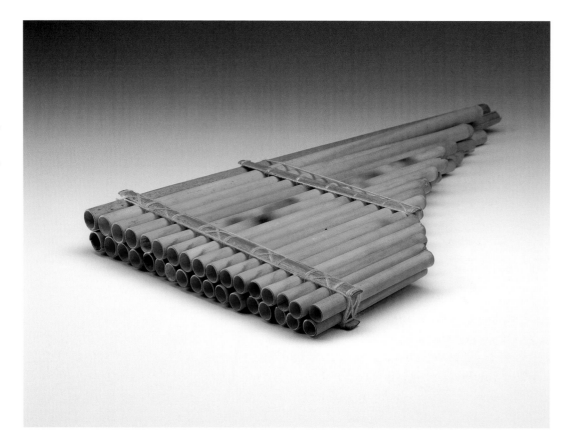

the valley for three to four weeks. The journey from the hatu to the valley on the Inka Road took between three and four days. Shepherds from the highlands of Cusco and Titicaca would also travel to neighboring valleys to trade their products and offer their services in exchange for corn and fruit. Many Aymara caravan drivers moved between the altiplano and the valleys and oases of Tarapacá and Arica, with each trip taking five to seven days (Nielsen 2011).

Researchers have also encountered Aymara respondents who journeyed from the Bolivian altiplano to the valleys of Arica, Tarapacá, and Calama in search of corn and work. Some caravan drivers from the Cusco highlands still journey to the mountain forests (*yungas*) of Paucartambo and the valley of Marcapata; similarly, shepherds of the mountains of Ayacucho travel down to Ayna and Apurímac. All of them

are in search of coca leaves, corn, and medicinal plants. One man who was interviewed in Pitumarca said that until the 1970s, farmers and ranchers would transport gold nuggets hidden in the *chipas*, small satchels made of leaves and plant fibers that are used to transport coca leaves by llama. All these journeys are made seasonally.

While shepherds from the high plateau may have replaced their llamas with horses, mules, or donkeys for transport, they have upheld their customs and have not forsaken their ancestral rituals. They continue to observe their indigenous traditions such as ayni, welcoming and leave-taking rituals, the use of the tampu for lodging, the apacheta (stone offering), and the exchange of gifts. The llama caravan drivers are known as *llameros*, *rescatiris*, *fleteros*, or *andarines*, while those who drive mules and horses are called *arrieros*, *troperos*, or *cargadores* (Núñez 2011). The use of different animals also implies differences in the complexity of the equipment used for the job, or *qqepi*. This is a culture of hauling, both on the backs of animals and people.

Preparing for each journey is a process that can take several days. Preparations include repairing and arranging harnesses, tack, *capachos* (implements of wood and fiber from which to suspend the load), bells and other ornamentation for the "captain" (lead) llama, and all the necessary ropes and bags. Then the drivers collect all the goods to be sold, traded, or simply used on the journey itself. These materials may include offerings for the *apus* (mountain spirits), the Achachilas, and apachetas; objects for the ayni; traveling clothes; *ojotas* (sandals); ponchos for sleeping; and cold meat and other food to be rationed throughout the journey.

On the eve of the journey, the ayllu, or extended family, gathers in the traveler's home to join in the rituals of farewell. Festivities include the sharing of food, alcoholic drink (*a'qa*, also called *chicha*), songs, and dance. The ayllu celebrates the traveler's return in the same way. The songs and prayers are dedicated to the road as a companion and to the sacred mountains as protectors.

For present-day Quechua, the concept of the journey has profound emotional, familial, and religious connotations. For the traveler, leaving home means leaving his family, his sacred space, his world; young people who travel for the first time, cry, kiss the Pachamama, and ask the apu for a speedy return. There are, however, communities of itinerants, such as the Cerro de Pasco Tusinos in Peru, traveling merchants who leave their villages during the harvest months, buying and selling along the way, and return home with the money and goods they have accumulated.

Minka and *chuta* continue to exist in Quechua and Aymara communities as traditional Andean forms of work. The minka is a cooperative that provides services and work for the benefit of the community or the family. Through the chuta, each ayllu commits itself to maintaining a portion of the road or canal that runs through its community. The ayllu leader, or *qollana*, summons the minka for the communal work; the leader also reminds the ayllu that it must comply with the chuta. These two forms of work are used for traditional activities, while the state regulates more modern projects.

The fact that today's engineers take advantage of the Qhapaq Ñan is often overlooked. From Colombia to Argentina and Chile, stretches of modern highway are constructed over the Inka Road. Among many well-known examples are Route 40, or the Inka Road in

A *sayhua* (road or astronomical marker). Pitumarca, near Ausangate, Peru, 2011. Photo by Ramiro Matos Mendieta, NMAI

Argentina; the Pan-American Highway, which extends along the coast from Ecuador to Santiago, Chile; and the Calle Real in Huancayo, Peru.

An ethnographic understanding of the Qhapaq Ñan makes it possible to comprehend its vast temporal and spatial complexity. The Inka road system continues to weave together ancient communities and alliances, much as it did in the past. Its purpose is intertwined with the landscape, cosmology, and service to people. It continues to be a unifying force, and a symbol of identity with a past that is always present through the road. It also functions independently of any modern geopolitical demarcations.

A traveler on the road leading to Pomata. Pomata, Lake Titicaca, Peru, 2006. Photo by Megan Son and Laurent Granier

facing: Modern Andean highways. Near Q'eswachaka, Canas Province, Peru, 2014. Photo by Doug McMains, NMAI

Unless otherwise noted, the words listed are in the Quechua language.

A

Acamama: The name for Cusco Valley before the arrival of Manco Capac and Mama Ocllo and the founding of Inka Cusco.

Achachila: Aymara word for ancestor or ancient, used to refer to the spirits of the ancestors. Usually, the word is used to say that the devil knows more for being older than for being evil. Just as older women are sometimes called Mamachas, older men are called Achachis.

aclla: Chosen women. On an annual basis the Inka collected as tribute the most beautiful and talented young girls from throughout the Empire. These chosen women were used for state purposes or dedicated to the state religion.

acllawasi: A building where the acllas lived and worked.

Almagro, Diego de: Francisco Pizarro's partner in the expedition to conquer Inka land.

Amaru Tupac Inka: Original designated heir to Inka **Pachacutic**. He was removed in favor of another son—**Tupac Inka Yupanqui**, or Topa Inka—because he was not viewed as being sufficiently gifted as a war leader.

amauta: A wise or learned person.

Ancasmayo River: River forming the northern boundary of the Inka Empire, near the modern border between Colombia and Ecuador.

Antisuyu: Inka name for the northeastern quarter of the Inka Empire, including the jungle lowlands.

apacheta: Offering places along the **Qhapaq Ñan** that are typically composed of conical piles of stones. Travelers along the road would leave a stone or another offering (coca leaves, liquid offering, or **c'halla**) as a sign of gratitude that the road, **Pachamama**, and/or the **apu** had brought them safely to that point.

apu: Mountain god or powerful mountain spirit. Also an honorific title given to the governors of the four **suyus** or to military officers of various ranks.

apusquipay: A general in command of a field army.

apusquipratin: A deputy commander of a field army.

Apurímac River: One of the major Amazon tributaries that ran through the Inka Empire. The name translates as *great speaker.*

a'qa: Fermented maize beer, called **chicha** by the Spanish. Important for **ayni** rituals.

arybalo (aríbalo in Spanish): Name (from the Greek) given by early scholars to the Inka pointed-bottom bottle, a unique Inka ceramic shape. Also see **makas**.

Atahualpa: Name of the last Inka ruler, who overthrew his brother in 1532 after a civil war that destabilized the Inka Empire. He was captured and executed by Francisco Pizarro in 1533.

auca: Warrior and enemy.

auqui: Inka prince, son of the Inka king.

Ayar: A title given to founding male ancestors.

Ayarmaca: An ethnic group native to the Cusco Valley and nearby areas that was a principal rival of the emerging Inka polity.

ayllu: The basic Andean social unit; based on genealogy, lineage, or kinship.

Aymara: One of the two principal surviving native languages in the Andes, it is spoken in southern highland Peru and Bolivia. The term is also used to refer to the modern ethnic group defined by the use of this language.

ayni: Reciprocity, the obligation for reciprocal labor.

aysana: The balance scale or handle on a ceramic.

B

Betanzos, Juan Diez de: One of the most important and reliable of the Spanish chroniclers. He married a former wife of **Atahualpa** and spoke Quechua fluently, which gave him access to the Inka version of their history.

Biru: A province reportedly discovered by the Spanish explorer Pascual de Andagoya while exploring the Peruvian coast. The name Peru derives from this word.

boleadora: A weapon made of two or three cords joined at one end with weights tied to the other ends. The device is thrown at the legs to entangle the prey.

C

cachi: Salt.

camarini: Creation, in the Aymara language.

camasca: Healers.

camayuc: Specialists in management or a particular trade, such as metalsmithing, weaving, or reading **khipus**.

Cañari: An ethnic group located in highland Ecuador that fiercely resisted the Inka.

Capac Yupanqui: Fifth ruler of the Inka dynasty (r. ca. AD 1320–50).

Capacocha: Ceremony at a sacred place, usually the summit of a glacier-capped mountain, during which Inka priests offered children as sacrifices to the **apus**.

Cayambi: A highland Ecuadorean ethnic group that was conquered by Huayna Capac.

cayaos: Close relatives of the Inka ruler: parents and siblings.

Ceja de selva: The edge of the jungle; the border between highland and lowland.

ceques: Sacred sightlines radiating out of the center of Cusco and possibly other **uchuys**, or second Cuscos, in the Inka empire.

ceque system: System of **ceque** lines that radiate outward from the **Qorikancha** temple in Cusco. The system organized the **wakas** of Cusco and the Inka ritual calendar.

chachacoma: An Andean plant.

chaka: Bridge.

chakacamayuc: The state official in charge of maintaining and monitoring bridges throughout the road network.

chakaruaq: Master bridge builder.

chakra: A cultivated piece of land.

chakiduro: The braided floor cables of the suspension bridge, made from three **q'eswaskas** (**chaki** = feet).

ch'alla: A liquid offering to Pachamama, or in a sacred place

champi: The preferred weapon of the Inka: a short club about sixty centimeters to one meter in length with a heavy weight on one end.

Chanka: The ethnic group living to the north of Cusco with whom the Inka fought at the beginning of their empire. The ninth Inka, **Pachacutic**, came to the throne after defeating the Chanka.

chaquitaqlla: The Andean foot plow.

charki: Freeze-dried meat. The English term for jerky, or jerked meat, derives from this term.

chaski: A runner who carried messages, **khipu**, or goods along the Qhapaq Ñan in a relay system.

chaskiwasi: The posts where **chaskis** waited to receive messages.

Chavín: An archaeological culture named for the site Chavín de Huántar in the north-central highlands of Peru.

chawpi: Center.

chicha: See **a'qa**.

Chimor: Spanish name for the Chimú kingdom, centered on the north coast of Peru, as well as the native language of the Chimú culture.

Chimú: The ethnic group controlling the Kingdom of Chimor.

Chinchaysuyu: Inka name for one of the four quarters of their empire; located to the north of Cusco.

Choquechaca River: The upper part of one of the two rivers between which Cusco lies. The part called Choquechaca extends to the Camino del Antisuyu, after which it is named the **Tullumayu**.

chullpa: Burial structures found in the highlands of Peru and Bolivia that often take the form of small towers.

chuñu: Freeze-dried potatoes.

Cieza de León, Pedro: A Spanish soldier who wrote an important account of the Inka based on his visit to Peru shortly after the conquest of the Inka.

Cobo, Bernabé: A Jesuit priest who wrote a history of the Inka and an account of their customs and religions early in the seventeenth century. Considered to be one of the most comprehensive and accurate accounts of the Inka.

coca: The plant whose leaves Andean people chew to fight fatigue, to heal, and for most rituals.

cocha: Bowl or container for liquid.

Collasuyu: One of the four quarters of the Inka empire; located to the southeast of Cusco.

colca: Granary or storage structure, an important infra-structural component of the Inka distribution system.

Colca Constellation: Quechua name for the Pleiades.

coluno: A non-Inka local road system in northern Ecuador.

Contisuyu: Inka name for one of the four quarters of their Empire; located to the southwest of Cusco.

Copacabana, Temple of: A major Inka religious shrine located at Lake Titicaca.

Copiapó: A mining site in Chile.

coya: The queen or a full daughter of the Inka king and queen.

cumpi: The finest quality of Inka cloth.

curaca: A regional ethnic leader.

curacazgo: The polity controlled by the **curaca**.

Cusco: Capital of the Inka Empire.

cuy: Guinea pig.

D

duro: Rope-bridge cables.

E

Early Horizon: Ca. 1500 to 370 BC.

Early Intermediate Period: 370 BC to AD 540.

Estete, Miguel de: One of Pizarro's soldiers, who wrote an eyewitness account soon after the conquest of Peru.

F

fanega: A measurement of grain, equivalent to about 1.5 bushels.

G

Garcilaso de la Vega: The first mestizo writer; known for his chronicle, he was the son of a Spanish captain and an Inka princess.

Guaman Poma de Ayala, Felipe: Native Peruvian author who wrote an illustrated letter to the King of Spain complaining of the maltreatment of the Indians in the early colonial period. His illustrations include images of the Inka dynasty and various activities that occurred under Inka rule.

guaranga: A unit of one thousand.

Guayara: An Inka festival during which all the **wakas** of Cusco were asked for an abundant year.

hahua Inka: Outer Inka, or Inka by adoption.

hanan: The upper half, or moiety, of the dual sociopolitical structure.

Hanancusco: Upper Cusco.

hap'inas: Suspension bridge handrails.

hapi'pakunas: Lateral **q'eswas** (literally, *holding tight*).

hatha: Aymara term for **ayllu**.

hatu: Place where goods are sold or exchanged.

hatun: Big.

hatun runa: The taxable male head of a household in the Inka social system. Literally, *big man*.

Hawkaypata: The central plaza in Inka Cusco; where the modern-day Plaza de Armas is located. From the Hawkaypata, the four principal roads to the four **suyus** extended out of the city and its suburbs into the rest of the empire.

Huacachaka: Sacred Bridge.

Huánuco Pampa: Major Inka administrative center in the Peruvian highlands north of Cusco.

Huascar: The twelfth Inka and the last independent, formally crowned Inka ruler before the Spanish Conquest. He ruled from AD 1525 to 1532 and was overthrown by his brother **Atahualpa**.

huauque: A statue made to represent an Inka ruler or high-ranking lord. The size, form, and material used to make the statue varied according to the whim of the person being represented. They could be made of many different materials, including stone, wood, or precious metals. The term also means *brother*.

Huayna Capac: The eleventh Inka; ruled from AD 1493 to 1525.

huayrur aclla: The second rank of **acllas**.

hunu: Unit of ten thousand.

hurin: The lower half, or moiety, of the dual sociopolitical structure.

Hurincusco: Lower Cusco.

ichhu: A type of puna grass used to build roofs and cables for bridges, such as the famous Inka suspension bridges (*Stipa ichu* is the scientific name).

illa: Amulet

Illapa: The Inka thunder god, believed to control the weather.

Inka Cusi Yupanqui: Name used by Inka **Pachacutic**, the ninth ruler, before his accession.

Inka Roca: The sixth ruler in the Inka dynasty.

Inkallacta: An Inka administrative province in Cochabamba, Bolivia.

Inkawasi: Literally, *Inka house*. It was a major Inka administrative center in the south coastal valley of Cañete. It is also used in modern times as a generic name for Inka ruins.

Inti: The sun god who was the special patron deity of the Inka.

Intihuatana: A carved stone at **Machu Picchu** that was used for solar observations. It is sometimes called *the hitching post of the sun*.

Intipunku: The archaeological site of the sun gate at Machu Picchu.

Inti Raymi: The Inka winter solstice festival, which is still celebrated.

kallanka: A large, niched hall.

kallapo: Wood sticks used the stabilize the bridge floor.

Kallawaya: A language and ethnic group from Bolivia; often they are traveling doctors.

kancha: An enclosure or group of houses. Typically a kancha takes the form of a central courtyard surrounded on all four sides by structures, with everything enclosed by a perimeter wall to create a single space. Each kancha is independent of those around it. It is the basic architectural unit of Cusco and other Inka settlements.

k'apa: Measurement used by the Inka; the size of a palm, roughly twenty centimeters.

kay pacha: Literally, *this world*, the middle level in the Inka cosmology.

khipu: A recording device and writing system that used knots on colored strings.

khipucamayuc: A specialist and state official who made and read **khipus**.

khococ: An Inka unit of measure; the distance from the elbow to the tip of the hand, about 45 centimeters.

Killke Style: A ceramic style found in the Cusco Valley and its environs; in use from approximately AD 1100 to the early Spanish colonial period.

L

Lake Titicaca: Name of the large high-altitude lake on the modern border between Peru and Bolivia. The site of the mythological origin of the creator god, Wiracocha, and (according to one version of the Inka origin myth) of the emergence of the first Inka couple, Manco Capac and Mama Ocllo.

Late Horizon: AD 1476 to 1532.

Late Intermediate Period: AD 900 to 1476.

league: A European measure of length, once commonly used in Latin America, that originally meant the distance a person could walk in an hour. The distance varied from country to country but usually was equal to about 5 kilometers, or 3.2 miles.

llacta: A hamlet, village, or town.

lloque: Left. It is also identified with the west and calm water as well as with the concepts of feminine and negative. Its complement is **paña**.

Lloque Yupanqui: Third ruler in the Inka dynasty.

Lupaca: Powerful kingdom located on the western side of Lake Titicaca, subjugated by the Inka.

M

macana: An Inka war club made of *chonta* palm wood and shaped like a sword, about 1.2 meters in length.

Machu Picchu: One of the royal estates of Inka **Pachacutic**, which became famous after the explorations of Hiram Bingham.

makas: The Quechua word for **arybalo**.

mallku: Aymara term for **curaca**.

mallqui: Mummy.

maki duros: Rope-bridge handrail cables made from two **q'eswaskas**.

mama: A title or honorific used by the Inka, equivalent to *lady*.

Mama Ocllo: One of the founders of the Inka dynasty who emerged, with her brother and husband **Manco Capac**, from **Tamputocco** or **Lake Titicaca**, depending on the Inka origin myth.

Mamacocha: The deity of standing water (lakes, the ocean, lagoons, etc.)

mamacona: Chosen women who became virgins of the sun.

Mamaquilla: Lady Moon, the moon, and moon goddess.

Mamasara: Ceremonial or ritualized maize.

Manco Capac: One of the founders of the Inka dynasty; also known as Ayar Manco. Emerged with his wife and sister **Mama Ocllo** from **Tamputocco** or **Lake Titicaca**, depending on the Inka origin myth.

Manco Inka: Second of the post-Conquest rulers. He reigned from AD 1533 to 1545 and led a general uprising against the Spaniards.

Manta: Town on the coast of Ecuador from which the creator god Wiracocha departed out to sea.

manta: Shawl.

Maras Tocco: One of the three caves at **Tamputocco**, the legendary Inka place of origin.

mascaypacha: The fringed royal headdress of the Inka ruler. The equivalent of a crown.

mast'a: The bridge floor mat made out of sticks and cord woven together.

Maule River: River in modern Chile that marked the southern boundary of the Inka Empire.

Mayta Capac: Fourth ruler in the Inka dynasty.

mestizo: Spanish term for persons of mixed European and native Andean parentage.

michi: An Inka official or judge.

Middle Horizon: AD 540 to 900.

mindalaes: Traditional itinerant merchants on the border between Colombia and Ecuador. They have no fixed marketplace.

minka: Calling upon exchange partners to perform labor that is owned.

mit'a: Rotational labor-tax service for the Inka state.

mitayuc (mitayo in Spanish): One who is engaged in **mit'a**.

mitmaq: Groups of people relocated within the Inka Empire by the government for state purposes.

mocha: An Inka gesture of reverence.

Moche: River valley on Peru's north coast. Also the name of an archaeological culture centered in this valley.

moiety: One half of a society ritually divided into two parts. Inka society was divided into an upper and a lower moiety.

Molina de Santiago, Cristóbal de: An eyewitness to the Spanish Conquest who wrote his account in AD 1556.

Montesinos, Fernando de: A Spanish chronicler who wrote an account of the Inka around AD 1642 that was notable for its inclusion of a lengthy and detailed list of Inka kings as well as those of earlier dynasties.

mullu: Quechua name for *Spondylus*, a genus of mollusks found in the warm coastal waters off Ecuador. The shell—which is characterized by long, sharp spines and a bright red or pink and white color—is highly valued by Andean peoples for offerings.

N

ñaña: Term that a woman would use in referring to her sister or female cousin.

napa: A pure white llama; symbol of the Inka Empire.

nina churasqa: Ceremonies and offerings during a rope-bridge renovation.

nusta: A princess, a daughter of the Inka king, or **auqui**.

O

ocllo: Pure woman.

Ollantaytambo: A royal estate of Inka **Pachacutic** located in the Urubamba Valley.

orco kawkachun: Mountain shoes made from a llama's neck.

orejones: Spanish name for the Inka nobles who wore large earplugs. Literally, *big ears*. Also see **pacayoqs**.

oroya: A device for crossing rivers consisting of a basket slung beneath a rope. Also known as a **waru waru** bridge.

P

pacarina: Birthplace of the people.

Pacariqtampu: Birthplace of the Inka, site of the emergence of the Inka's ancestors (the four Ayar brothers and their corresponding wives, led by Ayar Manco, or **Manco Capac**, and his wife **Mama Ocllo**) in one of the two Inka origin myths.

pacayoqs: The nobles who wore large earplugs.

pacha: Earth, time, or space.

pachaca: A unit of one hundred.

pachaca curaca: Inka administrative officer responsible for one hundred heads of household.

Pachacamac: A creator deity in the ancient Andean pantheon who was revered on the coast.

Pachacamac, Shrine of: One of the holiest shrines and oracles in ancient Peru, located just to the south of the modern city of Lima and dedicated to the creator deity of the same name.

Pachacutic: The ninth ruler of the Inka dynasty (r. 1438–71). He is credited with re-forming the Inka Empire and solidifying Inka territory in the Cusco Valley and from Cusco to Lake Titicaca. The name is also a word meaning *cataclysm* or *the overturning of earth, time, and space*.

Pachamama: The earth-mother goddess of the Andean people.

paco aclla: A class of **aclla** who were used by the Inka emperor to reward **curacas** and other important officials with wives.

palla: The daughter of an Inka noble.

paña: Right. It is also identified with the east and running water as well as with concepts of the masculine and positive. Its complement is **lloque**.

panaca: An Inka ruler's royal family and its descendent group. Excludes the Inka emperor's heir.

paqcha: Flowing liquid as well as a special container for liquid offerings.

paskana: Resting place.

pata: Terrace or platform.

Paullu Inka: Brother of **Manco Inka**. Installed as Inka by the Spanish after Manco led the rebellion against them. Paullu Inka ruled from AD 1537 to 1549.

payan: The grandfathers and their descendants.

Philip III, King of Spain: Spanish monarch at the time of the conquest of Peru.

Phuyupatamarca: Town that served as a way station and mountain worship site on the Inka road to Machu Picchu. Literally, *cloud terrace town*.

pirca: A structure made of rough fieldstone.

Pisac: Royal estate of Inka **Pachacutic** in the Urubamba Valley near Cusco.

pishca pachaca curaca: An Inka administrative official responsible for five hundred heads of household.

pishca waranga curaca: An Inka administrative official responsible for five thousand heads of household.

Pizarro, Francisco: Leader of the Spanish expedition to conquer the Inka Empire.

Polo de Ondegardo, Juan: An early Spanish colonial official at Cusco who wrote valuable observations of the Inka and their customs.

pukara: Fortress.

Pumachupan: *Tail of the puma*. It refers to the sector of Cusco that lies between the **Tullumayu** and **Saphi** Rivers, near their confluence.

Pumpu: A major Inka administrative center at Lake Junín in the central highlands of Peru.

puna: The high-altitude eco-zone above the tree line in the Andes.

punchao/Punchao: A twenty-four-hour day. Also the name of a golden idol of the sun kept in the **Qorikancha** temple in Cusco.

Puruauca: The stones that **Pachacutic** claimed turned into warriors to help him defeat the **Chanca** army at Cusco.

pututu: A trumpet made from a *Strombus* shell.

Q

qero: Wood. Also refers to drinking cups that have been made since pre-Inka times.

q'eswa: A single twisted cord made of **q'oya** or **ichhu** (grasses).

Q'eswachaka: The suspension bridge over the Apurímac River in Peru that has been maintained and renewed since the Inka period using traditional Inka methods (**q'eswa** = *twisted rope*; **chaka** = *bridge*).

q'eswaskas: The twisted rope that is made of thirty **q'eswas**—the building rope of **duros**.

qhapac: Chief, or person of the highest sociopolitical status.

Qhapaq Ñan: Road of the Lord, the road network built by the Inka.

Qhapaq Tocco: The central and most important of the caves at **Tamputocco**, from which the Inka's ancestors emerged at Pacariqtambo.

qollana: Traditional Andean community leader. During the Inka era, the word meant (1) genealogical and religious kinship to an Inka ruler, with affiliation to a **waka** on the **ceque** list, or (2) the great-grandfathers and their descendants.

Qorikancha: *Golden enclosure*, the temple of the sun located in the center of Cusco; also the center of the Cusco **ceque system**.

q'oya: One of the grasses used to make a suspension bridge.

Q'oylluriti: Site of the glacier ceremony now endangered by climate change.

Quechua: (1) Post-Conquest name for the Inka language, which was called **Runasimi** before the arrival of the Spanish. (2) The name of an ethnic group living northwest of Cusco at the beginning of the Inka expansion. (3) The warm, frost-free, lower valleys of the highland zone, excellent for the production of maize and other crops.

Quehuarkancha: The temple in Cusco where the Inkas kept a statue of the creator god Wiracocha.

Quispiguanca: Royal estate of **Huayna Capac** in the Urubamba Valley.

R

Raqchi: Location of the Inka temple of Wiracocha in the district of San Pedro de Cacha, about 110 kilometers southeast of Cusco.

rikra: Inka unit of measure equal to the distance of a man's outstretched arms; about 162 centimeters.

rok'ana: Inka unit of measure equal to a finger.

rumi: Bridge abutment (literally *stone*).

runakuna: Men.

Runasimi: The Inka language. It means *men's speech*.

Runtu Raccay: Archaeological ruin of an Inka way station on the road to **Machu Picchu**. Literally means *cave of eggs*.

Rutuchicoy: The Inka naming and first hair-cutting ceremony.

S

Santa Cruz Pachacuti Yamqui Salcamaygua, Juan de: A native Andean author who published an account of the Inka in AD 1615.

Sañu: Inka town where pottery was produced (its modern name is San Sabastián), located about five kilometers east of Cusco.

Saphi River: One of the two rivers between which Cusco lies. After it joins the **Tullumayu River**, it becomes the Huatanay River.

Saqsaywaman: An enormous megalithic structure on the hill just above the city of Cusco.

Sarmiento de Gamboa, Pedro: A Spanish author who wrote an account of the Inka at the command of the Viceroy Toledo.

sarpay: A priestess who spoke for the idol of the Apurímac **waka**.

Sausero: The sacred maize field dedicated to the sun and ceremonially planted at the beginning of the growing season.

saya: The moiety division of Inka society.

Sayacmarca: An Inka way station on the road to **Machu Picchu**.

sayhua: A route and/or territorial marker.

Sayri Tupac Inka: Younger son of **Manco Inka**, reigned after the Conquest from AD 1545 to 1558.

Saywite: Carved stone models that may be similar to maps and one of the keys to understanding Inka road planning. These rock carvings depict canals, stairways, roads, and other structures.

Saywiti: A large Inka installation close to **Machu Picchu** that is particularly famous for its curved stone.

Shapa Inka: The Inka emperor. It means *sole* or *unique Inka*.

sikya: An Inka unit of measure one half of the length of a **rikra**, about 81 centimeters.

sinche: An official or community war leader who is appointed temporarily in times of emergency.

Sinchi Roca: Second ruler in the Inka dynasty.

soncoyoc: Healer.

Spondylus: See **mullu**.

sucanca: Solar observation pillars or towers on the hills above Cusco.

suni: Andean ecological zone at 3,200 meters above sea level.

sunturpaucar: An elaborate tassel on a staff, one of the symbols of Inka royal authority.

Sutic Tocco: One of the three caves at **Tamputocco**, the Inka place of origin, according to one version of the creation story.

suyu: Geographic quadrant, or region. The whole of the Inka Empire (**Tawantinsuyu**) was made up of four **suyus**. Literally, *line*, *row*, or *road*.

T

Talca: The town at the Chilean terminus of the Inka coastal highway.

tambillo: A small hostel along the road, more modest than a **tampu**.

tampu (tambo in Spanish): A resting place or accommodation space along the Inka road and at other locations. The Spanish translated it as *inn*.

Tamputocco: Cave named in one of the Inka origin stories from which the four origin couples emerged.

taquik aclla: A class of **aclla**, or chosen women, selected for talent in playing music and singing. Their job was to entertain at royal festivals and feasts.

Tarpuntay: The Inka **ayllu** that provided priests of the sun. The name of this lineage became synonymous with the priesthood.

tarpuy: To plant.

Tawantinsuyu: The Four Parts Together, the Inka name for their empire. Also see **suyu**.

thatkiy: An Inka unit of distance measuring about 130 centimeters.

Thunupa: The name of the god of thunder and lightning in the altiplano region of southern Peru and Bolivia. The Inka called this god **Illapa**.

tiana: The low, carved wooden stool on which only the Inka emperor and his highest officials were allowed to sit.

tinga: The quantity of **q'eswa** (cord) each family must contribute toward rebuilding a rope suspension bridge. A **tinga** measures forty **brazada** (arm lengths) of **q'eswa**, which is the equivalent of 70 meters (230 feet).

tinkuy: The joining of two parts, such as the confluence of two rivers. Believed to be a sacred spot.

Tiqzi Wiracocha: The Andean creator god worshipped by the Inkas. This term also came to be applied to Europeans by Natives Andeans.

Titu Cusi: Sixth ruler after the Spanish Conquest. He ruled from 1558 to 1571 and led the resistance to the Spanish.

Titu Cusi Huallpa: Son and successor of **Tupac Inka Yupanqui** (also known as Topa Inka) who assumed the name of **Huayna Capac** upon accession to the throne.

Tiwanaku: Archaeological site at the southern end of **Lake Titicaca** in Bolivia. It was the capital of the Tiwanaku state during the **Middle Horizon**.

tucapu: The small, colorful square designs woven into garments worn by Inka royalty.

Tocori: The **waka** that presided over the irrigation systems of Inka Cusco.

tocoricoc: A top official of a **wamani**.

Toledo, Francisco Álvarez de: The viceroy who ruled Peru for the Spanish crown from 1569 to 1581.

Tomebamba: Northern capital of the Inka established near modern Cuenca, Ecuador, by the Inka **Huayna Capac**.

Topa Hualpa: First of the Inka rulers after the Spanish Conquest. He was placed on the throne by Pizarro in AD 1533 and died shortly afterward.

tora: Term used by a woman to refer to her brother or male cousin.

tukuyrikoq: Term meaning *he who sees all*. An Inka official inspector was chosen from close family members of the ruler and went about the empire checking on how well administrators were performing their jobs.

Tullumayu River: The lower part of one of the two rivers between which Cusco lies. The part called Tullumayu extends from the Camino del Antisuyu to its point of confluence with the **Saphi River**. After it joins the Saphi, it becomes the Huatanay River.

Tumbes: The place on the far north coast of Peru where Pizarro's expedition landed.

tumi: Ceremonial knife with a semicircular blade.

Tupac Amaru: Seventh and last ruler after the Spanish Conquest. He reigned from AD 1571 to 1572.

Tupac Inka Yupanqui: The tenth ruler of the Inka dynasty, who reigned from AD 1471 to 1493. Also known as Topa Inka.

tupu: (1) An Inka measure of distance of six thousand paces, or 7.8 kilometers. (2) An Inka measure of area of 25 **rikra** by 50 **rikra**, or about 3,280 square meters. (3) Spatulate-headed pins made of various metals that were used by Andean women to fasten their clothing.

U

uchuy: Second, or small.

ukhu pacha: Literally, *the world below*, or the underground; refers to the lowest of the three tiers in Inka cosmology.

Urubamba River: Major tributary of the Amazon River that flows through the Inka heartland.

ushnu: A stagelike platform structure found in the main plazas of Inka cities and towns from which the emperor of his surrogates could preside over ceremonies.

V

Vilcabamba: A wild part of the mountain region northwest of Cusco where the Inka resisting the Spanish Conquest built their last capital.

Vilcanota: Name of the river that becomes the **Urubamba** after it passes Cusco.

Vilcashuaman: Inka administrative center in the province of Vilcas, Ayacucho.

villac umu: The Inka head priest.

Viracocha Inka: The eighth ruler in the Inka dynasty, who reigned from 1410 until being overthrown by **Pachacutic** in AD 1438.

Vitcos: Town in the **Vilcabamba** region where Inkas resisting the Spanish sought refuge.

W

waka: A sacred object or space thought to contain animistic spirits. These could be mummies, stones, mountain peaks, or anything unusual in nature whether of great beauty or ugliness. Wakas served as guardians of people, places, or things.

wakapunku: Sacred door or entrance.

wamani: (1) The sacred spirit of a mountain peak. (2) An administrative division of the Inka Empire. (3) An Inka unit of distance consisting of 30 **topos** or 234 kilometers.

Wanakauri: (1) A mountain on the edge of the Cusco valley that was sacred to the Inka. (2) A sacred stone on this mountain believed to be the body of Ayar Ucho, one of the brothers of **Manco Capac**. (3) A sacred war idol carried into battle by Inka armies.

wanu: Guano, fertilizer.

waranqa curaca: An Inka administrative officer in charge of one thousand households.

Wari: (1) Sacred or revered. (2) The name of a pre-Inka archaeological culture centered at the site of the same name in Ayacucho. The Wari built road networks that were eventually incorporated into the Qhapaq Ñan under Inka rule.

Wari Wilka: The name of a famous oracle during the Inka period. It was located at an earlier temple belonging to the Wari Empire near the modern city of Huancayo, in the central Peruvian highlands.

waru waru: Pulley bridge

wayrana: An Andean kiln for melting metals.

X

Xerez, Francisco de: One of Pizarro's soldiers, who wrote an eyewitness account immediately after the conquest of the Inka.

Y

Yachaywasi: An Inka-era school in Cusco for the sons of both Inka and provincial nobility.

Yahuar Huaca: The seventh ruler in the Inka dynasty.

yana: A servant or a male/female couple.

yana aclla: A class of **aclla**, or chosen women, consisting of the least desirable girls, who became servants.

yanacona: A special class of people outside of the normal Inka hierarchy who were exempt from taxation and worked as retainers for the nobility.

yana phuyu: Dark clouds, the spaces between the constellations, in which the Inka saw objects and animals from their daily lives

yuku: An Inka unit of measure consisting of the distance between the thumb and forefinger of an outstretched hand; about twelve to fourteen centimeters.

yunga (maritime): Coastal valley in Peru between 500 and 2,500 meters in elevation.

yungas: A stretch of forest along the eastern slope of the Andes extending from Peru south through Bolivia and northern Argentina. A transitional zone between the Andean highlands and the Amazon rainforests.

yupay: To count.

yurac aclla: The highest-ranking chosen women, young women of Inka blood who were consecrated as virgins to Inti, the sun god.

yuya q'eswa: The rope used to bring **duros** across the gorge to the other side of the rope suspension bridge as it's being rebuilt.

overleaf: This *manta* (shawl) includes scenes of people and animals depicted in a Spanish style as well as bands of *tucapu* (small squares), an Inka design.

Colonial Inka woman's *manta* and detail, AD 1500–1700. Koati Island, Lake Titicaca, Bolivia. Cotton, camelid hair, silver metallic threads. 110.2 × 118.7 cm. 5/3773. Photo by Ernest Amoroso, NMAI

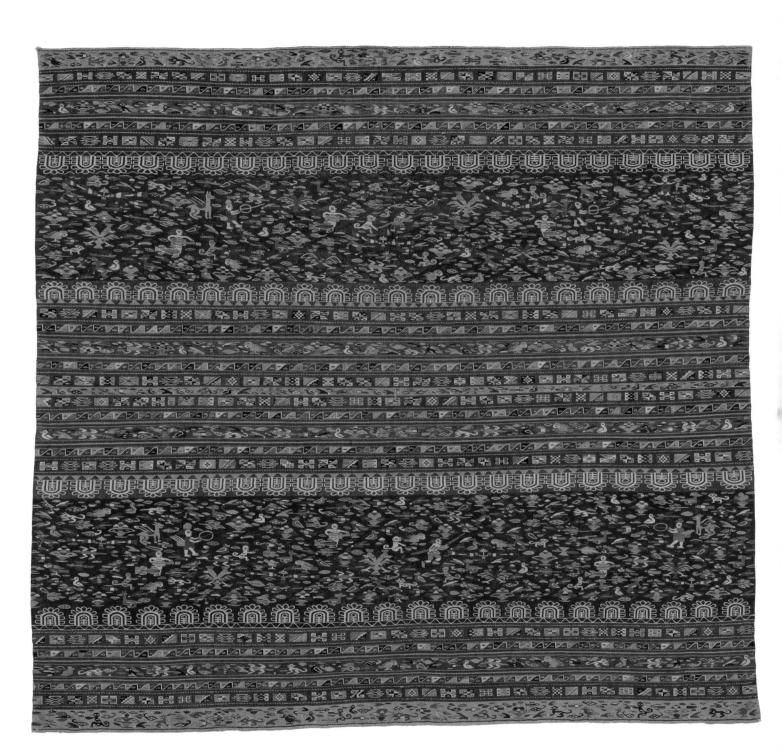

NOTES

Qhapaq Ñan and Its Landscapes VICTORIA CASTRO

1. For reasons of space, this essay refers only to the main mountain road.

2. This model can be applied to the entire western Andean slope, at least from Puno to the second region of Antofagasta in Chile.

Inka City Planning in Cusco
RICARDO MAR MEDINA & JOSÉ ALEJANDRO BELTRÁN-CABALLERO

1. Excavations carried out in Cusco have documented the presence of structures and levels from the Killke period in parts of the ancient city quite distant from one another (Bauer 2008, 157): in the Qorikancha (Rowe 1944), beneath the Hotel Libertador (González Corrales 1984), in Cusikancha on Calle Triunfo, in Colcampata and in Saqsaywaman (Rowe 1944).

2. Colonial sources specify that Cusco rivers were channeled and the city remodeled following a plan that Juan de Betanzos attributes to Pachacutic. Archaeological data confirm that the capital of Tawantinsuyu was the result of a planned operation and shows the coherent, uniform character of the river channeling and terrace construction.

3. There are doubtless other sacred places in the topography of Cusco, although the archaeological evidence is extremely limited. As Juan Polo de Ondegardo ([1571] 1990, 55) observes: "The City of Cusco was house and home to gods, and so, in all the city, there was no spring or byway, no wall that was not said to be mysterious and seen as manifestations of the temples of that City." The difficulties surrounding the identification of the Andean shrines that were inventoried by Cristóbal de Albornoz, Bernabé Cobo, and Polo de Ondegardo demonstrate the early efficiency of the Spanish as "eradicators of idolatry" (Zuidema 1964; Bauer 1998). Nevertheless, we have a relatively well-known *waka*, the Sapantiana waka, located at the edge of the ancient city of Cusco, which helps in restoring the form of places marked by the material presence of nature and imbued with a sacred quality.

4. Cristóbal de Albornoz ([1580] 1967, 26) cites "*Pucamarca quisuarcancha*, which was the house of the maker of thunder."

5. In the first book of the Casa de Cabildo: "Mayor Beltran de Castro was shown a plot of land in the houses where the so-called Ochullo adjoins the main church and the Plaza de Frontera and the Calle del Cacique on the other side" (Rivera Serna [1534] 1965; Farrington 2010).

6. Brian Bauer (2008, 211–66) provides a compilation of the innumerable literary references to all these buildings.

7. Pedro Cieza de León collected references to the state of the basin before the reestablishment of the city: "And they told particularly about the Valley of Cusco being barren and that the land they sowed never bore fruit." For that reason, "from within the great mountains of the Andes, they brought many thousands of loads of soil, which they spread over the entire [valley] . . . which [became] . . . very fertile as we now see it" ([1553] 1986, chap. 31, n. 101).

Mountains and the Sacred Landscape of the Inka
CHRISTIAN VITRY

1. A bivalve mollusk found in the warm Ecuadorean waters off the coast of Guayaquil, and off the coast of northern Peru. It was considered an element of social prestige and symbolic-religious power by prehistoric Andean societies. Pre-Hispanic priests used the mollusks to forecast the weather and were able to predict the rainy season four months in advance. The explanation for these predictions is based on the thermal sensitivity of the *Spondylus*. It is found exclusively in warm waters caused by marine currents. The entire Peruvian coast feels the cyclical influence of the cold Humboldt Current. However, as warm Ecuadorean currents advance over cold ones, they bring about a significant change in the meteorological conditions that affect agriculture. Today, this change in meteorological conditions is known as El Niño, which is characterized by an abundance of precipitation. If cold currents are more powerful, however, the opposite conditions will prevail, and it will be a very dry year. The priests knew all this because of the distribution and quantity of the mollusks gathered by specialists, who immediately spread the news. This allowed Inka leaders and administrators to postpone or cancel the sowing season, which either yielded abundant harvests or avoided big losses. We can only imagine the symbolic power that being the bearers of this predictive information gave to the Inka. In the eyes of the Andeans, it was possibly the most concrete evidence of the quasidivinity of the Children of the Sun (Vitry 2008).

2. *Lloke* is a thread with a reverse twist used in ceremonies. Some Andean communities believe that this type of thread is for the dead because, they say, the dead no longer have vital energy or strength. A similar sense of lethargy can be induced by spinning in reverse. In general, lloke thread was made with threads of contrasting colors, called dappled threads or *moliné*. It is currently used as an element of protection against evil spirits during the Pachamama feast, a time when participants wear lloke thread on their wrists and sometimes on their ankles.

3. Johan Reinhard was kind enough to send me a photograph of a shoe made in the same way as the one found in Ampato, but there are no studies of or publications about it.

Qhapaq Ñan and the Khipu: Inka Administration on the Road and along the Cord GARY URTON

1. See especially David Jenkins (2001).

2. For a discussion of place-values in the landscape, see Gary Urton (2012, 494–95).

3. Personal communication to the author, 2012.

Qhapaq Ñan: Andean Road System through the Collasuyu to the End of the Tawantinsuyu J. ROBERTO BÁRCENA

1. Numerous chronicles recount this event, including those attributed to Molina (known as El Chileno or El Almagrista [the Chilean or Follower of Almagro]) or to Bartolomé de Segovia. Both were priests who accompanied Almagro on his journey of exploration and conquest. The Molina/Segovia chronicle, *Relación de muchas cosas acaecidas en el Perú*, or *Account of Many Events That Occurred in Peru* (Molina/Segovia [1553] 1968), relates events that occurred before 1552.

2. Testimonies demonstrate another noteworthy fact: the expedition members are estimated to have numbered in the thousands, suggesting the massive supplies that such a mobilization would have required. At the start of the expedition, the Spaniards "removed a large number of sheep [mainly camelids such as llamas] from Cusco," [as well as] clothing and materials, which they carried with them (ibid., 84). During the course of the expedition, they secured additional supplies from the Native population.

3. Almagro had also sent Saavedra ahead, with the Spaniards who wanted to follow him, with the "assignment that . . . at one hundred thirty leagues from Cusco [he was] to lay siege to a town . . . which he did and stopped in the town of Paria one hundred thirty leagues from Cusco, and all the land of Collao went there and from the Charcas" (ibid., 84). Almagro himself finally reached Saavedra, in Paria, and continued ahead along the "Camino Real—the main Inka road through the mountains—toward the province of the Chichas, whose capital was the town of Topiza—present-day Tupiza, capital of the province of Sud Chichas in Bolivia—where . . . Paulo Topa Inga and Vila Oma [the *villac umu*] were awaiting him" (ibid., 84). When Almagro arrived in Tupiza, "by the royal road of the Inga which leads to the provinces of the Chichas," he asked Paullu Inka and Vila Oma "about the three Spaniards on horseback . . . and he was told that they had gone ahead and followed the road of the Inga, that went straight to the provinces of Chile" (ibid., 85).

4. "From there they left for the province of Chicoana, which was the home of the Diaguitas—a generic name for the indigenous people of the Period of Regional Development, or Chiefdoms of Northern Argentina and, by extension, similar areas of the Chilean Norte Chico—and since the Diaguitas knew about the things the Spaniards were doing, they indeed rose up and refused to allow them to pass in peace. . . . [Later they continued toward the] provinces of Copiapó [sic] . . . [which were] almost one hundred fifty uninhabited leagues away, a distance which Almagro traveled with difficulty because of the lack of towns and, if any were found, they were small and had nothing to eat. Nevertheless, Almagro and his people continued on to the valleys of Copiapó, a three-day journey through a deserted mountain pass, where, in the winter season, the road is knee-deep with snow, and when there is no snow, which was the case on Almagro's expedition, it is so cold that one night in the pass, which is five days from Copiapó, seventy horses and a large number of the service animals of the natives died from the cold" (ibid., 85).

The main road followed by the Spanish armies, as well as secondary routes in northern Argentina, were verified by archaeologists, who compared documentary sources (primarily Matienzo's letter) with the topography and archaeological remains. It was found that one could indeed repeat the journeys that had been carried out on foot with trains of llamas, horses, soldiers, and their paraphernalia, through the *tampus* linked by the Inka Road in the provinces of Jujuy, Salta, and Catamarca, from Calahoyo to El Moreno (tampus of Calahoyo, Moreta, Casavindo El Chico, del Llano, Rincón de las Salinas, and El Moreno), and from El Moreno to Tolombón (tampus of Buena Yerba, Corralito—the mountain pass to the Calchaquí Valley, de la Paloma, Pascoama, Chicuana, Guxuil, Angostaco, Cordova, or Talombones).

Qeros and Long-Distance Exchange   EMILY KAPLAN

1. *Qero* is a Quechua word meaning both *cup* and *wood,* but the word is often applied to vessels made of various materials from various cultures.

2. For example, Guaman Poma de Ayala ([1615] 1987) illustrates the use of qeros and Cobo ([1653] 1979) describes qeros as goods common to all households.

3. In separate studies, Miller (1997) and Carreras Rivery (1998) both identified *Escallonia* on most of the colonial qeros they examined and sampled; *Prosopis* and *Alnus* were identified on a small sample of Inka qeros. As all of these species grow throughout the Andes, varying in growth habits and ecological zones, the geographical sources of the woods have not been determined.

4. Since 1995 a group of conservators and conservation scientists have been examining and identifying the materials that were used to create colonial qeros; over time more collaborators have contributed data (Newman and Derrick 2002; Kaplan et al. 1999).

5. It is possible that the resin was exported to the south from Pasto, perhaps at the end of the Inka period, and used for qero production. There is no historical evidence of *Elaeagia* spp. elsewhere in the Andean region during the Inka and colonial periods, but today several species are widespread (Mora Osejo 1977; Botina 1990). Several YouTube videos show artists in San Juan de Pasto, Colombia, demonstrating and explaining the complex procedures involved in processing *Elaeagia* resin (known as *mopa mopa*). This video by Alonso Cano (Revista Andaluza de Arte) features artist Gilberto Granja: http://www.youtube.com/watch?v=s6ZjOB65krE&feature=youtube_gdata_player.

6. Known as the Giacomo Deposit, this ore body was offered for exploitation of titanium dioxide and silicon dioxide minerals.

Acosta, José de. (1590) 1962. *Historía natural y moral de las Indias*. 2nd ed. Mexico City: Fondo de Cultura Económica.

Advis Ataglich, Patricio. 2008. *El desierto conmovido: Paso de la hueste de Almagro por el norte de Chile*. Iquique: Ediciones Universidad Arturo Prat.

Agurto Calvo, S. 1980. *Cusco: Al traza urbana de la ciudad inca*. UNESCO. Lima: Instituto Nacional de Cultura del Perú.

———. 1987. *Estudios acerca de la construcción, arquitectura y planeamiento incas*. Lima: Cámara Peruana de la Construcción.

Albornoz, Cristóbal de. (1580) 1967. "Instrucción para descubrir todas las guacas del Pirú y sus camayos y haciendas." *Journal de la Société des Américanistes* 56 (1): 7–39.

Alcázar Molina, Cayetano. 1920. *Historia del correo en América*. Madrid: Biblioteca de Historia Hispanoamericana.

Aldunate, Carlos, and L. Cornejo, eds. 2001. *Tras la huella del Inka en Chile*. Santiago: Museo Chileno de Arte Precolombino.

Aldunate, Carlos, Juan J. Armesto, Victoria Castro, and Carolina Villagrán. 1981. "Estudio etnobotánica en una comunidad precordillerana de Antofagasta: Toconce." *Boletín del Museo de Historia Natural* 38:183–223.

———. 1983. "Ethnobotany of a Pre-Altiplanic Community in the Andes of Northern Chile. *Economic Botany* 37 (1): 120–135.

Allen, Catherine J. 2002. *The Hold Life Has: Coca and Cultural Identity in an Andean Community*. Washington, DC: Smithsonian Books.

Anglés Vargas, V. 1978. *Historia del Cusco incaico*. 2 vols. Cusco: Industrialgráfica.

Arellano Hoffmann, Carmen. 1984. *Notas sobre el indígena en la Intendencia de Tarma: Una evaluación de la visita de 1786*. Bonn: BAS 13.

———. 1988. *Apuntes históricos sobre la provincia de Tarma en la sierra central del Perú: El kuraka y los ayllus bajo la dominación colonial española, siglos XVI–XVII*. Bonn: BAS 15.

Arellano Hoffmann, Carmen, and Ramiro Matos Mendieta. 2007. "Variations between Inka Installations in the Puna of Chinchaycocha and the Drainage of Tarma." In *Variations in the Expression of Inka Power: A Symposium at Dumbarton Oaks, 18 and 19 October 1997*, edited by Richard Burger, Craig Morris, and Ramiro Matos Mendieta, 11–44. Washington, DC: Dumbarton Oaks Research Library and Collection.

Arguedas, José María. n.d. *Dos estudios sobre Huancayo*. Huancayo: Universidad Nacional del Centro del Perú.

Arriaga, Joseph de. (1621) 1968. *Extirpación de la idolatría del Perú*. Biblioteca de Autores Españoles, Book 209. Madrid: Ediciones Atlas.

Ascher, Marcia, and Robert Ascher. 1997. *Mathematics of the Incas: Code of the Quipu*. Mineola: Dover Publications.

Associated Press. 2005. "Bolivia's Morales Plans Referendum on Coca," NBCNews.com, December 20. http://www.nbcnews.com/id/10519611/ns/world_news-americas/t/bolivias-morales-plans-referendum-coca/.

Ávila, Francisco de. (1598?) 1966. *Dioses y hombres de Huarochirí*. Translated by J. M. Arguedas. Lima: Instituto de Estudios Peruanos.

Avilés, Sonia. 1998. "Caminos y arqueología. La ruta La Paz-Coroico vía Chucura." BA thesis, Universidad Mayor de San Andrés, La Paz.

Banderin, Francesco. 2004. *Tejiendo los lazos de un legado Qhapaq Ñan—Camino Principal: hacia la nominación de un patrimonio común, rico y diverso, de valor universal.* Lima: UNESCO.

Bárcena, J. Roberto, and Sergio Martín. 2009. *Modelos complementarios de la red vial inka en La Rioja: Nuevos aportes para la dominación inkaica del centro oeste Argentino.* Problemáticas de la arqueología contemporánea. Edited by Antonio Austral and Marcela Tamagnini. Book III, 83–93. Córdoba: Universidad Nacional de Río Cuarto.

Barreda Murillo, Luis. 1995. *Historia y arqueológia pre-inca.* Cusco: Instituto de Arqueológia Andina Machupicchu.

Bastien, Joseph W. 1978. "Mountain of the Condor: Metaphor and Ritual in an Andean Ayllu." American Ethnological Society, 64. St. Paul: West Publishing.

Baudin, Louis. 1955. *El imperio socialista de los Inkas.* Fourth edition. Santiago: Editorial Zig-Zag.

Bauer, Brian S. 1992. *The Development of the Inca State.* Austin: University of Texas Press.

———. 1998. *The Sacred Landscape of the Inca: The Cusco Ceque System.* Austin: University of Texas Press.

———. 2006. "Suspension Bridges of the Inca Empire." In *Andean Archaeology III: North and South,* edited by W. H. Isbell and H. Silverman, 468–93. New York: Springer.

———. 2008. *Cusco antiguo: Tierra natal de los Incas.* Translated by Javier Flores. Cusco: Centro Bartolomé de las Casas.

Bauer, Brian S., and Charles Stanish. 2001. *Ritual and Pilgrimage in the Ancient Andes: The Islands of the Sun and the Moon.* Austin: University of Texas Press.

Beltrán-Caballero, J. A., R. Mar, and D. Zapater. 2011. "Medio natural y gestión de recursos hidráulicos en América: La fundación del Cusco." In *Aquae sacrae: Agua y sacralidad en la antigüedad,* edited by A. Costa, L. Palahí Grimal, and D. Vivó, 313–41. Girona: Universidad de Girona.

Benson, Elizabeth. 1972. *The Mochica: A Culture of Peru.* New York: Praeger.

Benvenuto, Neptalí. 1952. *Historia de las carreteras de Perú.* Lima: Comisión Organizadora del V Congreso Panamericano de Carreteras.

Berenguer, José, ed. 2009. *Chile bajo el imperio de los Inkas.* Santiago: Museo Chileno de Arte Precolombino.

Berenguer, José, Carlos Aldunate, and Victoria Castro. 1984. "Orientación orográfica de las chullpas en Likán: La importancia de los cerros en la fase Toconce." Simposio Culturas Atacameñas (44th International Congress of Americanists), 175–220. Universidad del Norte, Antofagasta.

Berenguer, José, Iván Caceres R., Cecilia Sanhueza, and Pedro Hernández. 2005. "El Qhapaqñan en el Alto Loa, norte de Chile: Un estudio micro y macromorfológico." In *Estudios atacameños* 29: 7–39.

Betanzos, Juan de. (1551) 1880. *Suma y narración de los Incas.* Edited by Marcos Jiménez de la Espada. Madrid: M. G. Hernández.

———. (1557) 1987. *Suma y narración de los Incas.* Edited by María del Carmen Martín. Madrid: Ediciones Atlas.

———. (1557) 1996. *Narrative of the Inkas.* Translated and edited by Roland Hamilton and Dana Buchanan. Austin: University of Texas Press.

Bingham, Hiram. 1930. *Machu Picchu—A Citadel of the Incas.* New Haven: NGS and Yale University Press.

Bonavia, Duccio. 2008. *The South American Camelids.* Los Angeles: UCLA Cotsen Institute of Archaeology.

Botina, Jesus Rodrigo. 1990. *El barniz o mopa-mopa, Elaeagia pastoensis Mora (Rubiaceae): Estado actual de su conocimiento en Colombia.* Mocoa, Colombia: Corporación Autónoma Regional del Putumayo.

Bray, Tamara L., 2003. "Inka Pottery as Culinary Equipment: Food, Feasting, and Gender in Imperial State Design." *Latin American Antiquity* 14: 3–28.

Bray, Tamara L., Leah D. Minc, María C. Ceruti, José A. Chávez, Ruddy Perea, and Johan Reinhard. 2005. "A Compositional Analysis of Pottery Vessels Associated with the Inka Ritual of Capacocha." *Journal of Anthropological Archaeology* 24: 82–100.

Burger, Richard L., Karen L. Mohr Chávez, and Sergio J. Chávez. 2000. "Through the Glass Darkly: Pre-Hispanic Obsidian Procurement and Exchange in Southern Peru and Northern Bolivia." *Journal of World Prehistory* 14: 267–362.

Bustamante Carlos Inca, Calixto (Concolorcorvo). 1959. "El lazarillo de ciegos caminantes: Desde Buenos Aires hasta Lima." In *Relaciones Histórico—Literarias de la America meridional.* Real Academia Española [España]. Madrid: Ediciones Atlas.

Cabello de Balboa, M. (1586) 1951. *Miscelánea antártica: Una historia del Perú antiguo.* Lima: Universidad Nacional Mayor de San Marcos.

Canziani Amico, J. 2009. *Ciudad y territorio en los Andes: Contribuciones a la historia del urbanismo prehispánico*. Lima: Fondo Editorial, Pontífica Universidad Católica del Perú.

Cardona, Augusto. 2008. *Caminos prehispanicos de Arequipa/ Prehispanic Roads of Arequipa*. Bilingual edition. Arequipa: Cerro Verde y CIARQ.

Carreras Rivery, Raquel and Andrés Escalera Ureña. 1998. "Identificación de la madera de las vajillas de libación inca (keros) pertenecientes a la colección del Museo de América." *Anales-Museo de América* 6: 217–222.

Castro, Victoria. 1990. *Artifices del barro*. Santiago: Museo Chileno de Arte Precolombino.

———. 1997. "Huacca Muchay: Evangelización y religion andina en Charcas, Atacama La Baja." Masters' thesis, Universidad de Chile.

———. 2004. "Riqueza y complejidad del Qhapaq Ñan: Su identificación y puesta en valor," in *Tejiendo los lazos de un legado Qhapaq Ñan—Camino Principal: Hacia la nominación de un patrimonio común, rico y divers, de valor universal*. Lima, Peru: UNESCO.

———. 2006. "Ayquina y Toconce: Paisajes culturales del norte árido de Chile," in *Paisajes culturales de los Andes*, edited by Elias Mujica, Lima: UNESCO.

Castro, Victoria, and José Luis Martínez. 1996. "Poblaciones indígenas de la provincia de El Loa," in *Culturas de Chile*, Vol. 2, *Etnografia*, 69–109. Santiago: Editorial Andrés Bello.

Castro, Victoria, and Varinia Varela. 1992. "Así sabian contar." *Oralidad* 4: 16–27. Havana Regional Office of UNESCO.

———, eds. 1994. *Ceremonias de tierra y agua: Ritos milenarios andinos*. Santiago: Fondo de Desarollo de la Cultura y las Artes, Ministerio de Educación.

Chacaltana-Cortez, Sofía C. 2010. *El rol de los sistemas de almacenamiento de Camata Tambo y Camata Pueblo: Un tambo inca y una comunidad local adyacente ubicados en la región del Colesuyo, valle alto de Moquehua*. Lima: Pontificia Universidad Católica del Perú.

Chávez Ballon, M. 1970. "Ciudades incas: Cusco capital del imperio." *Wayka* 3: 1–14.

Christie, Jessica Joyce. 2008. "Inka Roads, Lines, and Rock Shrines: A Discussion of the Contexts of Trail Markers." *Journal of Anthropological Research* 64 (1): 41–66.

Cieza de León, Pedro de. (1553) 1962. *La crónica del Perú*. 3rd ed. Edited by Espasa Calpe. Madrid.

———. (1553) 1967. "El señorío de los Incas." *La crónica del Perú*, Book II, Chapter XV. Mexico City: Universidad Nacional Autónoma de México.

———. (1553) 1984. *La crónica del Perú: Primera parte*, 2nd ed. Lima: Pontificia Universidad Católica del Perú, Academia Nacional de la Historia.

———. (1553) 1986. *La crónica del Perú*. Biblioteca de la Historia No. 59. Madrid: Editorial Sarpe.

———. (1553) 1998. *The Discovery and Conquest of Peru*. Edited by A. P. Cook and N. D. Cook. Durham: Duke University Press.

———. (1553) 2000. *La crónica del Perú*. Cronicas de America, 5. Madrid: Las Rozas.

Cieza de León, Pedro de, and Franklin Pease. (1553) 2005. *La crónica del Perú: El señorío de los Incas*, 6th ed. Caracas: Biblioteca Ayacucho.

Cipolletti, María Susana. 1984. "Llamas y mulas, trueque y venta: el testimonio de un arriero puneño." *Revista andina* 2 (2): 513–38. Cusco: Centro Bartolomé de las Casas.

Cobo, Bernabé. (1653) 1890–93. *Historia del nuevo mundo*. Biblioteca de Autores Españoles, Books 2 and 4. Seville: Imprenta E. Resco.

———. (1653) 1956. *Historia del nuevo mundo*. Edited by Francisco Mateos. Biblioteca de Autores Españoles, vols. 91 and 92. Madrid: Atlas.

———. (1653) 1964. *Historia del nuevo mundo*. Edited by Francisco Mateos. Biblioteca de Autores Españoles. Madrid: Atlas.

———. (1653) 1979. *History of the Inca Empire*. Edited and translated by Roland Hamilton. Austin: University of Texas Press.

———. (1653) 1983. *History of the Inca Empire*. Edited and translated by Roland Hamilton. Austin: University of Texas Press.

———. (1653) 1990. *Inca Religion and Customs*. Austin: University of Texas Press.

Cook, N. David, ed. (1582) 1975. *Tasa de la visita general de Francisco de Toledo*. Lima: Universidad Nacional Mayor de San Marcos.

Cooke, Colin A., Holger Hintelmann, Jay J. Ague, Richard Burger, Harald Biester, Julian P. Sachs, and Daniel R. Engstrom. 2013. "Use and Legacy of Mercury in the Andes." *Environmental Science & Technology* (April 18). doi:10.1021/es3048027.

Cooke, Colin A., Mark B. Abbott, and Alexander P. Wolfe. 2008. "Late-Holocene Atmospheric Lead Deposition in the Peruvian and Bolivian Andes." *Holocene* 18, no. 2 (February 1): 353–59. doi:10.1177/0959683607085134.

Cummins, Thomas B. F. 2002. *Toasts with the Inca: Andean Abstraction and Colonial Images on Quero Vessels*. Ann Arbor: University of Michigan Press.

D'Altroy, Terence N. 1992. *Provincial Power in the Inca Empire*. Washington, DC: Smithsonian Institution Press.

———. 2002. *The Incas*. Malden, MA: Blackwell Publishers.

———. 2003. *Los Incas*. Barcelona: Ariel Editorial.

Dedenbach-Salazar Sáenz, Sabine. 1990. *Inca pachaq llamanpa willaynin: Uso y crianza de lo camélidos en la época incaica*. Bonn: Estudios Americanistas de Bonn, BAS 16.

Delgado Villanueva, Carlos. n.d. "Por el camino al Kontisuyu: Cusco-Velille." http://www.drc-cusco.gob.pe/dmdocuments/publicaciones/articulos/2011/kuntisuyu.pdf. Revised November 25, 2012.

Denevan, William M. 1966. *The Aboriginal Cultural Geography of Llanos de Mojos of Bolivia*. Berkeley: University of California Press.

Donnan, Christopher B. 1978. *Moche Art of Peru*. Los Angeles: Museum of Cultural History, UCLA.

Duviols, Pierre. (ca. 1582) 1967. "Un inédit de Cristóbal de Albornoz: La instrucción para descubrir todas las guacas del Pirú y sus camayos y haciendas." *Journal de la Société des Américanistes* 56 (1): 7–39.

Erickson, C. 2000. "Lomas de ocupación en los Llanos de Moxos." In *Arqueología de las tierras bajas*, edited by A. Durán Coirolo and R. Bracco Boksar, 208–26. Montevideo: Comisión Nacional de Arqueología.

Espada, Marcos Jiménez de la, ed. (1892) 2010. *De las antiguas gentes del Perú: Fraay Bartolomé de las Casas*. Puerto Rico.

Espinosa Reyes, Ricardo. 2002. *La gran ruta inka: El Capac Ñan*. Bilingual edition. Lima: Petroperu.

Espinoza Soriano, Waldemar. 1977. "Los cuatro suyos del Cuzco." *Bulletin de l'Institut Français d'Études Andines* 6 (3–4): 110–22.

Estete, Miguel de (attributed). (ca. 1540) 1918. "El descubrimiento y conquista del Perú." *Boletín de la Sociedad Ecuatoriana de Estudios Históricos Americanos* 1: 300–350.

Farrington, Ian. 2010. "The Houses and 'Fortress' of Waskar: Archaeological Perspectives on a Forgotten Building Complex in Inka Cusco." *Journal of Iberian and Latin American Studies* 16: 87–99.

Fejos, Paul. 1944. *Archaeological Explorations in the Cordillera Vilcabamba, Southeastern Peru*. New York: Viking Fund Publications in Anthropology.

Fisher, John, and Horst Pietschmann. 1994. "Wirtschaft, Handel, Geldwesen, Fiskus und Verkehr." In *Handbuch der Geschichte Lateinamerikas*, edited by Walther Bernecker, Raymond Buve, John Fisher, Horst Pietschmann, and Hans Werner Tobler, vol. 1, 400–453. Stuttgart: Klett-Cotta.

Flores Ochoa, Jorge. 1994. *Gold of the Andes: The Llamas, Alpacas, Vicuñas and Guanacos of South America*. Barcelona: Francis O. Patthey.

———. 2005. *El centro del universe Andino/The Centre of the Andean Universe*. Cusco: Municipalidad de Cusco.

Franquemont, Edward M. 1995. "The Bridge at Huanchiri: A Span across Time, Culture, and Technology." Presented at the 35th Annual Meeting of the Institute of Andean Studies, Berkeley, January 6–7, 1995.

Frantz, Tony, Ellen G. Howe, Emily Kaplan, Richard Newman, Ellen Pearlstein, Judith Levinson, and Odile Madden. n.d. "The Occurrence of a Cristobalite-Anatase-Bearing White Pigment on Wooden Andean Qeros." Unpublished manuscript.

Fresco, Antonio. 1983. "La red vial incaica en la sierra sur del Ecuador: Algunos datos para su estudio." *Cultura* 5 (15): 109–48.

———. 2004. *Ingañan: La red vial del imperio inca en los Andes ecuatoriales*. Quito: Banco Central del Ecuador.

Gade, Daniel W. 1981. "Bridge Types in the Central Andes." *Annals of the Association of American Geographers* 62: 94–109.

Galdos Rodríguez, Guillermo. 1987. *Comunidades prehispánicas de Arequipa*. Arequipa: Fundación M. J. Bustamante de la Fuente.

———. 1985. *Kuntisuyu: Lo que encontraron los españoles*. Arequipa: Fundación M. J. Bustamante de la Fuente.

Garcilaso de la Vega, El Inca. (1609) 1959. *Comentarios Reales de los Incas*. Lima: Universidad Mayor Nacional de San Marcos.

———. (1609) 1966. *Royal Commentaries of the Incas*. Translated by Harold V. Livermore. 2 vols. Austin: University of Texas Press.

———. (1609) 1976. *Comentarios Reales de los Incas*. Edited by Aurelio Miro Quesada. Caracas: Biblioteca Ayacucho.

———. (1609) 1994. *Royal Commentaries of the Inkas and General History of Peru*. 3rd ed. Translated by Harold V. Livermore. Austin: University of Texas Press.

Gasparini, Graziano, and Luise Margolies. 1977. *Arquitectura inka*. Caracas: Universidad Central de Venezuela.

Glave Testino, Luis Miguel. 1989. *Trajinantes: Caminos indígenas en la sociedad colonial, siglos XVI–XVII*. Lima: Instituto de Apoyo Agrario.

González Corrales, José. 1984. "Arquitectura y cerámica Killke del Cusco." *Revista del Museo e Instituto de Arqueológia* 23: 37–45. Cusco: Universidad Nacional de San Antonio Abad.

Gose, Peter. 1993. "Segmentary State Formation and the Ritual Control of Water under the Incas." *Comparative Study of Society and History* 35: 480–514.

Gregory, Herbert E. 1916. "A Geologic Reconnaissance of the Cuzco Valley." *American Journal of Science* 61 (24): 1–100.

Guaman Poma de Ayala, Felipe de. (1614) 1944. *El primer nueva crónica y buen gobierno*. Edited by Arthur Posnansky. La Paz: Editorial del Instituto Tihuanacu de Antropología.

———. (1615) 1956. *Nueva crónica y buen gobierno*. Edited by Luis Bustios Galvez. Lima: Editorial Cultura.

———. (1615) 1980. *El primer nueva crónica y buen gobierno*. Edited and with notes and commentary by John V. Murra and Rolena Adorno. Translated by J. L. Urioste. 3 vols. Mexico City: Siglo Veintiuno Editores.

———. (1615) 1987. *El primer nueva crónica y buen gobierno*. Crónicas de América 29, edited by John V. Murra, Rolena Adorno, and Jorge L. Urioste. Madrid: Historia 16.

Gutiérrez Álvarez, Secundino. 1993. *Las comunicaciones en América: de la senda primitiva al ferrocarril*. Coleccións realidades americanas 17. Madrid: MAPFRE.

Hanke, Lewis. 1967. *History of Latin American Civilization*. Vol. 1, *The Colonial Experience*. Boston: Little, Brown.

Harth-Terre, Emilio. 1961. *El historico puente sobre el río Apurímac*. Revista del Archivo Nacional del Perú, book 25, vol. 1, Lima.

Hastorf, C. A. 1987. "Archaeological Evidence of Coca (*Erythroxylum coca*, erythroxylaceae) in the Upper Mantaro Valley, Peru." *Economic Botany* 41 (2): 292–301.

Hemming, John. 1970. *The Conquest of the Inca*. New York: Harcourt.

Hernández Astete, F. 1984. "Los sistemas hidráulicos del valle del Cusco (prehispánicos)." BA thesis, Universidad Nacional de San Antonio Abad de Cusco.

———. 2008. "Las panacas y el poder en el Tahuantinsuyo." *Bulletin de l'Institut Français d'Études Andines* 37 (1): 29–45.

Hernández Príncipe, Rodrigo. (1621) 1986. "Visitas de Hernández Príncipe." In *Cultura andina y represión: Procesos y visitas de idolatrías y hechicerías Cajatambo, siglo XVII*, edited by Pierre Duviols, 461–507. Cusco: Centro de Estudios Regionales Andinos Bartolomé de las Casas.

Hodder, I. 1987. "Converging Traditions: the Search for Symbolic Meanings in Archaeology and Geography." In *Landscape and Culture: Geographical and Archaeological Perspectives*, edited by J. M. Wagstaff. Oxford: Blackwell.

Howe, Ellen G., and Ulrich Petersen. 1992. "Silver and Lead in Late Prehistory of the Mantaro Valley, Peru." In *Archaeometry of Pre-Columbian Sites and Artifacts*, 183–98. Los Angeles: UCLA Cotsen Institute of Archaeology and the Getty Conservation Institute.

Hyslop, John. 1984. *The Inka Road System*. Orlando: Academic Press.

———. 1984. *The Inka Road System*. London: Academic Press.

———. 1990. *Inka Settlement Planning*. Austin: University of Texas Press.

———. 1992. *Qhapaq Ñan. El sistema vial incaico*. Lima: Instituto Andino de Estudios Arqueológicos (INDEA).

———. 1993. "Factors Influencing the Transmission and Distribution of Inka Cultural Materials throughout Tawantinsuyu." In *Latin American Horizons*, edited by D. S. Rice, 337–56. Washington, DC: Dumbarton Oaks Research Library and Collection.

———. 1998. "Las fronteras estatales extremas del Tawantinsuyu." In *La frontera del estado inca*, edited by T. Dillehay and P. Netherley, 33–35. Quito: Fundación A. von Humboldt and Ediciones Abya-Yala.

Idrovo, Jaime. 1998. "Tomebamba, primera fase de conquista incásica en los Andes septentrionales: Los Cañaris y la conquista incásica del austro ecuatoriano." In *La frontera del estado inca*, edited by T. Dillehay and P. Netherley, 71–84. Quito: Fundación A. von Humboldt and Ediciones Abya-Yala.

Iñañez, Javier G. 2010. "Preliminary Report: Lead Isotope Analysis of Qero Samples by LA-MC-ICP-MS." Paper presented at the Smithsonian Museum Conservation Institute, University of Maryland, June 10.

Instituto Nacional de Cultura. 2004a. *Proyecto Qhapaq Ñan: Informe de Campaña 2002–2003*. Lima: Impresiones Fimart SAC.

———. 2004b. *Programa Qhapaq Ñan: Informe por cuencas hidrográficas del registro de tramos y sitios. Campañas 2003–2004*. Lima: Impresiones Fimart SAC.

Jacobsen, Nils, and Hans-Júrgen Puhle, eds. 1986. *The Economies of Mexico and Peru during the Late Colonial Period, 1760–1810.* Bibliotheca Ibero-Americana 34. Berlin: Colloquium Verlag.

Jenkins, David. 2001. "A Network Analysis of Inka Roads, Administrative Centers, and Storage Facilities." *Ethnohistory* 48 (4): 655–87.

Jones, Bradford, Cindy Klink, and Brian Bauer. 2004. "The First Inhabitants of the Cuzco Valley." In *Ancient Heartland of the Inca,* 65–77. Austin: University of Texas Press.

Julien, Catherine. 1991. *Condesuyu: The Political Division of Territory under Inka and Spanish Rule.* Bonn: BAS 16.

———. 2002. "Identidad y filiación por suyu en el emperio inkaico," *Boletín de arqueología* PUCP 6:11–22.

Kaplan, E., E. Pearlstein, E. Howe, and J. Levinson. 1999. "Análisis técnico de qeros pintados de los períodos inka y colonial." *Iconos: Revista peruana de conservación, arte, y arqueología* 2: 30–38.

Kaulicke, P. 2001. "La función cultural de las obras hidráulicos en el tiempo de los Incas." *Boletín de la Sociedad Geográfica de Lima* 114.

Korpisaari, Antti, Juan Faldin, Risto Kesseli, Jussi Korhonen, Sanna Saunaluoma, Ari Siiriainen, and Märtti Parssinen. 2003. "Informe preliminar de las investigaciones arqueológicas de la temporada 2002 en el sitio de La Fortaleza de Las Piedras." *Reports of the Finnish-Bolivian Archaeological Project in the Bolivian Amazon II.* Department of Archaeology, University of Helsinki, 7–33.

Larco Herrera, R., ed. 1934. *Cusco Histórico.* Lima: La Crónica/Variedades.

Lentz, D. L., ed. 2000. *Imperfect Balance: Landscape Transformations in the Pre-Columbian Americas.* New York: Columbia University Press.

Léons, Madeline Barbara, and Harry Sanabria. 1997. *Coca, Cocaine, and the Bolivian Reality.* Albany: State University of New York Press.

Llagostera, A. 1976. "Hipótesis sobre la expansion inkaica en la vertiente occidental de los Andes meridionales." *Anales de la Universidad del Norte* 10: 203–18.

———. 2010. "Retomando los límites y las limitaciones del 'Archipiélago Vertical.'" *Chungara* 42 (1): 283–95.

Locke, L. Leland. 1923. *The Ancient Quipu or Peruvian Knot Record.* New York: American Museum of Natural History.

López Campeny, S. 2007. "El poder de torcer, anudar y trenzar a través de los siglos: Textiles y ritual funerario en la puna meriodional Argentina." *Cuadernos del Instituto Nacional de Antropología y Pensamiento Latinoamericano* 21.

Lumbreras, Luis G. 1978. *The Peoples and Cultures of Ancient Peru.* Translated by Betty J. Meggers. Washington, DC: Smithsonian Institution Press.

———. 2006. "El Qhapaq Ñan—Camino principal andino: Plan de acción regional par un proceso de integración y cooperación," 11–13. Banco Interamericano de Desarrollo. Presentation prepared for UNESCO representation in Peru.

Mariño de Lobera, P. 1862. *Historia de Chile desde su descubrimiento hasta el año 1575.* Book 2, *Colección historiadores de Chile y documentos relativos a la historia nacional.* Santiago: Imprenta de Ferrocarril.

Mariscotti de Görlitz, Ana María. 1978. "Pachamama Santa Tierra: Contribucion al estudio de la religion autoctona en los Andes centro-meridionales." *Indiana:* Beiheft 8. Ibero-Amerikanisches Institut. Berlin: Gebr. Mann.

Martín Rubio, María del Carmen. 2009. "La cosmovisión religiosa andina y el rito de la capacocha/The Andean Religious World View and the Rite of the Capacocha." *Investigaciones sociales* 13 (23): 187–201.

Martín, S. 2002. "Factores de alteración geoambientales y antrópicos sobre el camino Inka en la Sierra de Famatina-La Rioja-Argentina: Consideraciones preliminares." *UNLaR ciencia,* Año 3 (2): 22–32.

———. 2005. "Caminos inkaicos 'principales' y 'secundarios' en la Sierra de Famatina (La Rioja-Argentina): actualización y revisión conceptual." *Revista Xama* 15.

Martínez C, José Luis. 2012. "El virrey Toledo y el control de las voces andinas coloniales." *Colonial Latin American Review* 21 (2): 175–208.

Martínez, Gabriel. 1976. "El sistema de los Uywiris en Isluga." In *Hominaje al Dr. Gustavo Le Paige S. J.,* 255–327. Santiago: Universidad del Norte.

———. 1983. "Los dioses de los cerros en los Andes." *Journal de la Societé des Americanistes* 69: 85–115.

———. 1989. *Espacio y pensamiento: Andes meridionales.* La Paz: Hisbol.

Matienzo, Juan de. (1566?) 1910. *Gobierno del Perú: Obra escrita en el siglo XVI por el licenciado don Juan Matienzo, oidor de la Real audiencia de Charcas.* Buenos Aires: Compañía Sud-Americana de Billetes de Banco.

Matos Mendieta, Ramiro. 1992a. *Pumpu: Centro administrativo inka de la puna de Junín*. Lima: Editorial Horizonte.

———. 1992b. "El camino real inca y la carretera moderna en Chinchaycocha, Junín," In *Estudios de arqueologia peruana*, edited by Duccio Bonavia. Lima: Fomciencias.

———. 2004. "Inca Ceramics." In *The Incas: Art and Symbols*. Lima: Banco de Credito del Perú.

McEwan, C., and M. I. Silva. 1989. "¿Qué fueron a hacer los Inkas en la costa central del Ecuador?" In *Relaciones interculturales en el area ecuatorial del Pácifico durante la época precolombina*, edited by J. F. Bouchard and M. Guinea, 163–85. Proceedings of the 46th International Congress of Americanists, BAR International Series 503.

McEwan, C., and Maarten van de Guchte. 1992. "Ancestral Time and Sacred Space in Inka State Ritual," In *The Ancient Americas: Art from Sacred Landscapes*, edited by Richard F. Townsend, 359–71. Art Institute of Chicago.

McEwan. Gordon F., ed. 2005. *Pikillacta: The Wari Empire in Cuzco*. Iowa City: University of Iowa Press.

———. 2006. *The Inkas: New Perspectives*. Santa Barbara, CA: ABC-CLIO.

McIntyre, Loren. 1973. "The Lost Empire of the Inkas." *National Geographic* 144 (6): 729–87.

Mellafe, Rolando. 1965. "La significación histórica de los puentes en el virreinato peruano del siglo XVI." In *Historia y cultura* 1:65–113.

Meyers, A. 2002. "Los Inkas: ¿bárbaros advenedizos o herederos de Tiahuanaco?" In *El hombre y los Andes*, vol. 2, edited by J. Espinoza and R. Gabai, 525–35. Lima: PUCP.

Meyers, A., and C. Ulbert. 1997. "Inka Archaeology in Eastern Bolivia: Some Aspects of the Samaipata Project." *Tawantinsuyu* 3:79–85.

Miller, Regis. *Identification of Qero Wood Samples*. Madison, WI: United States Department of Agriculture, Forest Products Laboratory, September 8, 1997.

Miño Garcés, L. 1994. *El manejo del espacio en el imperio inca*. Quito: Facultad Latino Americano de Ciencias Sociales.

Molina, Cristóbal de, "El chileno," and Bartolomé de Segovia. (1553) 1968. "Relación de muchas cosas acaecidas en el Perú." In *Crónicas peruanas de interés indígena*, edited by Francisco Estéve Barba. Biblioteca de Autores Españoles, 29: 57–95. Madrid: Atlas.

Molina, Cristóbal de, "El cuzceño." (1573) 1947. "Ritos y fábulas de los Incas." In *Colección Eurindia 14*. Buenos Aires: Editorial Futuro.

———. (1575) 1988. *Relación de la fabulas y ritos de los Ingas*. Edited by Henrique Urbano. Madrid: Historia 16.

Molina, Cristóbal de, and Cristóbal de Albornoz. (1575) 1989. *Fábulas y mitos de los Incas*. Edited by Henrique Urbano and Pierre Duviols. Crónicas de América 48. Madrid: Historia 16.

Mora Osejo, Luis Eduardo. 1977. "El barniz de Pasto." *Caldasia* 11 (55): 5–31.

Moreno, A., F. Molina, and F. Contreras. 1999. "La defensa de la ciudad como yacimiento arqueológico: Los proyectos de arqueología urbana." In *Actas: XXV Congreso Nacional de Arqueología*, 275–79.

Morris, Craig. 1967. "Storage in Tahuantinsuyu," PhD diss., University of Chicago.

Morris, Craig, and Donald Thompson. 1985. *Huánaco Pampa: An Inca City and Its Hinterland*. New York: Thames & Hudson.

Morris, Craig, and Adriana von Hagen. 2011. *The Incas*. London: Thames & Hudson.

Moseley, Michael E. 1992. *The Incas and Their Ancestors: The Archaeology of Peru*. New York: Thames & Hudson.

Muñoz, I. and J. Chacama. 2006. *Complejidad social en las alturas de Arica: Territorio, etnicidad y vinculación con el estado inca*. Arica: Ediciones Universidad de Tarapacá.

Murra, John V. 1972. "El 'control vertical' de un máximo de pisos ecológicos en la economía de las sociedades andinas." In *Visita de la provincia de León de Huánuco en 1562*, edited by J. Murra, 2: 429–76. Huánuco: Universidad Nacional Hermilio Valdizán.

———. 1975. *Formaciones económicas y políticas del mundo andino*. Lima: Instituto des Estudios Peruanos.

———. 1992. *La Visita de los valles de Sonqo en los yunka de coca de La Paz (1658–1670)*. Edicion a cargo de John Murra.

Murúa, Martin de. (1590) 2004. *Historia del origen y genealogía real de los reyes ingas del Pirú: De sus hechos, costumbres, trajes y manera de gobierno*. Facsimile edition. Madrid: Testimonio Editorial.

———. (1616) 1992. *Historia general del Perú*. Madrid.

National Research Council. 1989. *Lost Crops of the Incas: Little-Known Plants of the Andes with Promise for Worldwide Cultivation*. Washington, DC: National Academy Press.

Needham, Joseph. 1971. "Civil Engineering and Nautics." In *Science and Civilization in China,* vol. 4, part 3. Cambridge: Cambridge University Press.

Newman, Richard, and Michele Derrick. 2002. "Painted Qero Cups from the Inka and Colonial Periods in Peru: An Analytical Study of Pigments and Media." *MRS Proceedings.* vol. 712. http://journals.cambridge.org/abstract_S1946427400631482.

Newman, Richard, Emily Kaplan, and Michelle R. Derrick. (Forthcoming). "Mopa Mopa: Scientific Analysis and History of an Unusual South American Resin Used by the Inka and Artisans in Pasto, Colombia." *Journal of the American Institute for Conservation.*

Nielsen, Axel E. 2001. "Ethnoarchaeological Perspectives on Caravan Trade in the South-Central Andes." In *Ethnoarchaeology of Andean South America: Contributions to Archaeological Method and Theory,* edited by L. Kuznar, 163–201. Ann Arbor: University of Michigan Press.

———. 2003. "Por las rutas del Zenta: Evidencias directas del tráfico prehispánico entre Humahuaca y los Yungas." In *La mitad verde del mundo andino: Investigaciones arqueológicas en la vertiente oriental de los Andes y las tierras bajas de Bolivia y Argentina,* edited by Gabriela Oriz and Beatriz Ventura, 261–84. Jujuy: Universidad Nacional de Jujuy.

———. 2011. "El tráfico de caravanas entre Lípez y Atacama visto desde la Cordillera Occidental." In *En ruta: arqueología, historia y etnografía del tráfico surandino,* edited by Lautaro Núñez and Axel Nielsen, 83–110. Argentina: Encuentro.

Niles, S. 1999. *The Shape of Inca History: Narrative and Architecture in an Andean Empire.*

Nordenskiöld, E. 1924. Forschungen und Abenteuer in Südamerika. Stuttgart: Strecker und Schröder.

Núñez Srýtr, Marinka. 2011. "Rutas, viajes y convidos: Territorialidad peineña en las cuencas de Atacama y Punta Negra." In *En ruta: Arqueología, historia y etnografía del tráfico surandino,* edited by Lautaro Núñez and Axel Nielsen. Argentina: Encuentro.

Núñez, L., M. Grosjean, and I. Cartajena. 2005. "The Expansion of the Inka Empire into the Atacama Desert." In *23°S: Archaeology and Environmental History of the Southern Deserts,* edited by M. Smith and P. Hesse, 324–332. Canberra: National Museum of Australia Press.

Ochsendorf, John. 1996. "An Engineering Study of the Last Inca Suspension Bridge." In *Proceedings of the 13th Annual International Bridge Conference,* 398–404. Pittsburgh: Engineers' Society of Western Pennsylvania.

———. 2005 "Engineering Analysis for Construction History: Perils and Opportunities." International Congress on Construction History, Cambridge, United Kingdom.

O'Connor, Colin. 1993. *Roman Bridges.* Cambridge: Cambridge University Press.

Ogburn, Dennis E. "Evidence for Long-Distance Transportation of Building Stones in the Inka Empire, from Cuzco, Peru, to Saraguro, Ecuador." *Latin American Antiquity* 15 (4): 419–39.

Pärssinen, Märtti. 1992. *Tawantinsuyu: The Inca State and Its Political Organization.* Societas Historica Finlandiae/Studia Historica 43. Helsinki: SKS

Pärssinen, Märtti, and Antti Korpisaari. 2003. *Western Amazonia-Amazonia Ocidental. Multidisciplinary Studies on Ancient Expansionistic Movements, Fortifications and Sedentary Life.* Renwall Institute Publications 14. University of Helsinki.

Pärssinen, Märtti, and Ari Siiriäinen. 2003. *Andes orientales y Amazonia cccidental: Ensayos entre la historia y la arqueología de Bolivia, Brasil y Peru.* La Paz: Producciones CIMA.

Peñaherrera, Carlos. 2004. "Geografía." In *Enciclopedia temática del Perú.* Vol. 5. Lima: Editorial El Comercio.

Peters, Tom. 1987. *Transitions in Engineering: Guillaume-Henri Dufour and the Development of the Wire Cable Suspension Bridge in the Early Nineteenth Century.* Basel: Birkhauser Verlag.

Pizzaro, Pedro. (1571) 1921. *Relación del descubrimiento y conquista de los reinos del Perú.* Lima.

Platt, Tristan and Pablo Guisbert. 2008. "Tras las huellas del silencio: Potosí, los Inkas y el virrey Toledo." In *Minas y metalurgia en los Andes del sur desde la época prehispánica hasta el siglo XVII,* edited by Pablo Cruz and Jean-Joinville Vacher, 231–78. Sucre-Lima-Paris: Institut de recherche pour le développement, Insituto Francés de Estudios Andinos.

Polo de Ondegardo, Juan. (1571) 1916. *Informaciones acerca de la religion y gobierno de los Incas.* Colección de libros y documentos referentes a la historia del Perú, vol. 3. Lima: Sanmartí.

———. (1571) 1990. "Notables daños de no guarder a los indios sus fueros." In *El mundo de los Incas,* edited by L. González and A. Alonso. Madrid: Historia 16.

Ponce Sanginés, C. 1957. "La ceramica mollo." In *Arqueología boliviana: Primera mesa redonda,* edited by C. Ponce Sangines. La Paz: Biblioteca Paceña, Alcaldía Municipal de La Paz.

Pulgar Vidal, Javier. 1972. *Geografía del Perú: Las ocho regiones naturales del Perú.* 7th edition. Lima: Editorial Universo.

Ravines, Rogger, ed. 1978. *Tecnología andina.* Lima: Instituto de Estudios Peruanos.

Regal, Alberto. 1936. *Los caminos del Inca—En el antiguo Perú.* Lima: Sanmartí.

———. 1972. *Los puentes del Inka en el antiguo Perú.* Austin: University of Texas Press.

Reinhard, Johan. 1983. "Las montañas sagradas: Un estudio etnoarqueológico de ruinas en las Altas Cumbres Andinas." *Cuadernos de historia* 3: 27–62.

———. 1999. "At 22,000 Feet Children of Inka Sacrifice Found Frozen in Time." *National Geographic* 196 (5): 36–55.

Reinhard, Johan, and M. C. Ceruti. 2000. *Investigaciones arqueológicas en el volcán Llullaillaco: Complejo ceremonial inkaico de alta montaña.* Salta: Ediciones de la Universidad Católica de Salta (EUCASA).

Richardson III, James B. 1995. *People of the Andes.* Exploring the Ancient World, edited by Jeremy A. Sabloff. Washington, DC: Smithsonian Books.

Rivera Serna, Raúl, ed. (1534) 1965. "Libro primero de cabildos de la ciudad del Cuzco." In *Documenta* 4: 441–80.

Rivera-Sundt, O. 1979. "El complejo arqueológico de Samaipata." In *El fuerte preincaico de Samaipata*, edited by H. Boero Rojo and O. Rivera-Sundt, 41–103. La Paz: Editorial Los Amigos del Libro.

Rostworowski, Maria. (1988) 2009. *Historia del Tahuantinsuyu.* Lima: Instituto de Estudios Peruanos.

———. 2004a. "Incas." In *Enciclopedia temática del Perú.* Vol. 5. Lima: Editorial El Comercio.

———. 2004b. *Costa peruana prehispánica: Prólogo a Conflicts over Coca Fields in XVIth Century Peru.* Lima: Instituto de Estudios Peruanos Ediciones.

Rowe, John H. 1944. "An Introduction to the Archaeology of Cuzco." *Papers of the Peabody Museum of American Archaeology* 27 (2): 3–59.

———. 1946. "Inka Culture at the Time of the Spanish Conquest." In *Handbook of South American Indians*, vol. 2, edited by Julian H. Steward. Washington, DC: Smithsonian Institution.

Salazar, D. n.d. *Tras la senda del cobre atacameño: La historia minera de San José de El Abra.* Santiago: SCM El Abra.

Salcamayhua, Juan de Santa Cruz Pachacuti Yamqui, Pierre Duviols, and Cesar Itier. 1993. *Relación de antigüedades deste Reyno del Piru: Estudio etnohistórico y linguistic.* Cusco: Institut Francais d'Etudes Andines/Centro de Estudios Regionales Andinos Bartolomé de las Casas.

Sallnow, Michael J. 1987. *Pilgrims of the Andes: Regional Cults in Cusco.* Washington, DC: Smithsonian Institution Press.

Sancho, Pedro. (1543) 1917. *Relación para S.M. de lo sucedido en la conquista y pacificación de estas provincias de la Nueva Castilla y de la calidad de la tierra.* Translated by P. A. Means. New York: Cortes Society.

Santillán, Fernando (Hernando) de. (1563) 1968. "Relación del orígen, descendencia, política y gobierno de los Incas." In *Crónicas peruanas de interés indígena*, edited by Francisco Esteve Barba. 97–149. Madrid: Atlas.

Santoro, C. and I. Muñoz. 1981. "Patrón habitacional incaico en el área de Pampa Alto Ramírez." *Chungara* 7: 144–71.

Sanz, Nuria. 2004. "Qhapaq Ñan—Camino Principal Andino y el proceso de su candidatura como bien susceptible de ser inscrito en la Lista de Patrimonio Mundial." In *Tejiendo los lazos de un legado Qhapaq Ñan—Camino Principal: Hacia la nominación de un patrimonio común, rico y divers, de valor universal.* Lima: UNESCO.

Sarmiento de Gamboa, Pedro. (1572) 1907. *History of the Incas.* Translated and edited by C. R. Markham. Cambridge: Hakluyt Society.

———. (1572) 1947. *Historia de los Incas.* Edited by Angel Rosenblatt. Buenos Aires: Emecé.

———. (1572) 1960. "Historia Indica: Apéndice de Garcilaso de la Vega." In *Obras Completas*, t. IV, II parte. Biblioteca de Autores Españoles. Madrid: Atlas.

Schexnayder, Cliff, Manuel Celaya, Gerardo Chang Recavarren, Christine Fiori, and Edward J. Jaselskis. 2011. "Engineering with the Elements," *Journal of Construction Engineering and Management*, ASCE, 137, no. 10 (October 1): 755–61.

Schultze, Carol A., Charles Stanish, David A. Scott, Thilo Rehren, Scott Kuehner, and James K. Feathers. 2009. "Direct Evidence of 1,900 Years of Indigenous Silver Production in the Lake Titicaca Basin of Southern Peru." *Proceedings of the National Academy of Sciences* 106, no. 41 (October 13): 17280–83. doi:10.1073/pnas.0907733106.

Serrera Contreras, Ramón María. 1992. *Tráfico terrestre y red vial en las Indias españolas.* Barcelona: Lunwerg Editores.

Sherbondy, J. 1982. "The Canal Systems of Hanan Cuzco." PhD thesis, University of Illinois at Urbana-Champaign.

Siiriäinen, Ari. 2003. "Towards the Chronology of the Las Piedras Fortress in the Bolivian Amazon: Four Radiocarbon

Datings." *Reports of the Finnish-Bolivian Archaeological Project in the Bolivian Amazon II*, 1–6. University of Helsinki.

Siracusano, Gabriela, and Ian Barnett. 2011. *Pigments and Power in the Andes : From the Material to the Symbolic in Andean Cultural Practices, 1500–1800*. London: Archetype Publications.

Skewes, J. C., D. Guerra, P. Rojas, and M. Mellado. 2011. "¿La memoria de los paisajes o los paisajes de la memoria?" *Desenvolvimento e meio ambiente* (Editora UFPR) 23: 39–57.

Squier, Ephraim G. 1877. *Peru: Incidents of Travel and Exploration in the Land of the Incas*. New York: Harper and Brothers.

Stanish, C., and B. Bauer. 2011. "Peregrinaje y geografía del poder en el estado inka." In *Estudios arqueológicos sobre los Inkas*. Cusco: Centro Bartolomé de los Casas, Archivos de Historia Andina 47.

Stehberg, R. 1995. *Instalaciones incaicas en el norte y centro semiárido de Chile*. Santiago: Dirreción de Bibliotecas, Archivos y Museos.

———. 2012. "Mapocho incaico." *Boletín del Museo Nacional de Historia Natural* 61: 85–149.

Stehberg, R., and M. T. Planella. 1997. "Intervención inka en un territorio de la cultura local Aconcagua de la zona centro-sur de Chile." *Tawantinsuyu* 3: 58–78.

Stothert, Karen. 1967. *Pre-Colonial Highways of Bolivia, Part 1: The La Paz-Yungas Route Via Palca*. La Paz: Academia Nacional de Ciencias de Bolivia 17.

Strube Erdmann, León. 1941. "Antiguos fortines y fortalezas indígenas en el N.O. Argentino." In *Boletín del Instituto de San Felipe y Santiago de Estudios Históricos de Salta*. Vol. 2. Salta.

———. 1943. "Los pucaras del N.O. Argentino son de filiación incaica." In *Congreso de historia Argentina del norte y centro*. Vol. 1. Córdoba: Editorial Litvack.

———. 1963. *La vialidad imperial de los Inkas*. Serie Histórica 33. Córdoba: Instituto de Estudios Americanistas

Tamayo Herrera, J. 1992. *Historia general de Cusco*. Vol. 1. Cusco: Editorial Mercantil.

Taylor, Gerald. 1999. *Ritos y tradiciones de Huarochirí*. 2nd rev. ed. Edited and translated by Gerald Taylor. Lima: IFEA/Banco Central de Reserva del Perú/Universidad Particular Ricardo Palma.

Tilley, Christopher. 1994. *A Phenomenology of Landscape: Places, Paths, and Monuments*. Oxford: Berg.

Trimborn, H. 1967. "Der skulptierte Berg von Samaipata." In *Archäologische studien in den kordilleren boliviens*, vol. 3.

Baessler-Archiv, Beiträge zur Völkerkunde, NF 5 Berlin: Baessler Institut.

Tripcevich, Nico. 2007. "Quarries, Caravans, and Routes to Complexity: Prehispanic Obsidian in the South-Central Andes," PhD diss., University of California at Santa Barbara.

Uribe, M. 1999–2000. "La arqueología del Inka en Chile." *Revista Chilena de Antropología* 15: 63–97.

Uribe Rodríguez, M., and B. G. Cabello. 2005. "Cerámica en el camino: Los materiales del río Loa (Norte Grande de Chile) y sus implicaciones tipológicas y conductuales para la comprensión de la vialidad y la expansión del Tawantinsuyu." *Revista española de antropología americana* 35: 75–98.

Urton, Gary. 1981. *At the Crossroads of the Earth and Sky: An Andean Cosmology*. Austin: University of Texas Press. Published in 2006 as *En el cruce de rumbos de la tierra y cielo* (Cusco: Centro de Estudios Regionales Andinos Bartolomé de las Casas).

———. 1990. *The History of a Myth: Pacariqtambo and the Origin of the Incas*. Austin: University of Texas Press. Published in 2004 as *Historia de un mito* (Cusco: Centro de Estudios Regionales Andinos Bartolomé de las Casas).

———. 2003. *Signs of the Inka Khipu: Binary Coding in the Andean Knotted-String Records*. Austin: University of Texas Press.

———. 2012. "Recording Values in the Inka Empire." In *The Construction of Value in the Ancient World*. Edited by John K. Papadopoulos and Gary Urton, 475–96. Los Angeles: UCLA Cotsen Institute of Archaeology.

Urton, Gary, and Carrie J. Brezine. 2005. "Khipu Accounting in Ancient Peru." *Science* 309: 1065–67.

Vaca de Castro, Cristóbal de. (1543) 1908. "Ordenanzas de tambos." In *Revista histórica* 3: 427–92, edited by Antonio Rodriguez Bonilla. Lima: Instituto Histórico del Perú.

Valcarcel, L. E. 1933. "Sajsawaman redescubierto" *Revista del Museo Nacional,* 3 (1–2): 3–36.

Valencia Zegarra, A., and A. Gibaja Oviedo. 1991. *Marcavalle: El rostro oculto del Cusco*. Cusco: Instituto Regional de Cultura de la Región Inka.

Valera, Blás. (1585) 1950. "De las costumbres antiguas de los naturales de Pirú." In *Tres relaciones de antigüedades peruanas*, edited by M. Jiménez Espada. Asunción: Editorial Guarani.

Vargas Paliza, E. 2007. *Kusikancha: Morada de las momias reales de los Inkas*. Cusco: Instituto Nacional de Cultura.

Vilá, Bibiana. 2012. *Camélidos sudamericanos*. Buenos Aires: Eudeba.

Villagrán, Carolina, and Victoria Castro. 2004. *Ciencia indígena de los Andes del norte de Chile.* Programa de Biodiversidad Universidad de Chile. Santiago de Chile: Editorial Universitaria.

Villanueva Urteaga, H., and J. Sherbondy. 1980. *Cusco: Aguas y poder.* Cusco: Centro de Estudios Regionales Andinos Bartolomé de las Casas.

Vitry, Christian. 1999. "Las Momias de Salta." *Revista miradas* 21, June–July.

———. 2000. *Aportes para el estudio de caminos inkaicos: Tramo Morohuasi-Inkahuasi, Salta-Argentina.* Salta: Editorial Gofica.

———. 2008. "Los espacios rituales en las montañas donde los Inkas practicaron sacrificios humanos." In *Paisagens culturais: Contrastes sul-americanos,* edited by Carlos Terra and Rubens Andrade, 47–65. Rio de Janeiro: Universidade Federal do Rio de Janeiro.

———. 2014. *Los calzados de montaña de los Inkas.* Argentina: Palloni Ediciones.

Vivar, G. de. (1558) 1979. *Crónica y relación copiosa y verdadera de los reinos de Chile.* Edited by L. Sáez-Godoy. Bibliotheca Ibero-Americana. Berlin: Colloquium Verlag.

Von Hagen, Adriana. 1996. "The Incas," *Secrets of Lost Empires. Reconstructing the Glories of Ages Past.* Edited by Michael Barnes. 180–221. London: BBC Books.

Von Hagen, Victor W. 1955. *Highway of the Sun.* New York: Duell, Sloan and Pearce.

Wilder, Thornton. 1927. *The Bridge of San Luis Rey.* New York: HarperCollins.

Zapata, J. 1988. "Los cerros sagrados: Panorama del periodo formativo en la cuenca del Vilcanota, Cuzco." *Boletín de arqueología* PUCP 2: 307–36.

Zárate, Augustin de. (1555) 1862. *Historia del descubrimiento y conquista de la provincia del Perú.* Biblioteca de Autores Españoles, book 2, chap.12. Madrid 483.

Zecenarro, G. 2001. *Arquitectura arqueológica en la quebrada de Thanpumach'ay.* Cusco: Municipalidad Provincial del Cusco.

Zuidema, R. Tom. 1964. *The Ceque System of Cuzco: The Social Organization of the Capital of the Inca.* Leiden: E. J. Brill.

———. 1973. "Kinship and Ancestor Cult in Three Peruvian Communities: Hérnandez Príncipe's Account of 1622." *Bulletin de l'Institut Français d'Etudes Andines* 2 (1): 16–33.

———. 1986. *La civilisation inca au Cuzco.* Edited by F. Héritier. Paris: Presses Universitaires de France, Collège de France.

———. 1989. *Reyes y guerreros: Ensayos de cultura andina.* Edited by Manuel Burga. Lima: Fomciencias.

———. 1991. *La civilización inca en Cuzco.* Mexico City: Fondo de Cultura Económica.

———. 1993. "De la Tarasca a Mama Huaco: La historia de un mito y rito Cuzqueño." In *Religions des Andes et langues indigènes équateur-Pérou-Bolivie avant et après la Conquête Espagnole.* Actes du Colloque III d'Études Andines. Edited by Pierre Duviols. Aix-en-Provence: Publications de l'Université de Provence.

———. 1995. *El sistema de ceques del Cuzco: La organización social de la capital de los Incas.* Translated by Ernesto Salazar. Lima: Fondo Editorial PUCP.

———. 2011. *El calendario inca: Tiempo y espacio en la organización ritual del Cuzco; La idea del pasado.* Lima: Fondo Editorial del Congreso del Perú/Fondo Editorial Pontificia Universidad Católica del Perú.

Zuidema, R. Tom, and Deborah Poole. 1982. "Los límites de los cuatro suyus incaicos en el Cusco." *Bulletin de l'Institut Français d'Études Andines* 11 (1–2): 83–89.

overleaf: These beads are made from the shell of *Spondylus*, a genus of mollusk found off the coast of Ecuador. Called *mullu* in Quechua, the shell was a sacred material closely controlled by the Inka state.

Shell beads, AD 1000–1500. Tembladera, Cajamarca region, Peru. *Spondylus* shell. Largest: 6.2 × 2 × 0.9 cm; smallest: 4.8 × 1.8 × 0.9 cm. 24/1017. Photo by Ernest Amoroso, NMAI

CONTRIBUTORS

Donato Amado Gonzales is a doctoral candidate in Andean studies at Pontificia Universidad Católica del Perú and a member of the National Academy of History. He earned a BA in history from the Universidad Nacional de San Antonio Abad del Cusco and an MA in history from the Pontificia Universidad Católica del Perú. Amado is a specialist in Andean rural history of the sixteenth through the nineteenth centuries. His research focuses on the Andean highway system, the Qhapaq Ñan Cusco Project, the *ceque* system, and land tenure in the valley of Cusco and Machu Picchu.

Carmen Arellano Hoffmann studied history and archaeology at the Pontificia Universidad Católica del Perú and received her PhD in cultural anthropology from the University of Bonn. Her research has focused on the ethnohistory of Peru's central highlands during Inka and colonial times, Andean notation systems, and indigenous world view. She has conducted archaeological and anthropological fieldwork in Peru, Mexico, Guatemala, Chile, Argentina, and Brazil. Formerly the director of Peru's National Museum of Archaeology, Anthropology, and History, she has served since February 2013 as the academic secretary of that country's National Academy of History.

Joaquín Roberto Bárcena has a doctorate in geography and history with a specialization in prehistoric studies. He was a senior researcher at the National Scientific and Technical Research Council (CONICET) in Argentina and an associate professor at Universidad Nacional de Cuyo, in Mendoza, Argentina. Between 2010 and 2014, he served as the director of the Institute of Human and Environmental Sciences (INCIHUSA). Recognized as an honorary member of Argentina's National Commission for Museums, Monuments, and Historical Sites, Bárcena is currently the director of the Archaeological and Ethnological Institute at the Universidad Nacional de Cuyo.

José Barreiro (Taíno), PhD, is the assistant director for culture and history research and the director of the Office for Latin America at the National Museum of the American Indian. A developmental figure in Native American journalism and publishing, Barreiro was an early voice in American Indian outreach to the United Nations and developed indigenous hemispheric coverage for the international journal *Akwesasne Notes*. At Cornell University (1984–2002) Barreiro helped establish the American Indian Program and served as the associate director of the creative workshop Akwe:kon Press, which published the award-winning journal *Native Americas*. Recent books include *Thinking in Indian: A John Mohawk Reader* (2010) and the novel, *Taíno: The Indian Chronicles* (2012).

José Berenguer received his PhD in anthropology from the University of Illinois at Urbana-Champaign. He is the chief curator of the Chilean Museum of Pre-Columbian Art, the editor of *Boletín del Museo Chileno de Arte Precolombino*, and a specialist in the prehistory of the Atacama Desert. The long-term emphasis of his research has been in the spatial, social, and ritual aspects of human interaction in the south-central Andes at a local, regional, and interregional level. Currently he works to understand the role of visual culture in the development of desert societies.

José Alejandro Beltrán-Caballero is an architect and an associate researcher at the Seminary of Ancient Topography at Universitat Rovira i Virgili in Tarragona, Spain. He received his PhD in architecture from Universitat Politècnica de Catalunya–Escola Tècnica Superior d'Arquitectura, Barcelona. His work focuses on the study of ancient settlements in relation to water management and the interpretation of the landscape in ancient cities. He has also worked on virtual reconstruction projects in Europe and South America.

Victoria Castro is professor emeritus at the University of Chile. She is an activist in the struggle for the recognition of indigenous communities and in the pursuit of Chile's identity as a multiethnic and multicultural country. She was a consultant to the UNESCO panel that designated the Inka Road a World Heritage site and an advisor to the team that created the National Museum of the American Indian's exhibition *The Great Inka Road: Engineering an Empire*.

Gerardo Chang Recavarren is a professor in the Civil Engineering Department at Universidad de Piura, Peru. He holds degrees from Pontificia Universidad Católica del Perú. Since 1992 he has taught construction engineering and structural engineering courses at the university. Prior to that, he worked with a construction company.

Christine M. Fiori is the associate director of the Myers-Lawson School of Construction at Virginia Tech. She received her PhD in civil engineering, with a concentration in geotechnical engineering, from Drexel University. Her interest in ancient construction led to a National Science Foundation grant to explore the construction techniques of the Inka, specifically the Inka Road in Peru. She has also led student teams to Vietnam, Kenya, Belize, and Haiti to complete community engagement programs.

Samantha Pary Ghayour McKnew has a degree in anthropology with a specialty in cultural discourse in Latin American policies. As a researcher from 2010 to 2014, she was integral to the development of the National Museum of the American Indian exhibition *The Great Inka Road: Engineering an Empire*. Her experience includes fieldwork in Latin America and diaspora communities in the Washington, DC, area. She is currently completing her graduate work.

Emily Kaplan has been an objects conservator at the Smithsonian National Museum of the American Indian since 1996. She specializes in preventive conservation and in technical studies of the museum's Latin American collections, with a particular interest in pigments and plant materials.

Ricardo Mar Medina is a professor of archaeology at Universitat Rovira i Virgili, Tarragona, Spain. He is an archaeological architect with a PhD from Universitat Politècnica de Catalunya, Barcelona. He has been a guest professor at universities in England, Italy, the United States, Colombia, and Peru. Mar has worked and managed projects in Spain, Portugal, Italy, France, Morocco, Tunisia, Colombia, and Peru.

Sergio Martin has a doctorate in archaeology and history from Universidad Nacional de Cuyo in Argentina. Currently he works as a researcher at the National Institute of Anthropology and Latin American Thought (INAPL) and as an adjunct professor at the National University Arturo Jauretche of Buenos Aires. Since 1999 he has studied the Inka Road and the Inka presence in the Argentine province of La Rioja.

RAMIRO MATOS MENDIETA (Quechua), a curator at the National Museum of the American Indian, holds a doctorate in archaeology and ethnology from Universidad Nacional Mayor de San Marcos in Lima. A leading archaeologist of Andean cultures, Matos has served as a visiting professor at the University of Texas; University of California, Los Angeles; George Mason University; University of Maryland at College Park; University of Bonn; and University of Copenhagen. An emeritus professor at the Universidad Nacional Mayor de San Marcos, he has received postdoctoral and research grants from the John Simon Guggenheim Foundation, the Smithsonian Institution, Dumbarton Oaks, the National Geographic Society, and the Mellon Foundation. He is the author of numerous articles and books.

AXEL E. NIELSEN earned a doctorate in history at Universidad Nacional de Córdoba, Argentina, and a PhD in anthropology at the University of Arizona. For the past thirty years he has conducted archaeological and ethnographic research in the Andes of northwestern Argentina and southern Bolivia. His main research interests include Andean religions, pre-Columbian political processes, interregional interaction (trade and war), and ethnoarchaeology. Currently he is a principal researcher at Argentina's National Scientific and Technical Research Council (CONICET) and works at the National Institute of Anthropology and Latin American Thought.

JOHN OCHSENDORF is the Class of 1942 Professor of Architecture and Engineering at the Massachusetts Institute of Technology. He has been researching the history and technology of Inka suspension bridges since his undergraduate thesis on the topic at Cornell, where he majored in structural engineering and minored in archaeology.

JOSÉ LUIS PINO MATOS has an archaeology degree from Universidad Nacional Mayor de San Marcos, and is a doctoral candidate in archaeology at Pontificia Universidad Católica del Perú in Lima. His specialization is in Inka archaeoastronomy, with a focus on sites within Cusco, Huánuco Pampa, Pumpu, Tarmatambo, and Aypati. He also served as one of the coordinators for the Qhapaq Ñan Peruvian Program of the Ministry of Culture.

MARIO A. RIVERA is executive director of the program Identity End of the World: Patagonia, Tierra del Fuego, and Antarctica at Universidad de Magallanes, Chile. He is also a research associate at the Field Museum in Chicago. Rivera is a researcher and consultant in Andean cultural heritage issues, the archaeology of complex societies, and environmental archaeology. A former director of the Institute of Anthropology and the San Miguel de Azapa Archaeological Museum in Arica, Chile, Rivera holds MS and PhD degrees in anthropology from the University of Wisconsin, Madison.

CLIFFORD SCHEXNAYDER is the Emeritus Eminent Scholar at Arizona State University's Del E. Webb School of Construction. He holds degrees from the Georgia Institute of Technology and Purdue University and has taught construction engineering at Universidad de Piura and Ricardo Palma Universidad in Peru. Before entering academia he worked with major heavy/highway construction contractors.

MAURICIO RODRÍGUEZ URIBE is an associate professor at the University of Chile, where he received his BA in anthropology and his MA in archaeology, and where he has been working since 1998. He is currently completing his PhD at the University of Buenos Aires, and he serves on the advisory committee of Argentina's Archaeological Heritage National Monuments Council. His research focus is the Andean cultures of the Atacama Desert in northern Chile.

GARY URTON is Dumbarton Oaks Professor of Pre-Columbian Studies and chairman of the Department of Anthropology at Harvard University. His research focuses on a variety of topics in pre-Columbian and early colonial Andean intellectual history. His books include *At the Crossroads of the Earth and the Sky* (1981), *The History of a Myth* (1990), *The Social Life of Numbers* (1997), *Inca Myths* (1999), and *Signs of the Inka Khipu* (2003). A MacArthur Fellow (2001–2005), Urton is the founder/director of the Harvard Khipu Database Project.

EDMUNDO DE LA VEGA MACHICAO is an archaeologist from Universidad Católica Santa María de Arequipa, in Peru. He has participated in various archaeological research projects in Arequipa, Cusco, Moquegua, and Puno. His research interests have focused mainly on the late and intermediate periods of the Bolivian site Tiwanaku. He has authored and coauthored several publications in Peru, the United States, and South Korea. He currently teaches at the Professional School of Anthropology at the National University of the Altiplano, Puno, Peru.

CHRISTIAN VITRY is an archaeologist, a professor of geography and biological sciences, and a professional mountain guide. For two decades he has been investigating high-mountain archaeological sites in the Andes and on Inka roads. He is a professor and researcher at National University of Salta, Argentina, an instructor in the Mountain Guides' Association, and is the director of the Qhapaq Ñan Program-Andean Vial System (UNESCO) in the Province of Salta.

ALEXEI VRANICH is a research professor at the Cotsen Institute of Archaeology at UCLA. He received his BA from the University of California, Berkeley, and his doctorate in anthropology from the University of Pennsylvania. Working as an archaeologist in South America since 1995, Vranich collaborates with contemporary indigenous communities to develop strategies for increasing tribal stewardship over their archaeological and cultural resources. His current research focuses on the ancient Inka capital of Cusco, and on Machu Picchu.

KENNETH R. WRIGHT, a consulting engineer, is the founder of Wright Water Engineers of Denver, Colorado. His company has been involved in paleohydrological research in Peru, Mesa Verde, southern France, Pompeii, Olympia, Thailand, Cambodia, and China. In Peru he and his wife, Ruth, have focused on the hydrology and hydraulics of Machu Picchu, Tipon, Moray, and currently, Ollantaytambo. Wright has been awarded four honorary degrees from universities in Lima and Cusco, including an honorary doctorate from Universidad Nacional de Ingeniería.

RUTH M. WRIGHT is the vice president of Wright Paleohydrological Institute and is active in water resources policy and field research. As a former member of the Colorado House of Representatives, including six years as the House minority leader, she supported the wise use of natural resources. She is a graduate of Marquette University and earned her JD from the University of Colorado Law School. She was awarded honorary professorships in 2008 from Universidad Nacional San Antonio de Abad and in 2009 from Universidad Nacional de Ingeniería.

KARINA A. YAGER is an anthropologist and climate change researcher whose work focuses on the Andean peoples and the mountain regions of Peru and Bolivia. She is currently a visiting professor of sustainability studies at SUNY-Stony Brook. Yager works with NASA and the Earth Vision Institute. She applies interdisciplinary methods to her research, which includes the remote sensing of land cover and land-use change, ethnographic fieldwork with pastoral societies, and the ecological study of high-altitude vegetation. Her current research focus is the impact of disappearing glaciers on pastoral agriculture in the Central Andes.

R. T. ZUIDEMA studied at universities in Leiden, Netherlands, and Madrid, Spain. From 1955 to 1964 he was the curator of the South and North America and Siberia sections at the State Museum of the Netherlands. He has taught anthropology at the University of Huamanga in Ayacucho, Peru, and he was a professor of anthropology at the University of Illinois at Urbana-Champaign. His most recent book, *El calendario inca: Tiempo y espacio en la organización ritual del Cuzco: La idea del pasado,* was published in 2011.

ACKNOWLEDGMENTS

The Smithsonian National Museum of the American Indian (NMAI) exhibition on the Inka Road, which is called the Qhapaq Ñan, or Way of the Lord, in the Quechua language, was born in 2008 as an initiative suggested by photographer Megan Son. She gained the support of NMAI leaders Kevin Gover, Tim Johnson, Karen Fort, and Kerry Boyd, who agreed to implement it as a major project. Shortly after the meeting with Megan, I was invited to assume the honored position of lead curator. I accepted the challenge and was accompanied by José Barreiro as co-curator. I take this opportunity to thank Megan for bringing this important initiative to the NMAI, and to thank directors Gover, Johnson, Fort, and Boyd for accepting the proposal and trusting me with this transcendent responsibility.

The Inka Road Project (IRP) is of international dimension and large scale, involving six Andean countries, the heirs of the Inka Empire: Colombia, Ecuador, Peru, Bolivia, Chile, and Argentina. We started the project at a time of great sensitivity regarding the Qhapaq Ñan. UNESCO officially coordinated two investigations in these six countries with a view to designating the Inka Road as a World Heritage site. Although our attempts to make contact with those involved in the multinational project were unsuccessful, national leaders responded very generously to our communications.

The IRP's first action was to travel to the Andean countries to communicate personally with their ministers of culture and directors of cultural heritage. Our goal was to discuss the scope and objectives of the exhibition and deliver draft text outlining the project. Everyone with whom we met greeted us kindly and offered full support. We also visited the Qhapaq Ñan offices in the six countries, agreeing with each on mutual collaboration. Finally, we visited many traditional communities—the contemporary users of the Inka Trail—where we received great hospitality and unconditional support for the Inka Road Project.

In addition, we contacted colleagues in the field and in museums who were studying the Inka road system. At each location, we received generous help in developing the project. In our seven years of fieldwork with scholars, government officials, and Quechua and Aymara leaders, we encountered no problems. What prevailed during our journey was the support and collaboration of our colleagues—students of archaeology and anthropology—who spared nothing in sharing their study materials with us. We have benefited from innumerable publications, unpublished manuscripts, maps, drawings, and photographs as well as from approximately fifteen theses. Indigenous leaders also opened their doors, responding to all our concerns. We collected from them abundant oral histories, ethnographic observations, and photographs. To these honorable Andeans and distinguished academics, we extend our special gratitude. Without them it would have been impossible to gather so much of the information that is now stored at the NMAI.

On our journey through six countries, we received unexpected attention. In Colombia, we visited Ipiales and Pasto, where artisans working with the *Elaeagia* resin, also known as *mopa mopa* or Pasto varnish (material used in painting Inka *qeros*), patiently explained their technology. In Ecuador, we received help from Jorge Marcos, José Echevarría, Mónica Bolaños, Jaime Idrovo, Benigno Malo and many Native informants in Caranque, Otavalo, Yahuarcocha, Ambato, Cuenca (Canar), Saraguro, Loja, and Guayaquil. These Quechua speakers are the modern Andean users of the Inka Road. In Peru, we benefited from tips and information from Carmen Arellano Hoffmann, Donato Amado Gonzáles, Jorge Flores Ochoa, José Pino Matos, Edmundo de la Vega Machicao, María Eugenia Muñiz, Antonia Miranda, Roxana Abril, Bertha Vargas, Ricardo Ruiz Caro, Ernesto García Calderón, Fernando Astete Victoria, Marco Marcés, and many others who generously shared their time and data. We would also like to thank our contributors from Chinchaycocha, Warautambo, Huánuco Pampa, Ancash, Vilcashuaman, Andahuaylas, and the Cusco and Puno communities. At Andahuaylas we were guided by Daniella Kurin, who is perfectly familiar with that region and a new Quechua speaker.

During his 2013 visit to Peru, G. Wayne Clough, who was then the secretary of the Smithsonian, signed an agreement with Susana Baca, then the Peruvian minister of culture. Officials Paloma Carcedo and Luisa Vetter as well as Carmen Arellano Hoffmann, the director of the National Museum of Anthropology, Archaeology, and History, all gave their personal and institutional support to the IRP; for them our deepest appreciation.

In Bolivia, we received the support of Minister Pablo Groux, José Estévez, Marcos Michel, and Walter Alvarez (Kallawaya), who kindly guided us along the paths of Charazani, as well as of María de los Ángeles Muñoz de Cochabamba and many Aymara people from the Titicaca basin. Carmen Beatriz Loza and Claudia Condarco generously gave us their research on the Tambo de Paria. In Argentina, we were the fortunate recipients of assistance

from Christian Vitry, Roberto Bárcena, Sergio Martin, Axel Nielsen, Myriam Tarragó, Verónica Williams, as well as from communities linked to the Inka Trail in Huamahuaca, Salta, Jujuy, Mendoza, and La Rioja. Bárcena drove us to visit his excavations and showed us the site of Uspallaqta, while Vitry accompanied us to several locations in Salta and Humahuaca. In Chile, we benefited from the support and advice of Victoria Castro, José Berenguer, Mauricio Uribe, Mario A. Rivera, and Calogero Santo, augmented by information from users of the road in Calama, Atacama, and Arica. We wish to highlight the support of CONICYT-PIA, Anillo: Código SOC 1405, Chile, for Victoria Castro's research. From Spain, we received tremendous academic and technical support from Ricardo Mar Medina and José Alejandro Beltrán-Caballero, whose studies and 3-D relief of the Inka city of Cusco were the basis for building the model that occupies the central section of the exhibition.

Our American colleagues were very generous in sharing their advice and data. We very much appreciate the support and solidarity of Gary Urton at Harvard University, Colin McEwan at Dumbarton Oaks, Charles Stanish, the director of the Cotsen Institute of Archaeology at UCLA, Tom Dillehay at Vanderbilt University, Christine M. Fiori at Virginia Tech, John Ochsendorf at MIT, Clifford Schexnayder at Arizona State University, Ruth M. and Kenneth R. Wright of Wright Water Engineers, Tamara L. Bray of Wayne University, Terence D'Altroy of Columbia University, the Metropolitan Museum's Joanne Pillsbury, Alexei Vranich at the Cotsen Institute, Dennis Osborg at the University of North Carolina, Ann Rowe at the Textile Museum in Washington, DC, Nancy Rosoff of the Brooklyn Museum, Sumru Aricanli of the American Museum of Natural History, Jorge Arellano of the Anthropology Department at the Smithsonian's National Museum of Natural History, Jeffrey Splitstoser at the Pre-Columbian Society of Washington, DC, NASA fellow Karina A. Yager, and many others, to each of whom we express our sincere thanks.

We express our special gratitude to secretary emeritus of the Smithsonian Institution G. Wayne Clough for his support, stimulation, and encouragement during our

2013 trip to Peru; to Richard Kurin, the under secretary for history, art and culture, for his constant encouragement as we were developing the IRP; to NMAI director Kevin Gover for his consistent support and advice; and to NMAI associate directors Tim Johnson and David Penney as well as assistant director Kerry Boyd for their advice and watchful tutelage. I am also indebted to the entire exhibition project team, ably led by project manager Amy Van Allen and exhibition manager Jennifer Tozer, including the teams responsible for the exemplary design and fabrication of the exhibition gallery.

I would like to highlight the professionalism and editorial work of NMAI publications manager Tanya Thrasher and her staff, primarily Sally Barrows and Ann Kawasaki; to them, my deepest gratitude. I am also grateful for the professionalism of NMAI's Photo Services staff, led by Katherine Fogden, especially for the work of Ernest Amoroso, whose high-quality photos make the book. The conservation staff deserves special appreciation: Marian Kaminitz, the head of the Conservation Office, whose leadership is augmented by the great professionalism and careful work of objects conservators Emily Kaplan and Kelly McHugh, textile conservator Susan Heald, contractor Lisa Anderson, and Mellon Fellows Fran Ritchie, Caitlin Mahoney, Cathleen Zaret, and Kate Blair in addition to intern Amanda McCleod. I would also like to thank mountmakers Shelly Uhlir and mount-making contractors William Bowser and William Mead. In addition, I would like to acknowledge the work and contributions of Veronica Quiguango, Gail Joice, Anthony Williams, Fiorella Casavilca, and José Montaño.

On the media team, the leadership and professionalism of Daniel Davis is well worth mentioning. He is supported by Mark Christal, Doug McMains, and Erin Weinman; to all of them our special appreciation. Thanks, too, to contractor Ralf Oberti and to Dan Cole from the National Museum of Natural History for their contributions. We also thank Juanita Wrenn (WrennWorks); Dave Schaller (EduWeb); Jim Spadaccini (Ideum); Tim Songer, the president of Interactive Knowledge; Antonio Jordan; Cheryl Wilson; Laurie Swindull; and Deanna Wood for their valuable contributions to the Media and Web teams. In addition, we would like to acknowledge the work of the contractors in charge of photography and images.

Within the museum's Education Office, our thanks to education manager Clare Cuddy (now retired); education specialists Vilma Ortiz-Sanchez and Suzanne Davis; acting education manager Edwin Schupman, and contractor Isabel Hawkins. Also thanks to archivist Heather Shannon and librarian Elayne Silversmith for their consistent support of the project.

The Inka Road Project has been fortunate to have outstanding research assistants such as Lucia Abramovich, Samantha Pary Ghayour McKnew, and Diana Marcela Hajjar. We started the project with Lucia, consolidated and organized the project's written and photographic documentation with Samantha, and currently are privileged to count on Diana Marcela, who has sorted the project files, pulled everything together, and responded with great professionalism to the requirements of the project in its final phases. With their language skills, talent, and dedication, each of them successively has played a key role in implementing and organizing the narratives and data scripts. To them we express our deepest appreciation, especially to Diana Marcela, who has most recently carried a heavy load in meeting the project's demands.

Finally I want to thank NMAI associate director Jane Sledge for her technical and administrative support of the exhibition and Richard Freeman, Roger Belton, and Bryan Kennedy in the Information Technology Office, who were quick in responding to our requests. Many thanks, too, to our colleagues Cécile Ganteaume, Antonio Curet, Paul Chaat Smith, and Ann McMullen in the Curatorial Department; and to José Barreiro and RoseMaría Estévez in the NMAI's Office for Latin America, who were always supportive of the Inka Road Project.

RAMIRO MATOS MENDIETA

The Great Inka Road: Engineering an Empire

Director: Kevin Gover (Pawnee)

Associate director for museum programs: Tim Johnson (Mohawk)

Associate director for museum scholarship: David Penney

PUBLICATION

General editors: Ramiro Matos Mendieta (Quechua) and José Barreiro (Taíno)

Publications manager: Tanya Thrasher (Cherokee Nation)

Assistant publications manager: Ann Kawasaki

Project editors: Sally Barrows, Christine T. Gordon, Cecilia I. Parker

Designers: Julie Allred, BW&A Books; Steve Bell

Editorial, research, and translation assistance: Eriksen Translations, Inc.; Samantha Pary Ghayour McKnew; Indexing Partners, LLC; Diana Marcela Hajjar; Katharine Martinek; Jane McAllister; Arwen Nuttall (Four Winds Band of Cherokee); Jessica Phippen

Map illustrations: Nancy Bratton Design; Daniel G. Cole, Smithsonian Institution

Administrative assistance: RoseMaria Romero Estévez (Zapotec), Carol Gardner, Tionna Moore

Permissions: Wendy Hurlock Baker, Ann Kawasaki, Diana Marcela Hajjar, Jessica Phippen

Photography and photo services: Ernest Amoroso, Katherine Fogden (Akwesasne Mohawk), Doug McMains, R.A.Whiteside

Photo archives: Michael Pahn, Heather Shannon

Prepress: Bill Whitcher, Smithsonian Enterprises

EXHIBITION

Co-curators: Ramiro Matos Mendieta (Quechua) and José Barreiro (Taíno)

Curatorial research assistants: Lucia Abramovich, Fiorella Casavilca, Samantha Pary Ghayour McKnew, Diana Marcela Hajjar, Katharine Martinek, Jessica Phippen

Librarian: Elayne Silversmith (Navajo)

Executive project manager: Amy Van Allen

Exhibition manager: Jennifer Tozer

Exhibition design manager: Kerry Boyd

Script editing: Rosemary Regan

Translation: MariaCristina Moro and Laura Temes

Exhibition design: Chris Arnold

Exhibition graphic design: Elizabeth Hunter

Exhibition fabrication: Pat (John) Chirichella, Craig Huzway, Jay (Jerry) Jarvis, Robert Patterson, Kon Rhyu, Elias Stern

Collections conservation: Susan Heald, Marian Kaminitz, Emily Kaplan, Kelly McHugh, NMAI Andrew W. Mellon Fellows, and interns

Exhibition mountmaking: Shelly Uhlir

Registration: Kara Hurst, Rajshree Solanki

Collections management: Victoria Cranner, Gail Joice, Veronica Quiguango (Kichwa), Christina Oricchio

Exhibition media: Mark Christal, Daniel Davis, Doug McMains

Website: Katharine Martinek, Holly Stewart, Laurie Swindull, Cheryl Wilson, Deanna Wood

Information technology: Walter Plush, Dwight Schmidt, Jane Sledge, James Smith, Emmanuel Udoumoh, Erin Weinman, Randel Wilson

Development: Cameron McGuire, Elaine Webster, Gerald Zavala

Executive planning office: Wayne Smith, Christa Stabler

Education: Clare Cuddy, Suzanne Davis, Gaetana DeGennaro (Tohono O'odham), Edwin Schupman (Muscogee), Vilma Ortiz-Sanchez

Cultural arts: Janet Clark, Hayes Lavis, Shawn Termin (Lakota)

Seminars and symposia: Elizabeth Kennedy Gische

Public affairs: Leonda Levchuk (Navajo), Claudia Lima, Eileen Maxwell

Special events: Arley Donovan, Denise Robinson Simms, Hannah Wendling

Interpretive services: Mandy Foster (Cheyenne River Sioux), Sharyl Pahe (Navajo/San Carlos Apache), Adrienne Smith (Cherokee/Muscogee-Creek Nations of Oklahoma), Ami Temarantz

Special thanks to our dedicated project representatives in Restaurant Associates, Smithsonian Enterprises, Smithsonian Gardens, Smithsonian Latino Center, Smithsonian Office of Facilities Engineering and Operations, and the Smithsonian Office of the Chief Information Officer's Digitization Program.

We are grateful for the expertise of the numerous consultants and contractors involved in developing the exhibition and related products, and for the skill and dedication of the National Museum of the American Indian administrative personnel who helped to make this project possible.

overleaf left: Some Native Andeans place ceramic statues, frequently churches or bulls, on the roofs of their homes. Quechua roof ornament in the shape of a church, 1971–1972. Quinua, Peru. Ceramic, paint. 44.5 × 23.5 × 15.9 cm. 26/3405. Photo by Ernest Amoroso, NMAI

overleaf right: This coca bag has llama designs woven into its body and red fringe, a sign of the high status of its owner. Inka coca bag, AD 1450–1532. South coast of Peru. Cotton. 50.2 × 17.2 × 2.5 cm. 24/7967. Photo by Ernest Amoroso, NMAI

INDEX

Inka empire enabled by, 53–54, 59; technological exchange of suspension bridges, 57–58; types of, 121. *See also* Q'eswachaka suspension bridge

Cabana people, 120

Cabanaconde, 120, 125

Cachapoal River, 100

Cajamarca, 5, 79, 80, 81, 83, 157

Cajatambo, 89

Calahoyo, 106, 180n4

Calama, 106

calendar, 84; December solstice, 89; November procession, 87–88; September, Inka month of sowing, 85–86

Callalli, 123, 125

Callo, 82

Camana, Peru, 121, **122**, 126

Camarones Valley, 96, 98

Camino de Calderas (Road of the Hot Springs), 125

Camino de la Costa (Royal Coast Road), 96. *See also* Camino Real de los Llanos, Camino Inka Costero

Camino del Choro, Bolivia, 15

Camino Inka Costero (Coastal Inka Road), 15. *See also* Camino de la Costa, Camino Real de los Llanos

Camino Real (Royal Road), 141, 153, 156, 179n3

Camino Real de la Sierra, 97

Camino Real de los Llanos (Royal Valley Road), 96, 97, 126. *See also* Camino de la Costa, Camino Inka Costero

canals, 3, 5, 33, 75, 78, 80, 133, 161

Cañari rebels, 104

Cano, Alonso, 180n5

Capac Yupanqui (fifth Inka), 54, 120, 121

Capacmarca, 122

Capacocha (ceremonial child sacrifice), 2, 16, 35–37, **35–37**, 100, 108, 119

Carangas people, 96

Carapacho people, 130

caravans, **2**, 17, **17**, 70–72, 160–62. *See also* llamas

Caravelí valley, 120

Carreras Rivery, Raquel, 180n3

Casa del Cabildo (Council House), 32, 178n5

Casaurco (Arch of Ticatica), 22

Castro, Beltran de, 178n5

Castro, Victoria, 2, 7

Catamarca province, 106, 180n4

Catarpe, San Pedro de Atacama, **91**

Catequil (deity-oracle), 80

Catunqui, 22

cave paintings, 120, 153

caves, 47

Caxas, 81

Caylloma, 123

Ccapi, 121

Ccora, 121

Ccorawire Mountain, 77

ceques (sacred sightlines), 84–85, **86**, 88, 89, 119

ceremonial spaces. *See kanchas; ushnus*

Cerro Cuevas Pintadas, Argentina, **72**

Cerro de Esmeralda, Iquique, 100

Cerro de Pasco Tusinos (Peruvian traveling merchants), 161

Cerro El Plomo. *See* El Plomo

Cerro Verde mining camp, 98

Chacabuco Mountains, 97

Chachani Volcano, 35, 119, 125

Chachapoyas, Peru, *xiv*, 130, 133

Chaco region, 129, 132

chakacamayucs (bridge-keepers), 56–57, **57**

Chakamarca, 79

Chanapata culture, 25

Chanca, 121

Chañi Volcano, 36

Chanka peoples, 3, 54, 75

Charazani, Bolivia, xiii

chaskis (runner-messengers), 4, 7, 15, 17, 63–64, **64, 68**, 68–69, 122, 136, 142, 144; bag of, **69**; footwear of, **69**

chaskiwasis (relay posts for message runners), 15, 69, 92, 144

Chawaytiri (Quechua community), 1

chawpi (center of Inka Empire), 3, 7, 120. *See also* Cusco

Chena fortress, 100

chicha. See a'qa

Chicoana, 106, 180n4

Chile, xv, 14, 15, 16, 71, 95–100, 142, 153, 158, 161

Chilque people, 120

chimpus (llama decorations), **70**

Chimú people, 17, 103; *balsa* vessel, **124**; stirrup-spout bottle in form of puma, **28**; *tumi* (ritual knife), **94**

China (ancient) suspension bridges, 52

Chincha people, 17, 75, 78, 88

Chinchaysuyu, 1, 7, 8, 21, 61, 75–83, **76,** 89, 126

Chinchero, 33

Chiriguanos people, 131, 133

Chivay, 120, 125

Choquechaca (also called Tullumayu) River, 21, 28

Choquequirao, 76

Christianity: Catholic church built over Inka structure, **148**; crosses, **22, 152,** 153–54; Feast of Corpus Christi, 89

chúa (serving dish), 99

chuclla (chaski huts), 63

Chuichui settlement, 116

Chumbibilcas, 54

Chumbivilca people, 120

Chumpivillca, 54

Chuquiabo (La Paz), 15

Chuquibamba valley, 120, 123

Chuquicamata mining camp, 98

Chuquisaca, 149

Church of San Cristóbal, Cusco, 27

Chuscha Mountain, 36

Cieza de León, Pedro, 13, 57, 178n7

Cipolletti, María Susana, 158

civil engineering, 2, 3, 5, 6, 10, 15, 55–56, 104, 109–12

Cobo, Bernabé, 6, 19, 54, 56, 63, 122, 178n3, 180n2

coca, 130, **136–37**, 136–38, 141, 145, 157, 160; bags for carrying (*chipas*), **138**, 160, **203**

cocha (ritual vessel), **20, 26**

Cochabamba valley, 132, 133, 135

Cochacajas, 77, 80

Colca Canyon/River, **i, 12, 15,** 123, 125, **125**

Colca-Majes-Camaná basin, 123

colcas (state warehouses), 7, **44**, 63, **64,** 66, 91, 98, **125**

Colla people and region, 103, 114

Collagua people, 120

Collahuasi smelting, 98

Collao, 15, 104, 106, 108, 179n3

Collasuyu, 1, 7, 8, 15, 21, **23,** 35, 62, 69, 83, 89, 95, **101,** 103–8, 115, 126

Colombia, 14, 16, 138, 161

colonial period, 25, 28, 30, **30,** 33, 58, 72, 90, 104, 106, 133, **140,** 141–48, 157; *qero* artists, 150, **151**

Colquemarca, 122

Comecaballos, 106

Confluencia, 108

CAPTIONS FOR IMAGES PAGES 211–214:

p. 211: This *aquilla* is a special type of cup made specifically for *a'qa* (also known as *chicha*, or maize beer). The carved face and prominent beak are reminiscent of a condor.

Inka *aquilla* (cup), AD 1470–1532. Cusco region, Peru. Silver. 29.1 × 10.2 cm. 16/9875. Photo by Ernest Amoroso, NMAI

pp. 212–13: A mountain in Peru's central highlands, near the Cordillera de Chila, 2014. Photo by Doug McMains, NMAI

p. 214: This figurine demonstrates the blending of Andean and European technologies and traditions. The filigree technique is a European import and the subject, the llama, is an important Andean animal.

Wanka Quechua llama figurine, 1900–1930. Ayacucho, Peru. Silver alloy. 7.5 × 4.8 × 1.3 cm. 15/9401. Photo by Ernest Amoroso, NMAI